ORGANIZATION IN VISION

Foreword by Paolo Legrenzi and Paolo Bozzi

ORGANIZATION IN VISION

Essays on Gestalt Perception

GAETANO KANIZSA

PRAEGER

PRAEGER SPECIAL STUDIES • PRAEGER SCIENTIFIC

Library of Congress Cataloging in Publication Data

Kanizsa, Gaetano.
    Organization in vision.

    Bibliography: p.
    Includes index.
    1. Gestalt psychology. 2. Visual perception.
I. Title.
BF203.K29   150.19'82   79-11851
ISBN 0-03-049071-5

PRAEGER PUBLISHERS, PRAEGER SPECIAL STUDIES
383 Madison Avenue, New York, N.Y., 10017, U.S.A.

Published in the United States of America in 1979
by Praeger Publishers,
A Division of Holt, Rinehart and Winston, CBS Inc.

9 038 987654321

Printed in the United States of America

FOREWORD

Paolo Legrenzi and Paolo Bozzi

Trieste is a city that has long been related to psychology in many ways. The names of two Trieste-born scholars will be familiar to English-speaking readers. Edward Weiss, the original researcher and therapist, concluded his career as a psychoanalyst in the United States. And Italo Svevo, who also lived in Trieste, wrote books that were understood and discussed in England and North America earlier than in Italy—books that present fundamental models of the interrelation between psycho-analysis, literature, and phenomenology in everyday life.

The connection between Trieste and experimental psychology may be less familiar to the English-speaking reader. Vittorio Benussi, the most important and complex figure in the early development of experimental psychology, was a native of this city. An exceptionally imaginative experimenter, Benussi was a student of Alexius Meinong at Graz, and after World War I was awarded the chair of psychology at the University of Padua. Despite his discoveries of new phenomena in the fields of perception, of movement, of form, of color, and especially of temporal structures, Benussi remained faithful to Meinong's concep-tion of an analysis of direct experience in which it is necessary to distinguish two levels: that of sense data and that of the organization of sense data in perception.

Cesare Musatti, Benussi's pupil at Padua, overcame many of the theoretical difficulties encountered by his teacher while working within the framework of gestalt psychology. He made extensive use of gestalt in his research, during which he discovered, among other things, kinetic depth effects. His students Fabio Metelli and Gaetano Kanizsa, both from Trieste, followed this theoretical line.

Therefore we believe that this volume, which presents the work of Gaetano Kanizsa, is interesting for two reasons. His research is worth consideration not only for its central interest in the field of visual perception and for the wealth of theories attached to it, but also because it reveals a fruitful style of doing research that is derived from the Central European cultural tradition—tradition that, in our opinion, explains many of the typical aspects of Kanizsa's experimental work.

A description of Kanizsa's stylistic peculiarities may prove useful to readers with a background in the most recent psychology, which is unrelated to the traditional European experimental effort. Indeed, Kanizsa's research may cause some adaptational problems for readers not accustomed to his style.

A fundamental aspect of Kanizsa's explorations is the immediate evidence of the phenomena that particularly attract him. Only rarely do the visual facts that he discovers and analyzes need indirect demonstrations through refined applied quantitative analysis. He works on clear and visible, though unexpected, facts. Likewise unequivocal are the effects that occur under experimental conditions. One may imagine that Kanizsa would have been able to obtain similar results even on a desert island—provided, of course, he had paper and the materials with which to draw and paint, plus a rudimentary apparatus for mechanically projecting movements and lights (but without the help of experimental subjects).

By closely following his work methods, one receives the distinct impression of research carried out directly on the phenomena. Whereas most psychologists accept that a certain object is red because 27 people out of 30 call it "red," the phenomena with which Kanizsa works are so evident that it is possible to say that 27 people out of 30 call an object "red" because it *is* red.

This is very important, because the visual properties studied by Kanizsa are not limited to extremely controlled and simplified laboratory situations. They can be repeated anywhere, without special devices. In other words, they can be encountered in everday life.

In a paper published in the 1950s, Kanizsa stated that although it may seem paradoxical, a phenomenon is very seldom seen in its purity, "and thus to determine it in its authenticity and to realize the related problems is often not less difficult than to solve them."

The truth of the matter is that Kanizsa discovers the problems to be studied in the laboratory during the observation of daily occurrences. An example is his research on gamma movement (see Chapter 6), which started when Kanizsa, sitting in a café, noticed the peculiar movement of the intermittent light of a neon sign consisting of two adjacent parts, one flashing and one continuous. Immediately he went to the laboratory, here was a new phenomenon to investigate. Undoubtedly many psychologists had seen it in a world full of neon signs. But the phenomenon had not been recognized as relevant, and our knowledge in the field of apparent movements had not been expanded. This is the nature of discovery.

In the world of research, the prevalent experimental method consists of a set of controlled operations determined by hypotheses suggested by theoretical models. The chain "model—verification—correction of the model—reverification—formulation of alternative models—reverification" is the basic structure, and probably constitutes the only scheme for progress in science. However, it is unavoidable that this method occasionally produces results entirely irrelevant to people with larger concerns, as U. Neisser claims in the third chapter of his last book (Neisser 1967).

At times it becomes necessary to break this paradigmatic circle and to seek the natural, primary source of the phenomena: the visual experience of ordinary seeing. Although the researchers who enjoy this way of exploring are not very numerous, in the past a great part of fruitful psychological research developed in this fashion.

Obviously, the discovery of facts relevant to a theory of perception from the experience of daily life is not a matter of simply looking around. The capacity to discover, in the sense employed here, depends as much on the capacity of observation as on keeping in mind a well-defined theory: those phenomena that appear not to support the theory probably can be analyzed profitably in the laboratory. The scheme thus can be outlined as "theory—observation of everyday experience—discovery—laboratory verification—correction of theory." The former scheme (which is "normal" today— may figure as a "subroutine" of the penultimate step, between laboratory verification and correction of the theory.

This procedure characterizes many of Kanizsa's most successful investigations, for very often he has made discoveries similar to that of gamma movement.

The idea of a "veridical perception" has been reintroduced into many theoretical discussions because some new points of view are built upon models derived from the information theory. Kanizsa does not leave room for such questions because the problem he tries to solve is not concerned with the degree of information that perception gives us about some external reality but, rather, with the intimate structure of the visual world. Thus perceptual experiences, to him, are all equally true because they are as they appear.

Following this line of reasoning, it may seem that there is not much to do, in perception, but to conduct an intense inspection of the environment, which ought to be sufficient to understanding the structure of the visible world. However, if you ask Kanizsa about it, he will respond—as he always does—that we probably know less than 10 percent of the properties of the visual world, no matter how long the list of discoveries made in the last century may be. Many psychologists work as if the catalog of relevant phenomena were already complete, so that the actual task consists only in building models to be verified in ever more sophisticated ways; for this reason the papers in the journals of experimental psychology are generally more concerned with verifying hypotheses than with discovering new phenomena. How, then, to refute this prevailing presumption? We know only the already discovered phenomena, not those that remain to be discovered. Kanizsa's assumption is based on his proved ability to see new and problematic facts where others look but do not see.

Since this operation is easy for him, Kanizsa concludes that there is a great deal more to discover. We must remember that, in addition to his work as an experimental psychologist, Kanizsa has, since the 1950s, also been a painter; he employs an idiosyncratic technique of griffonage by which he creates volumes, surfaces, textures, spaces. Certainly, as an artist, he does not proceed by consciously developing a preconceived project based on the laws of perception; rather, as he has often remarked, he paints with immediacy and imagination.

This by now automatic competence in utilizing complex microstructures in order to create variously formed spaces and bodies testifies to Kanizsa's intimate confidence in the functional relations that interconnect visual objects. He combines the conceptualizing confidence of the scientist with the instinctual control that, as an artist, he exerts on materials.

The general demonstration that comes out of the book through a series of particular ones is that the pleasure of looking at ordinary events, without being obsessed by theoretical micromodels, favors the construction of theories. Of course, this is true if, and only if, it still holds that theory has only debts toward facts, and that facts have only rights on theory.

ACKNOWLEDGMENTS ━━━━━━

Without the invaluable help of Nicholas Pastore of New York and Paolo Legrenzi of Trieste this book would not be what it is. I also want to thank Mike Riegle, who translated the articles, and Sandro Bertoli for the execution of the drawings.

I am grateful to the following journals and publishers for permission to use selections from my published articles: *Psychologische Forschung, Archivio di Psicologia Neurologia e Psichiatria, Italian Journal of Psychology, Acta Psychologica, Psychologische Beiträge*, and the Steinkopff Publishing Company.

CONTENTS ────────────────────────

LIST OF TABLES

ORGANIZATION IN VISION

1

TWO WAYS OF GOING BEYOND THE INFORMATION GIVEN

PRIMARY PROCESS AND SECONDARY PROCESS

When I look around an unfamiliar place or under limited conditions of visibility, I try to make sense of the things that I see, to recognize them; I hypothesize on their nature, checking such hypotheses by examining the characteristics of what is being observed; I predict behavior and adjust my original conjectures according to the results of these checks. This process, which takes time, but which can also occur in a fraction of a second, is not a mere passive *recording* of information impressed upon my sensory organs by the environment. Rather, it consists of an active *construction* by means of which sensory data are selected, analyzed, and integrated with properties not directly noticeable but only hypothesized, deduced, or anticipated, according to available information and intellectual capacities. Beginning with sensory input and leading to a coherent and significant phenomenal world where I can behave securely and appropriately, this entire process may be, and has been, called "perception." The term avoids an excessively distinct separation between vision and thought, since in this process it is difficult to determine the point where the sensory aspect ends and the mental processes begin.

If "thought" is taken to mean processes such as categorizing, grasping relationships, and reasoning by induction and deduction, one can maintain that it is present in all phases of the process described above. Indeed, the simple "identification" of a visual object (even seeing it as a blur, for example) implies an elementary logical process

1

(the placing of the object in one identity category rather than another). In the other phases, the involvement of mental processes, particularly those relying on inference, becomes even more noticeable. Therefore, although "vision" and "thought" are concepts that we normally differentiate, the possibility of strict separation becomes problematic when one analyzes the concrete interaction of an organism with its environment.

We may be tempted to overcome this difficulty by maintaining that in fact these two activities are not distinguishable because they form part of a continuum that it is senseless to break. In this case "pure" perception has no more meaning than "pure" thought.

This position is understandable, but one cannot escape the impression that in some way this procedure avoids a major problem that had been laboriously unearthed but, because of the avoidance, is in continual risk of being pushed out of sight.

It is clear that even the simplest of the cognitive processes mentioned above presupposes a "certain something" that must be identified—that is, it must be assigned an equivalence class. This operation allows one to infer other probable characteristics and is the basis for all the more complex cognitive processes.

The lack of recognition or the insufficient recognition of the logical necessity of this required step is, in my opinion, at the root of the ambiguities and misunderstandings of the term "perception" and of the recurring disagreements about the theories proposed to explain it. Actually, the existence of the problem is generally acknowledged, but the resulting consequences are not always noted. Even J. Bruner, who supports a radically panlogical theory, admits: "Surely, one may argue (and Hebb has done so effectively) that there must be certain forms of primitive organization within the perceptual field that make possible the differential use of cues in identity categorizing. Both logically and psychologically the point is evident." However, having made this admission, he adds, "Yet it seems to me foolish and unnecessary to assume that the sensory 'stuff' on which higher order categorizations are based is, if you will, of a different sensory order than more evolved identities with which our perceptual world is normally peopled." He concludes with the peremptory statement "All perceptual experience is necessarily the end product of a categorization process" (Bruner 1957a, p. 125).

The problem that continually tends to be overlooked is that of the formation of those "primary units" to which the inferential activity of the cognitive process can apply. These are the data beyond which "perception" goes, the cues that are interpreted and surpassed. A study of the perceptual process that takes for granted the existence of the primary units and concentrates on a description of the steps the mind uses to process these data in order to make them more significant for the perceiver is both valid and of great importance, but it clearly limits itself to a single phase of the overall process. This phase may be defined as a "secondary process," to distinguish it from a "primary process"— that which U. Neisser calls the "preconscious process" and B. Julesz, "pure perception." Through the latter the sensory input is transformed into segregated units whose characteristics are then analyzed by the secondary process.

For one who studies the secondary process, the formation of cues is not a problem: they are a given starting point and are accepted as such. They become a problem if one realizes that the sensory input from which the cues are derived is always equivocal and that consequently the passage from input to organized units is the product of a necessary preliminary process. In my opinion this problem is no less valid or important a subject of study than the secondary process is. As is well known, the gestaltists have concerned themselves with the primary process. They have proposed a field model in which, by means of the dynamic self-distribution of the effects of the sensory input, phenomenological units or objects are generated with all their properties of color, size, shape, three-dimensionality, movement, and expressiveness. Their phenomenological analyses have established certain principles or laws that this self-distribution follows. Although today gestalt theory does not have much credit as an explanatory theory, it is undeniable that the principles of perceptual organization discovered by gestaltists are facts that must be taken into account.

Currently much more widespread is the cognitive model in its numerous variants developed under the influence of information theory and computer science. This model is brought to bear on the explanation of what happens in the primary process, applying to it the principles that seem valid in the operation of the secondary process. Accordingly, even the mechanism that processes the entering information (the sensory stimuli or, as we might say, first-degree information) functions with the logic of the secondary process, thereby classifying, analyzing, forming hypotheses, verifying them, and making decisions— decisions that may be wrong. But although in the case of the secondary process it is meaningful to speak of errors, since the aim of the perceiver is to reach veridical conclusions—that is, to determine whether the phenomenological objects correspond to "real" ones—it does not make much sense to attribute this intention to the primary mechanisms of elaboration, which simply function according to their own set rules, without specific aims.

I have nothing against the construction or even the proliferation of models—with the proviso, however, that such models account for all the phenomena they were built to explain, even those that may appear to be "errors." How do certain authors of inferential models behave when the "logic" of the primary process brings outcomes that are discordant with those foreseen on the basis of the "logic" of the secondary process? Examples of such discrepancies are numerous and well-known. Even so, many researchers are inclined to label them curiosities or exceptions, continuing to insist that the primary process must function according to the logic of the secondary. For instance, Bruner (1957a) admits: "Let it be plain that no claim is being made for the utter indistinguishability of perceptual and more conceptual inferences. In the first place, the former appear to be notably less docile or reversible than the latter. . . ." He cites the inefficaciousness of knowledge on the appearance of the Ames room and on the length of the lines in the Müller-Lyer illusion, then hastens to add: "But these differences, interesting in themselves, must not lead us to overlook the common feature of inference underlying so much of cognitive activity.' And R. L. Gregory states:

> The perceptual system does not always agree with the rational thinking cortex. To the cortex the distance of the moon is a quarter of a million miles; to the visual part of the brain it is a mere few hundred yards. Though in this instance the cortical view is the correct one, the striate area is never informed, and we still see the moon as though it lay almost within our grasp. The visual brain has its own logic and preferences which are not understood cortically. (Gregory 1966, p. 224).

But when it comes to explaining optical illusions or the formation of anomalous surfaces, for example, Gregory attributes to the optical system such mechanisms as "constancy scaling" and "object hypothesis," whose "inappropriate" applications are supposed to account for the illusory phenomena. The latter are explained as the result of errors committed by the optical system in "reasonings," "judgements," and "inferential processes" of the same type as those found in the reasoning proper.

No exceptions may be allowed in a sound scientific theory. Unless exceptions are explainable by the theory, it becomes untenable and must be modified or replaced. If one is faced with phenomena indicating that a part of the system that processes entering information does not function according to the model's predictions, I find it damaging to call them exceptions for the sake of saving the model. It would be far more productive to consider these phenomena as precious indicators of the actual functioning of the system—that is, as "natural experimental situations" that can suggest the "logic" according to which the system works.

I shall return to this argument later, but first I would like to examine a little more closely the real meaning of "to go beyond the information given," to see whether this expression can be applied with the same significance to all the phases of the cognitive process.

TWO WAYS OF GOING BEYOND THE INFORMATION GIVEN

In the secondary process there are two ways of going beyond the information given. The first consists of making an identification or recognition. Ascribing a given object to a set of functionally equivalent objects allows one to know something more about the object itself. In this sense we can say that categorizing is the simplest way of going beyond the information given. The second way of going beyond the information given is literally called making an inference. This may be of a statistical or of a formal type, and consists of interpolating the missing elements when two or more elements are given.

One also can find two ways of going beyond the information given in the "primary" process. First, since the primary process cannot be considered a passive, mechanical recording of distant stimuli, but consists of an organization of proximal stimulation, in this case too we may speak of a process that goes beyond the information given. Naturally the term "information" here refers to something different from that discussed so far. It refers to the proximal stimulation, to the distribution of the elementary stimuli on the receiving organ that the optical system processes and organizes, transforming an unrelated set of elements (which theoretically could be unified in an infinite number of ways) into a certain number of segregated units with precise spatial and temporal relationships of similarity, size, functional dependence, and so on. These organized units are the second-degree data upon which all the successive cognitive activities operate. Since the organization is not contained in the stimuli (even if the latter contain the conditions), but is added by the organism, one may also say in this case, if one wishes to speak in these terms, that the primary process goes beyond the information given.

How it goes beyond the information is a question of research that must be approached empirically, and not by affirmations of theoretical preferences. Hermann von Helmholtz's hypothesis of "unconscious judgments," in its many currently fashionable reincarnations, is one of these theoretical options. To insist that it is "foolish and unnecessary" to make other assumptions is to take for granted the solution of problems that still await exploration.

There is a second way in which one can say that the brain goes beyond the information given in the primary process. This may be called perceptual interpolation. In both primary and secondary processes we have phenomena of totalization, of completion, of integration, of "filling in the gaps"—that is, of making present that which is absent.

The interpolation in the primary process can be modal or amodal. Examples of modal completion are in stroboscopic β movement, in the continuation of the visual field in the region corresponding to the blind spot, and in the formation of anomalous contours and surfaces. In all these cases the filled-in parts have the characteristics of visual modality and are phenomenally indistinguishable from those that have a counterpart in the stimuli.

Much more numerous are the cases of amodal completion. By "amodal presence" we mean that type of perceptual existence (not only imagined but also "encountered"; see Metzger 1954) that is not verified by any sensory modality (see Chapter 12, second footnote). It may seem to be a phenomenon worthy of note, but of not central importance in the construction of our phenomenal world. In fact, when A. Michotte first examined it in 1951, he called it "a *new* enigma of perception." Formerly it was seen only in terms of three-dimensional vision, as one of the "pictorial" cues of depth (interposition or overlapping).

However, amodal completion is a much more universal phenomenon, and merits much more attention than it receives. One need only recall the fundamental fact of figure-ground segmentation in the construction of the phenomenal world, in which the articulation always implies the completion (precisely amodal) of the continuous background existing behind the figure. And not only does every phenomenal object taken as a figure appear against a background amodally present behind it; it also possesses, phenomenally, its own back side. Although not visible, this posterior part is nonetheless phenomenally present. Indeed, this part does not have an arbitrary form that can be modified by the imagination, as G. Tampieri's research has shown (1956). Moreover, every phenomenal object seen three-dimensionally has an interior. This, too, is a real phenomenal presence ("encountered," not simply "imagined"), even if amodal.

Therefore, the optical system always fills gaps, goes beyond the information given through perceptual interpolation. This must be considered not simply as an interesting phenomenon, curious or worthy of note, but, on the contrary, as a norm of visual perception, a universal fact that happens every time we find ourselves in front of a field organized as figure and background, every time a phenomenal object exists. This conviction is also expressed by S. Ullman (1976).

In my view, the phenomena of amodal completion are of special interest because they constitute an area particularly adapted for studying *how* the optical system goes beyond the information given. If we

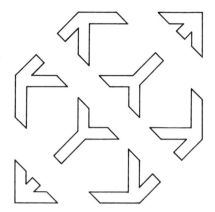

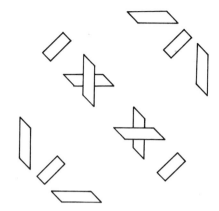

Figure 1.1a Seeing and thinking are clearly distinguishable activities. With these "pieces" we can *imagine* a cube, but it is very difficult to *see* it.

Figure 1.1b These also are fragments of a cube that is actually invisible.

consider amodal completion as the result of a process of inference (even though I doubt the utility of this identification), the analysis of the ways in which this is realized may allow us to discover the "logic" that these inferential processes follow. Or, as I would prefer to say, the logic of the phenomenal construction of reality. Such "logic" is perhaps not the same as the logic that the mind employs in making true inferences.

Let us look at Figures 1.1a and 1.1b. The first can be described as a group of eight angular figures and the second as ten parallelograms and rectangles, some of which overlap. If one says that both are Necker cubes from which parts have been removed (each is missing the parts of the other), this information may serve for "imagining" the two cubes, albeit with considerable difficulty; however, it remains almost impossible to "see" the two cubes.

However, by superimposing the patterns of Figure 1.2a, it becomes very simple to see the cubes. Thus one arrives at Figures 1.2b and 1.2c, in each of which one clearly sees a cube covered by three stripes. These two visual cubes are therefore the product of amodal completion. Through this mechanism the primary process goes beyond the information given, while with the same fundamental elements the secondary process is unable to construct the cube even by inference.

Or compare Figures 1.3a and 1.3b. At first sight they seem to have little in common, because the four pairs of black sectors (Figure 1.3c), present in both, are completed in different ways. In Figure 1.3a they make four disks under rectangles (Figure 1.3d)—that is, the nearest sectors go together—while in Figure 1.3b the completion operates as in Figure 1.3e—that is, the farthest-apart sectors go together. This completion depends directly on the type of figure-ground articulation that

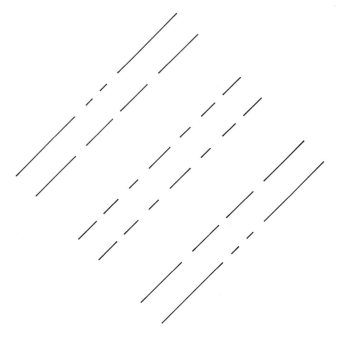

Figure 1.2a Adding these segments to the Figures 1.1a and 1.1b makes the cube visible.

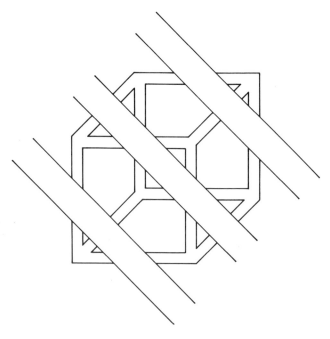

Figure 1.2b The cube is amodally completed behind the three opaque stripes and becomes perceptually *present*.

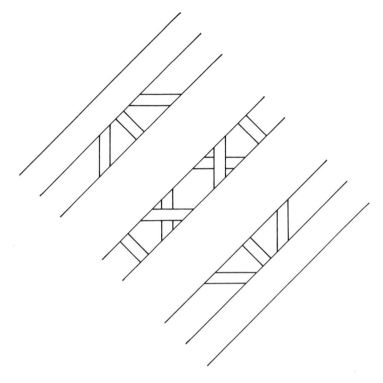

Figure 1.2c Amodal *presence* of the invisible cube of Figure 1.1b.

operates in each case: it is always realized behind the part of the field that takes the character of a figure. This happens even if the figure is produced by the completion of other regions and therefore lacks "real" contours, as in Figures 1.4a and 1.4b.

The same phenomenon occurs in Figures 1.5a and 1.5b. The four groups of black figures (Figure 1.5c) are unified in the four squares of Figure 1.5a (see Figure 1.5d) and in the disk and parts of the disk of Figure 1.5b (see Figure 1.5e).

All of these examples demonstrate that the interpolations of missing parts among given elements that are easy—even compelling— to make on the perceptual level do not take place when the same fundamental elements must be integrated through cognitive inference. Such visual interpolations obey their own precise rules, which cannot be modified by the intervention of inferential operations in the secondary process. One cannot see black disks in Figure 1.5a or a square in Figure 1.5b, just as one does not see the cube in Figures 1.1a and 1.1b. Herein lies the enormous difference between the two ways of going

Figure 1.3a Four black disks partially hidden by rectangles (see Figure 1.3d).

Figure 1.3b A black square partially hidden by a cross (see Figures 1.3c and 1.3e).

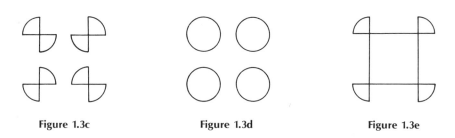

Figure 1.3c   Figure 1.3d   Figure 1.3e

beyond the information given: in the secondary process, going beyond the information given never implies a true perceptual effect.

If this is true, it seems to me that the convention of calling this type of inference "perceptual" is a dubious one. This type of inference is "perceptual" only in the sense that it operates on material present in direct visual experience. When I see PS.CHOL.GY and I easily read the word PSYCHOLOGY, I go beyond the given information by making a typical inference or cognitive interpolation. This does not, however, let me *see* the missing Y and O. Why, then, call this inference *perceptual* when it contains nothing perceptual? Probably because it mentally integrates a perceived fact, and because we are reluctant to admit the difference between *seeing* a letter, seeing it with our eyes, and merely imagining it.

But what do we gain by ignoring or underrating this difference? To "read" the configuration of Figure 1.6a as a number or a letter, according to the categorical set of the moment, does not visually transform the figure (a black vertical bar and a curve composed of two parts of a circle). I am dealing with the categorization or interpretation

Figure 1.4a Covering surfaces may be anomalous. In this figure, as well as in Figure 1.4b, the four patterns of Figure 1.3c are in isolation—that is, not adjacent to any "real" contour.

Figure 1.4b Here too the patterns of Figure 1.3c are amodally completed behind an anomalous surface, with a very different outcome than in Figure 1.4a.

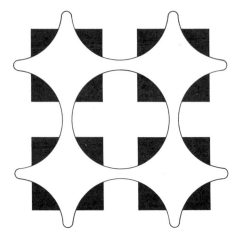

Figure 1.5a Amodal completion creates four black squares (see Figure 1.5d).

Figure 1.5b With the same black elements (see Figures 1.5c and 1.5e) only circular patterns are seen.

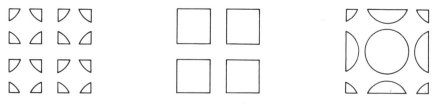

Figure 1.5c   **Figure 1.5d**   **Figure 1.5e**

of an already formed figure—that is, of something segregated in the visual field about which I can ask myself: what is it? what do I do with it? what do I call it? where do I put it? and so on. But whatever my answers, the visual gaps of the configuration remain as they are, while the effect of a filling-in based on the primary process will be characterized by a real amodal presence (Figure 1.6b).

The famous experiment of J. Bruner and A. Minturn (1955), and especially the use made of it, demonstrate that, sixty years after Max Wertheimer, the problem of visual organization, of the construction of phenomenal objects, is still not fully grasped and that many psychologists face it, even today, "first at the level of the next-higher story, that is, too late" (Metzger 1966; Arnheim 1969). To start from the next-higher story—that is, to study the secondary process—means not to be directly involved with perception, but with how thinking affects perceived objects. In other words, it means taking for granted the visual presence of objects that in the secondary process are analyzed, interpreted, and given significance, but to which nothing visual is added by this process.

That thinking operates in and upon perceived reality is a truism that hardly needs demonstration. But to affirm from this that perceived reality is also a product of thinking, seems to me not only an unauthorized but also a useless and perhaps even dangerous leap. To refuse to make distinctions because distinctions are difficult exposes one to the continual risk of creating confusion. And confusion is never useful.

Figure 1.6a A configuration that can be read either as the numeral 13 or as the character B (Bruner and Minturn 1955).

Figure 1.6b When amodal completion occurs, the outcome is more unambiguous: a partially covered B.

SEEING AND THINKING

If, therefore, the means of going beyond the information given are of two types—visual and nonvisual—does this mean that the rules that govern them also are different? As I have already stated, it seems to me that we must approach this question without presuppositions. To see and to think are normally two very distinct activities from a phenomenal point of view; we all know, for example, that it is one thing to look at an object and another to mentally solve an arithmetic equation. They are two activities that we experience very differently. In philosophical thinking there has often been a correspondence between this phenomenal difference and a sharp separation between these two fields of cognitive activity, involving a hierarchical distinction: perception gathers the raw material that thought elaborates, orders, and classifies, and from which it extracts the concepts that it uses in its various operations.

In opposition to this tendency to dichotomize there have been various attempts to eliminate or minimize the drastic distinction between perception and thought through the demonstration that, at least in principle, their functioning is analogous. One can, for example follow Jean Piaget by seeing perception as the matrix of thought, in the sense that the perceptual activity would be a primordial phase of the activity of thought. Or one can affirm, as R. Arnheim does, that all the typical procedures of thought, such as the comprehension of relationships, inferences, and formations of concepts are implicit in the act of seeing. And thus for Helmholtz and the neo-Helmholtzians of today, perceptions may be considered the *result* of the activity of thought, particularly of inferential processes or of unconscious judgments.

This way of approaching the relation between perception and thought undoubtedly has its fascination, and can play a heuristic role in the construction of a reasonable theory of cognitive processes. But it also presents certain risks, the greatest of which is that in giving a primary place to the undeniable analogies between the two processes, one may undervalue the equally obvious differences. In this way we run the risk of not seeing the true problems that belong to either field.

I shall try to demonstrate by means of concrete examples how an excessive preoccupation with what is common to the two processes, or an excessive faith in their common rules, can lead one to overlook some genuine problems.

To show how every act of seeing implies a visual judgment, Arnheim refers to the example of the disk set off-center in a square (Figure 1.7). One can prove that the disk is off-center by measuring its distance from each of the four sides, but these measurements and their analysis are basically useless, because the eye sees directly that the disk is not at the center of the square. One need not "think"; it is enough to "look." In the seeing a judgment is already implicit.

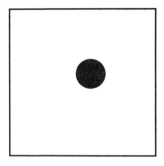

Figure 1.7   There is no need for any measurement in order to "see" that the point is off-center (Arnheim 1974).

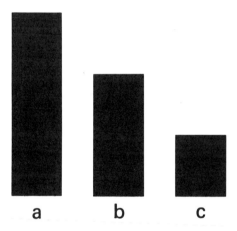

Figure 1.8   We see directly that A>C, without any need of considering the premises A>B, B>C.

Likewise, in the case of three objects of different sizes (Figure 1.8), I can reach the conclusion that A > C by comparing A > B and B >C. However, by perception this judgment is immediate: I "see" that A > C, without need of any intermediate stages.

In these cases, which can be multiplied infinitely, thinking and seeing lead to the same conclusions, and it therefore seems that they are capable of the same operations and that they function according to the same principles. But there are situations in which perception leads to results different from those of thinking, situations that thus suggest that the rules governing perception may not be the same as those governing thinking.

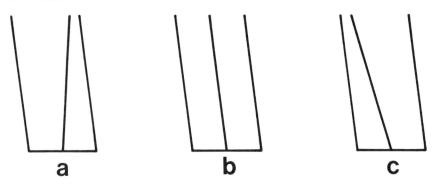

a   b   c

Figure 1.9 From Goldmeier (1972).

The definitions of the basic concepts in the two fields offer a useful means of comparison. Let us take as an example similarity, an important concept in both fields. In perception this is considered one of the principal factors of unification or grouping; similar elements tend to constitute a unity, to be experienced as belonging to the same group. But what, exactly, does "similar" mean? One can give several definitions that, in order not to be tautological, make use of some criterion that is not similarity itself. For example, two figures are more similar the greater the number of equal parts or elements they have in common and the fewer the differences between the unequal parts. Naturally such differences must always be determinable quantitatively.

Figure 1.10 From Goldmeier (1972).

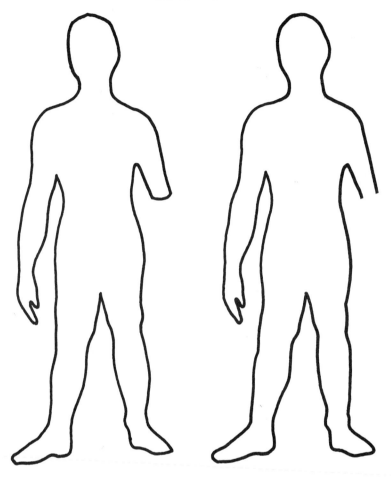

Figure 1.11a A complete picture of an incomplete man.

Figure 1.11b Here the incompleteness is on the perceptual level.

However, to offer a single example from E. Goldmeier (1972), if one is asked which of the two figures B and C, in Figure 1.9 bears a greater resemblance to Figure A, most observers agree that C is the more similar, even though, according to the definition, it bears the lesser resemblance.

Thus the criterion of partial identity does not always apply. One could perhaps propose a more comprehensive criterion, such as the identity of relationships or of proportions. But not even such an extended criterion always applies. If one must choose, in Figure 1.10, whether B or C is more similar to A, the choice normally falls on C and not on the rigorously proportional variant B.

From situations like these, where the logic of seeing does not seem to correspond exactly to that of thinking, Goldmeier constructed a series of splendid experiments for studying the conditions that determine the impression of greater or lesser similarity. Through them he discovered that to define phenomenal similarity as partial identity or as identity of proportions is not sufficient; it is necessary to resort to concepts, such as phenomenal goodness, that refer to essential—even if not quantifiable—properties of the perceived reality, and as such cannot be ignored simply because we are not yet capable of giving them a precise mathematical formulation or an elegant rational definition.

Another concept important for the discussion of both perception and thinking is completeness. The meaning of "complete" or "incomplete" can vary as one moves from one field to the other. Figure 1.11a represents a man without an arm—an incomplete man. But visually the drawing is complete; we see a man with an amputated arm. Figure 1.11b, however, is visually "incomplete" and lacking on the perceptual level; it is not finished. Figure 1.12a is incomplete as regards the concept of a face, while from a perceptual point of view one could not call it incomplete, since in what there is, everything is there. In Figure 1.12b there is also a perceptual incompleteness; the face tends to continue, to complete itself.

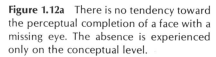

Figure 1.12a There is no tendency toward the perceptual completion of a face with a missing eye. The absence is experienced only on the conceptual level.

Figure 1.12b The face is *incomplete* on the perceptual level; from that arises the tendency to completion.

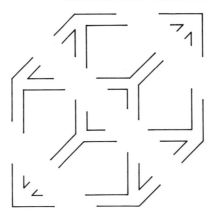

Figure 1.13 The *subtraction* of some parts from the patterns of Figure 1.1a makes them "incomplete"; that is, forces are released that allow the completion of the patterns. Now the cube has perceptual *presence*.

That the criteria of completion that are valid as regards thinking need not coincide with those active in perception is further demonstrated by comparing Figure 1.1a with Figure 1.13, which is constructed from the former by removing a certain number of line segments. By this means one has the anomalous appearance of three opaque stripes superimposed on a Necker cube, which in Figure 1.1a could not be seen. The formation of these anomalous planes is the consequence of the amodal completion of the interrupted contours of the cube. Obviously the patterns of Figure 1.1a are "complete" on the perceptual level—that is, they are white areas contoured by a black outline, and do not demand further completion. Thus they do not create those anomalous surfaces that in Figure 1.13 indicate an incompleteness on the perceptual level. From similar situations J. M. Kennedy (1974) and D. Piggins (1975) arrive at rather different conclusions.

Here, then, is another case in which it is clear that if we do not take account of the different meanings that "complete" and "incomplete" can assume in the realms of perception and thought, but, rather, take as valid for both only the meaning that applies to thinking, we risk remaining blind to the real perceptual problem.

A third concept is symmetry. An extremely strong tendency toward symmetry exists in thought, so much so that man discovers nature to be dominated entirely by laws of symmetry, even if, in many cases, one must suspect that he discovers what he himself puts there. In perception the tendency to symmetry, as an aspect of regularity, was assigned a role of primary importance by Wertheimer. Only recently has it been

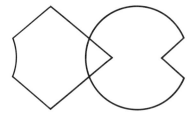

Figure 1.14a If the tendency toward maximal symmetry had the same relevance in perception as in thinking, this configuration would be seen as the juxtaposition of the two symmetrical patterns of Figure 1.14b.

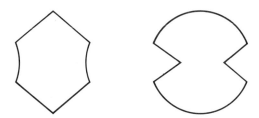

Figure 1.14b Figure 1.14a is formed by these two symmetrical patterns. Why is it so difficult to see them?

shown that this factor is perhaps less strong than it previously seemed, and that it is easily overcome by "continuity of direction" or "tendency to convexity" (see Chapter 5).

Figure 1.14a is experienced spontaneously as two superimposed figures, one round and the other angular. Why does one not also realize the equally possible solution of two perfectly symmetrical figures juxtaposed? (See Figure 1.14b.) Likewise, as the five crosses of Figure 5.10a are put near each other (Figure 5.10b), the original symmetry disappears. The continuity of direction yields a result that, in terms of the symmetry criterion, is much less satisfying than the first.

Evidently the tendency for symmetry is not so powerful in determining the organization of perceptual reality as one might suppose from the importance that it assumes in the realm of thought. Nonetheless, presuppositions derived from thought have managed to influence our expectation to find symmetry in perceptual phenomena, in a way that disguises the real problems of this area.

To the thesis that I have tried to suggest here—that it is epistemologically incorrect, and for the researcher even dangerous, to transfer to visual problems schemes explicitly drawn from the realm of thought—it may be useful to add some considerations regarding the "impossibilities" that exist in only one of the two fields.

First, what is possible in seeing may not be possible in thinking. Consider L. S. and R. Penrose's "impossible objects" (Figures 1.15, and 1.16). One has an impression of paradoxicality in observing them. But the impossibility does not concern perception—the figures, as a matter of fact, are seen. What is impossible is to imagine them realized in three-dimensional space, this space being considered from the standpoint of the logic of geometry. Therefore their proper name should be "unthinkable figures." The same is true of our perception of "impossible movements," such as those illustrated by Cesare Musatti (1924) with the display of Figure 1.17. If one spins the disk around its center, one sees the little circle turn around the large circle, even though there is not enough room for the passage of the little circle between the circle and the edge of the disk. Once again the impossibility consists in thinking that the little circle, while remaining on the plane of the disk, can turn around the large circle. But that is what one sees.

Second, it may be impossible to see what is easy to think. Here the examples are infinite, and I limit myself to one in which the separation between the two fields is particularly evident. In Figure 1.18a, which is the reproduction of a verticle rectangle of black thread set partly on a black horizontal rectangle, I succeed in seeing only the contrary: a black horizontal rectangle set on an outline rectangle that passes behind it. But I find no difficulty in "thinking" that the vertical rectangle is placed, as in fact it is, on top of the black horizontal rectangle. The same impossibility continues even if I break the surface of the horizontal rectangle and thus completely isolate the two sides of the vertical rectangle, as in Figure 1.18b. Here too the vertical rectangle passes phenomenally behind the striped rectangle, even when it is completely uncovered, as one can prove by tracing its perimeter with a finger or a pencil.

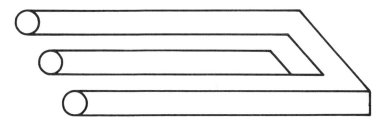

Figure 1.15 "Unthinkable" figure (L.S. and R. Penrose 1958).

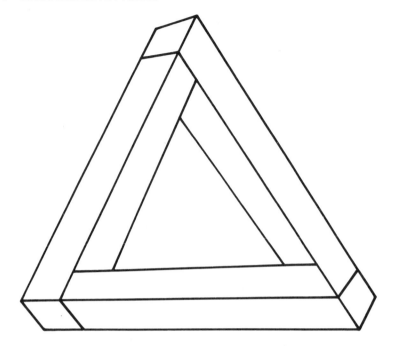

Figure 1.16 "Unthinkable" triangle (L.S. and R. Penrose 1958).

Figure 1.17 One sees what is impossible to conceive (Musatti 1924).

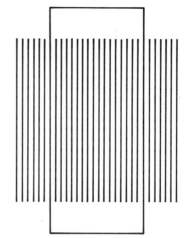

Figure 1.18a Why is one unable to see the rectangle outlined in black that is superimposed on the horizontal rectangle?

Figure 1.18b The vertical rectangle passes behind the striped rectangle.

Once again, showing the separation between what is possible in thought and impossible in perception can make us aware of the existence of a specific problem in perception: the conditions that determine the stratification of the visual field in several overlapping planes, a problem that risks not being recognized if one takes for granted an identical functioning of thought and perception.

At this point I would like to add a clarification. I do not want to give the impression of wishing to go back to the clear separation and hierarchical distinction between thinking and seeing that I stated earlier. The fact that seeing and thinking are two very different activities on the phenomenal level need not mean that we may not discover that fundamentally they share the same principles in their functioning. But finding cases in which the two activities seem to follow the same laws does not mean that these similarities are confirmed. The fact that one can indicate other cases in which these similarities do not occur can suggest that the similarities, even if they are more numerous than the differences, represent fortuitous coincidences, and that in fact the two fields are regulated by different laws.

The examples that I have offered seem to indicate that the eye reasons—if one should wish to say that it reasons—in its own fashion. And it seems to me of dubious value to expand the meaning of a concept (in this case, that of "reasoning") beyond certain limits. Apart from possible—but by no means certain—advantages of economy or of conceptual elegance that may derive from considering the functioning of the two activities in the same way, there are the possibly greater disadvantages existing in a certain loss of heuristic capacity and in failing to point out important problems.

2

PERCEPTION, PAST EXPERIENCE, AND THE "IMPOSSIBLE EXPERIMENT"

The effect of past experience on the interpretation of our perceptual world is beyond question. The familiarity that objects have for us, the special meaning they have in a person's private world, and above all their demand character are the result of the number and kinds of experiences we have had with them—that is, of our differing personal histories. There is, however, less agreement about the influence that past experience exerts on other characteristics of phenomenal objects, such as their shape, color, size, movement, and, even more basically, their formation into objects as such—that is, on the processes that articulate the multiplicity of stimuli into distinct perceptual objects.

There are two important contrasting theses regarding the influence of past experience. According to the first, past experience as such exerts a determinant influence on perceptual organization; the second limits considerably the role of this "empirical" factor. Neither of the two theses has clearly prevailed over the other, and the situation is still far from clear. Some have tried to "solve" the problem once and for all by declaring that it does not exist. Cesare Musatti (1964) has provided a brilliant line of reasoning in this regard. He claims that if this were a real scientific issue, sooner or later it would be solved in the way that all such problems are solved: by appealing to facts and experiment. But,

Gaetano Kanizsa. 1969. "Perception, Past Experience, and the 'Impossible Experiment'." *Acta Psychologica* 31: 66–96.

according to him, it is illusory to believe that such a solution is forthcoming on this question because there are no "crucial experiments" that can be appealed to. The person who persists in trying to find an answer at the empirical level has not yet understood that crucial experiments regarding this problem are impossible, not because of practical difficulties but in principle.

Musatti goes on to point out that if we consider the case of the perceptual "constancies," we must agree, because they are facts that we can verify empirically, that we see objects through the mediation of what is projected on the retina; that these projections are continuously changing in shape, size, intensity, and other characteristics; and that, in spite of all this, we experience a world of objects that, far from behaving like their corresponding retinal projections, are relatively constant and stable. We might assert that the disposition to see the objects of the world as "constant" is "learned," because the objects that surround us from birth are in fact stable with respect to their various characteristics; but we might also affirm the opposite: that these constancies are due to an innate tendency to select from the continuous flow of changing stimuli that which is "invariant" and, thus, makes possible the formation of phenomenal objects that are permanent in time and constant in properties.

According to Musatti, the decision between these two abstract alternatives is a matter of personal preference, because in order to perform the "impossible" crucial experiment, we would either have to create a world in which there were no "constant" objects or have to modify ourselves so as to perceive the world in a different way. Both alternatives are evidently unrealizable. Musatti concludes that the problem as posed is actually a pseudo problem, one of the many insoluble antinomies that fill the history of philosophical and scientific thought.

I cannot agree with such a radical conclusion, first of all because it results from a line of reasoning whose premises do not seem to me to be completely well-grounded, and second, because it is refuted by facts. The premises are not well-grounded because the hypothesis of greatly modifying the usual conditions under which we perceive objects, creating an environment in which there are not solid and steady objects and where the other typical conditions of perception (acoustic, kinesthetic, gravitational, orientational) are also deeply altered, is not absurd and impossible to carry out. Attempts to perform experiments of this sort have been made, from the *Ganzfeld* of W. Metzger (1930) to the more recent ones of J. E. Hochberg, W. Triebel, and G. Seaman (1951); from the experiments on systematic disorientation and distortion of the visual field done by I. Kohler (1951) to the "stabilized" images of R. M. Pritchard, M. Heron, and D. O. Hebb

(1960); and from the imposing amount of research on sensory deprivation to the experiments on the effects of hallucinogenic drugs.

Musatti's conclusion is also refuted by the facts, because a great number of experimental situations where empirical and autochthonous factors are brought into conflict with very clear results can be found not only in gestalt work, but also in that of Musatti himself, as well as that of P. Renvall (1929), K. von Fieandt (1938; 1949), and A. Ames (1946), to name but a few.

The fact that there are wide differences of opinion about the meaning of these experiments does not, in my opinion, allow us to conclude that they are not valid. We cannot, of course, claim that these experiments are decisive or crucial. In science *experimenta crucis*, an invention of philosophers, do not exist, just as absolute certitudes do not. In science we proceed by successive approximations, and experiments serve not to prove that a hypothesis is correct but rather, more modestly, that it is not false. In what follows I want to present and comment briefly upon some new situations that I believe show that (a) in this field significant, if not crucial, experiments are possible, and (b) the results of these experimental situations do not seem to be compatible with an extreme empiricist explanation of perceptual organization.

HOW OBJECTS ARE MADE INVISIBLE

Animal mimicry and camouflage, used in wartime to hide soldiers, vehicles, or buildings from enemy attack, offer a great number of examples of how an object can be completely masked, even when it is "out in the open" and, so to speak, "under the nose" of those who are searching for it. Metzger dedicates two chapters of his *Gesetze des Sehens* (1974) to an analysis of different principles according to which animals camouflage themselves, and he shows that in all cases visual rules are operating that favor a segmentation of the observer's field in such a way that other objects appear in the place of what is being sought. But such cases of camouflage, amazing as they are, are not, in and of themselves, decisive evidence against empiricist explanations of perceptual structure, because even though the "hidden" objects are parts of our everyday experience (animals, for instance), so are the objects that are seen in their place (tree trunks, leaves, and rocks, for instance). Nevertheless, the masking of familiar figures has been used by many authors to criticize explanations of perceptual organization that are exclusively empiricist.

A classic example of these demonstrations is the researches of K. Gottschaldt (1926), but Max Wertheimer (1923) had already shown how

Figure 2.1a Five white squares on a black background or four black arrows on a white background?

Figure 2.1b The arrows of Figure 2.1a in a situation that is no longer reversible.

a well-known word can be perfectly masked by placing its mirror image just above or below it. Figures 2.1a, 2.2a, and 2.3 are constructed according to such principles.

Figure 2.2a Symmetrization masks well-known letters and numerals. (See Figure 2.2b).

Figure 2.2b

Figure 2.3 Here too the use of mirror images of letters make words invisible.

If we analyze the conditions in which masking of well-known shapes occurs, we find that the masking does not depend on the fact that the figures are presented in an unusual context or on the mere addition of extra lines. In fact, in Figure 2.4 the letter R and the numeral 3, and in Figure 2.5 the printed words, are all perfectly recognizable, even though in unusual contexts and crossed by a number of irrelevant lines. This is not the case in Figures 2.2a and 2.3, in which the masking is complete. We must conclude from this that familiar shapes are masked when the addition of other lines creates conditions that favor the formation of other unities based on such nonempirical factors as closure, symmetry, and good continuation.

Figure 2.4 The unusual context is not responsible for the masking.

WITHOUTMOTIVATION

Figure 2.5 The words of Figure 2.3 are now visible even though they overlap.

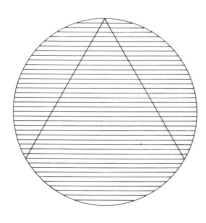 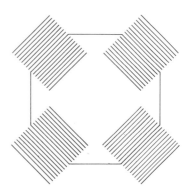

Figure 2.6a The base of the triangle is "swallowed up" by the homogeneous array of horizontal parallel lines (Galli and Zama 1931).

Figure 2.6b The masking of an octagon (Galli and Zama 1931).

Some very effective masking situations were devised by A. Galli and A. Zama (1931) on the basis of the patterns used by Gottschaldt. Two particularly impressive examples are reproduced in Figures 2.6a and 2.6b. In Figure 2.6a the base of the triangle, although it remains in place and is not crossed by other lines, disappears as the "base," thus destroying the triangle as a visual object. What happens here could be called a case of "social conformity of a line"; it is detached from the triangle, absorbed by the array of parallel lines, and obliged to change completely its function and phenomenal appearance. The same may be said about the sides of the octagon, which are so well absorbed by the parallel lines that a square appears, the vertexes of which are amodally completed "under" the parallel lines, as if the situation were that shown in Figure 2.7.

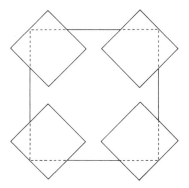

Figure 2.7 The *perceptually real* square that replaces the *physically real* octagon of Figure 2.6b.

In some situations that I devised (Figures 2.8a, 2.9a and 2.10a) the same principle prevails as in the patterns of Galli and Zama. The little church is no longer seen as soon as the overlay with the black outline is removed (see Figures 2.8b, 2.9b and 2.10b). It is literally "split up" because each of its elements enters a different "society" of parallel or radial lines.

These examples offer some advantages over those described earlier. In Figures 2.1a, 2.2a, and 2.3 the "hidden" objects are not generally seen by a naive observer, though once their presence is known, these familiar shapes are easily abstracted from their larger context. This is very difficult in the examples from Galli and Zama and from Gottschaldt. In the latter, however, the "hidden" figures do not have the advantage of being more familiar than the equally regular and familiar figures that phenomenally appear instead. Neither of these objections applies to my examples. In fact, (a) it is impossible to "see" the little

Figure 2.8a It is impossible to "see" the (known) outline of the church embedded in the (never seen before) configuration.

church even after having been repeatedly shown the place where it is, once the overlay with the outline is removed; and (b) what is seen instead of the church is neither more "familiar" not more "regular" than the church; on the contrary, what appears instead has probably never been seen before.

Thus, while from an atomistic point of view all the conditions are present for the perception of a familiar shape, the field is so organized

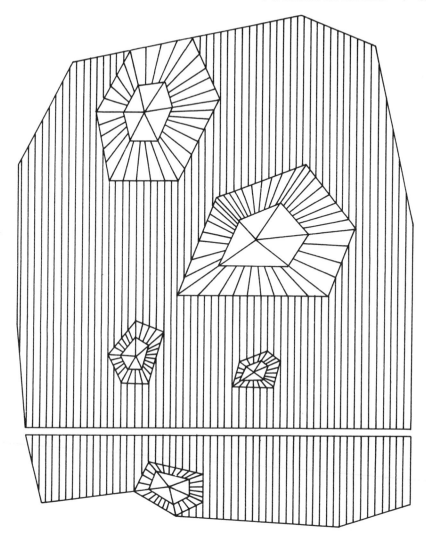

Figure 2.8b

that an unknown, somewhat bizarre pattern is seen, a pattern that is neither orderly nor symmetrical. It is not true, therefore, that a perceptual structure, in order to be stable and compelling, must be geometrically regular and symmetrical. This is a very common misconception. Perceptual order is not geometrical order. In fact, most of the objects in our phenomenal world are quite stable and unambiguous even though they are not regular in a geometrical sense.

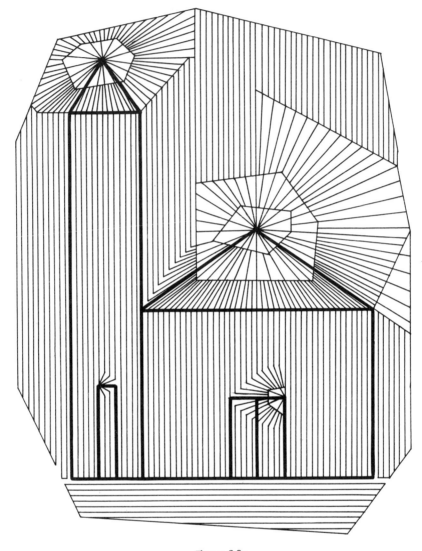

Figure 2.9a

WHAT IS IN FRONT AND WHAT IS BEHIND?

In a situation like that shown in Figure 2.11, which can be described in physical terms as an irregular, chromatically homogeneous zone, observers usually see the zone as split into two figures, a square and a triangle, one in front of the other. This "in front of/behind" relationship is relatively indeterminate. As in other reversible situations, the

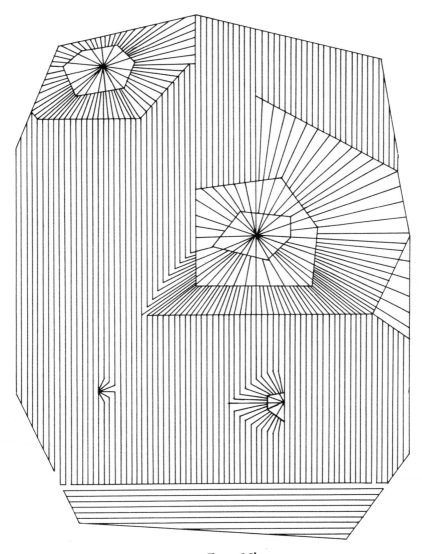

Figure 2.9b

square is in front for some observers and behind for others, and the relationship sometimes alternates periodically for a given observer, either spontaneously or through a modification in attention. Is it possible to find situations in which such reversibility is eliminated and the perceptual effect is thus more stable? This problem has been experimentally analyzed by G. Petter (1956), who succeeded in isolating the principal conditions that determine this relationship between

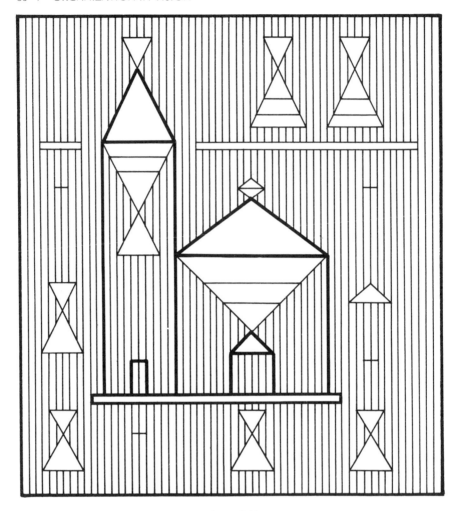

Figure 2.10a

figures. He did this by using regions of stimulation that were physically homogeneous but phenomenally split into two regions, one in front and one behind. He also proposed a very convincing hypothesis to explain the phenomenon by showing that, other conditions being equal, the figure that is larger, less articulated, and in motion is perceived as being "in front of" the other.

Thus, in Figure 2.12 the large rectangle is seen by most observers as in front of the annulus and of the ribbon.

According to the hypothesis suggested by Petter, the perceptual organization of our visual field is determined by the "ease" with which amodal and anomalous contours are formed. The latter require a

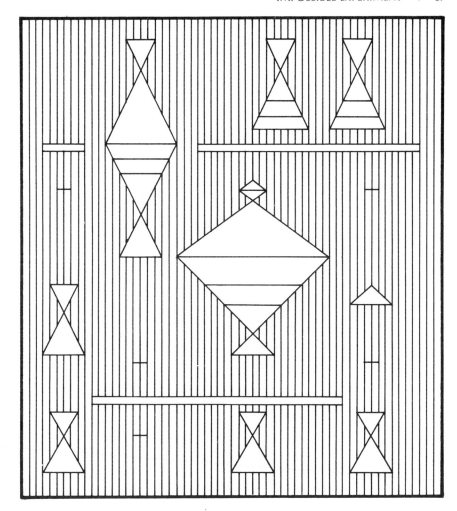

Figure 2.10b

greater amount of energy than the former; therefore, the figure that requires the relatively smaller anomalous completion is seen as being in front. Generally that figure is the relatively larger, as can be seen in Figure 2.14.

We can see how strong the Petter effect is in Figures 2.15–2.18, which I have prepared. They help to show that it is not impossible to study experimentally the effect of past experience on perceptual organization.

In these situations past experience and autochthonous factors of perceptual organization are put directly into conflict (which is not the case with the squares, disks, and crosses used by Petter, all of which are

Figure 2.11 Modal contours cross a chromatically homogeneous zone. Visual lines can emerge without a corresponding discontinuity in stimulation. The triangle can lie in front of the square or vice versa.

Figure 2.12 The situation is no more reversible; the annulus and the ribbon pass behind the rectangle.

Figure 2.13 Another instance of the splitting of a homogeneous region into two overlapping surfaces. Thinner ends pass behind thicker ones.

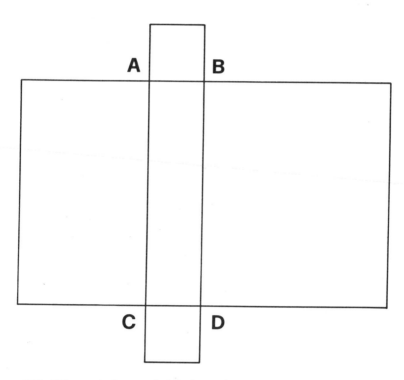

Figure 2.14 If the vertical rectangle is in front, the *modal* contours are AC and BD, and the *amodal* contours are AB and CD—that is, the length of modal contours is greater than the length of amodal contours. The contrary is true if the horizontal rectangle is in front (AC + BD < AB + CD). The latter organization is perceptually privileged.

Figure 2.15 The fishing rod passes behind the sail.

Figure 2.16 The fencer's sword pierces the referee.

Figure 2.17 The man and the woman are entangled in the fence.

more or less equally familiar and regular). The fishing rod, contrary to the expectations that we may have had on the basis of our past experience and to any efforts we may make to "set" ourselves accordingly, refuses to pass in front of the sail. Yet, since the chromatic zone that represents the two different objects (sail and rod) is homogeneously colored, nothing prevents them from splitting according to our experience and expectation.

This way of splitting does not occur, because what is decisive in this case, as in the others, is not past experience but the forces of organization described in Petter's hypothesis. The fishing rod is thinner than the sail, so it is "forced" to pass behind even though it suggests a humorous effect to the observer; similarly the fencer's sword pierces the referee several meters away, the umbrella is threaded through the girl's hair, and the man and the woman are strangely entangled in the fence. All these figures seem absurd, but this does not change the in front of/behind relationships imposed by the figural conditions. The past experience factor is unable to exert sufficient influence to render the figures more sensible.

PARADOXICAL TRANSPARENCY

The problem presented by situations where the impression of transparency occurs is similar to that presented by the superposition

Figure 2.18 The umbrella is threaded through the girl's hair.

relationships discussed in the preceding section. Petter repeated his experiments by projecting light gray, rather than black, shadows. To do this he pasted patterns made of nearly transparent celluloid on the lenses of the projector. When the two shadows are not superimposed, they appear to be two opaque, gray surfaces. But as soon as they are partially superimposed, one of them loses its opaqueness and appears to be transparent and in front of the other.

In this case as well the problem arose of which of the two surfaces is on top of the other and, consequently, becomes transparent. According to the observations made by Petter, the conditions determining the phenomenal transparency of one surface rather than the other are practically the same as those determining the in front of/behind relationship with respect to opaque surfaces (in which a chromatically homogeneous region split into two superimposed planes).

Therefore it should be possible to put these factors of transparency into conflict with experiential factors, and thus to compare their relative strength in the organization of our perceptual environment. If the factors pointed out by Petter are stronger than our past experience, it should be possible to create situations in which objects become transparent even though we "know" from experience that they are opaque, and vice versa.

Figures 2.19 and 2.20 show just such situations. In fact, many observers see the knife and the leaves as transparent and in front of the glass and the bottle. They also have an impresssion of oddity and absurdity, because the effect is both unexpected on the basis of everyday experience and in conflict with the perspective information on depth given by the figure. As in the situations discussed in the preceding section, the impression of absurdity is strong evidence that in these cases the perceptual organization imposes itself against expectation and past experience. The object made out of opaque material

Figure 2.19 The transparent knife.

Figure 2.20 Transparent leaves.

becomes transparent because on structural/figural grounds it must be in front, even though from an experiential point of view the opposite should be the case.

The surprise of the observers and their saying, as they did in the case of the fisherman and of the fencer, that there must be some mistake in the picture are evidence for the genuineness of the effect. Of course these observations are valid only in those situations in which the other variable, which Fabio Metelli (1967) has shown to be important in the occurrence of impressions of transparency (namely, the brightness relationships between the surfaces of the two objects and the common or "shared" region in which they are superimposed), is held relatively constant and favorable to the paradoxical effect. But this factor too is a nonexperiential one, and thus entirely in line with the principal point of this study, the relative importance of autochthonous structural factors in comparison with so-called experiential factors when the two are put into conflict.

EUROPE UPSIDE DOWN

The experiment involving Figure 2.21 was conducted with 49 university students. This configuration (50 by 70 centimeters) was hung on a classroom wall near the professor's desk during the first period in a

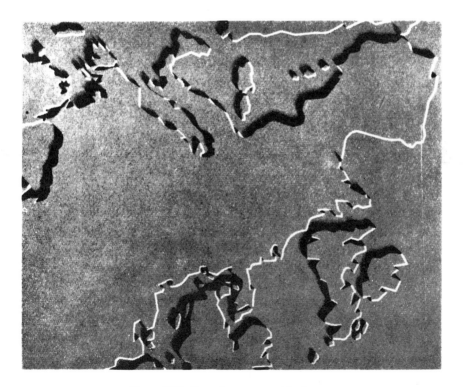

Figure 2.21 Turn the page upside down.

psychology course. At the end of the lesson the students were asked to write a description of this figure that they had had the opportunity to observe during the previous hour.

Only seven of the subjects recognized the figure as being a map of Europe turned upside down, with the seas and oceans, rather than the continents and islands, in relief: "I see a map of Europe. The water, rather than the land, is in relief. This reminds me of the negative of a photograph. I was struck by it as soon as I came into the room. The white line could be misleading."

Twenty subjects had the impression that it was a map, but were not able to say what it represented because they perceived the bodies of water as being land masses as a result of their being in relief: "This design looks like an aerial photograph of a coastal region. The coast is very jagged, with lots of lagoons and small bodies of water." "I see a map at the center of which there is a large body of water. At the periphery there are numerous peninsulas with lakes or inland seas." "It's a map of a sea, its jagged coastline, the sort having a lot of fjords." "Some irregular figures whose borders are represented by white lines or by shadows (perhaps in relief). To better describe the form of the design, I might add that the appearance is that of a monochromatic map."

In the descriptions by the remaining 22 subjects, not only is there no reference to Europe, but it seems that the figure was not even seen as a map: "Gray background crossed by thin, irregular white lines and by lines of variable thickness that are somewhat wider than the white lines. These lines give rise to surfaces in relief." "Gray rectangle with jagged white lines crossing, at various points, long black zones of differing forms and sizes." "It's a piece of dark gray paper on which appear some black and white lines; some of them broken, some closed, and others open. The lines, being very marked, give the impression of a drawing in relief." "There is a rectangular piece of gray plastic in relief. The form is quite jagged with prominences, indentations, and protrusions. In the middle, however, there is a rather large, flat, irregular surface."

These results may be variously interpreted, but it is clear that, given the scholastic level of the subjects and the considerable amount of observation time that they were allowed, the occurrence of recognition in only 7 out of 49 cases (less than 15 percent) does not lend much support to past experience as a determinant factor in the structuring of our perceptual world.

It might be held that the lack of recognition is essentially due to the upside-down orientation of the map, and thus to the lack of familiarity with such configurations. But it certainly cannot be claimed that the other configuration, in which the seas and the land masses exchange roles, is any more familiar. How, then, are we to explain the fact that 42 subjects, even not seeing Europe, saw a precise configuration, though they said they had never seen it before?

Once again the explanation is not to be sought in subjects' greater or lesser familiarity with the material but, rather, in the forces that determine the figure-ground relationships of the field—that is, in the forces that give the character of an "object" to certain areas (which are thus delimited by a margin and have a form) while leaving other areas "empty," without margins or form, in the background.

In the present situation the parts in relief become the "objects" or "figures," with a well-defined, though completely unfamiliar, form, whereas all the rest of the configuration is simply the background, or the environment, in which the "objects" are found. Being background, then, subjectively it has no form and thus is not "recognizable," even though objectively it has a form that should be quite familiar.

The problem remains of determining which factors in these situations lead to the perception of surface relief and depression, and to their sudden reversal when the configuration is turned upside down. Wertheimer considered situations of this type of be evidence for the existence of an "empirical factor" in perceptual organization. Von Fieandt (1938), who did a great deal of experimental research on this problem, and Metzger (1974), in his interpretation of L. Lauenstein's (1938) results, do not seem to share Wertheimer's opinion.

However, leaving aside for the moment the problem of what causes the relief structure, the fact remains that when this structure is presented in such a way that the bodies of water are in relief and the land masses are concave, for 85 percent of the subjects a map of Europe, well-known, familiar, seen thousands of times, does not exist in their phenomenal experience.

The upside-down position certainly exerts some influence on the perceptual result, giving the configuration the appearance of a set of irregular and unfamiliar lines that have never been seen before. But this result depends only in small part on lack of familiarity. What is much more important is the physiognomic transformation that disorientation on the retina produces in certain meaningful configurations (see Chapter 13).

This research must be continued by separating these two variables, the upside-down position and the inversion of conventional relief, which in Figure 2.21 act in the same direction. Thus it will be necessary to construct a plastic model of Europe and photograph it with illumination coming from a direction exactly opposite that in Figure 2.24, so as to obtain a configuration in which the landmasses are seen as concave and the bodies of water as in relief when this map is shown in the usual orientation, and vice versa when it is presented upside down.

Figure 2.22a The device seen from in front:
A = two coaxial pivots (see the details in Fi-
gure 2.23) on which fixed objects move in
opposite directions.
B = swinging pivot.
C = box for the electric motor.

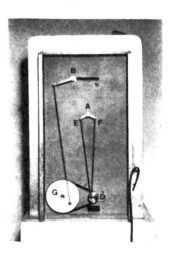

Figure 2.22b The device seen from behind:
D = driving pulley with eccentric.
E and F = swinging arms jointed with
the coaxial pivots in A.
G = pulley with eccentric for the
swings of pivot B.
The amplitude of the oscillations of
the pivots in A can be varied by modifying the eccentric's position and the
length of the arms E and F.

Figure 2.23 Details of the two pulleys
that bear the objects fixed to the coaxial
pivots in A. The pulleys can be fixed to
the pivots in order to obtain every
combination of oscillations of the two
objects (see Figure 2.24).

THE DANCING OSTRICH

The experiment that we will now examine is rather difficult to describe. With the apparatus shown in Figures 2.22a, 2.22b, and 2.23, two objects ("legs") can be made to oscillate on the coaxial pivots at A such that they move in opposite directions, the one passing in front of the other. At the same time two other objects, fixed on pivot B, can also be oscillated.

With this apparatus it is possible to vary the frequency of oscillation over a wide range (from 26 to 100 oscillations per minute) as well as the amplitude (see Figure 2.22b). In addition, by changing the point at which the objects are fixed on their respective pivots, it is possible to modify the relative position of their trajectories (see Figure 2.24).

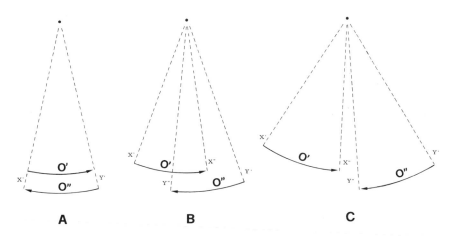

Figure 2.24 Three possible combinations of the oscillations of the two pivots and their respective objects:

> a = the trajectories completely superposed: when O_1 is in X_1, O_2 is in Y_1; when O_1 is in Y_1, O_2 is in X_1.
> b = the trajectories partially superposed: O_1 and O_2 leave X_1 and Y_1 at the same time and arrive in X_2 and Y_2 at the same time.
> c = the trajectories have no point of contact; and the objects never superpose. When O_1 is in X_1, O_2 is in Y_1; when O_1 is in X_2, O_2 is in Y_2.

We may attach the two "legs" on pivot A as shown in Figure 2.25a and the two "arms" on pivot B (see Figure 2.24B) and, finally, the "jacket" so that it appropriately covers the region between the two arms and the point at which the two legs are attached (Figure 2.25c).

If this apparatus is set into motion, the little man begins to move his arms and legs, and one would expect to see him "walk" more or less

Figure 2.25a

Figure 2.25b

Figure 2.25c

rapidly. Instead, a rather strange thing happens: he does not walk but, rather, begins to strike his legs together rhythmically, as if he were dancing. In other words, even though both of his legs objectively perform complete trajectories (as shown in part A of Figure 2.24), phenomenally they seem to do something quite different: each seems to return to the end point of the path from which it began after encountering the other leg at the midpoint. Thus, one leg appears to remain permanently on the left side and the other permanently on the right (Figure 2.26).

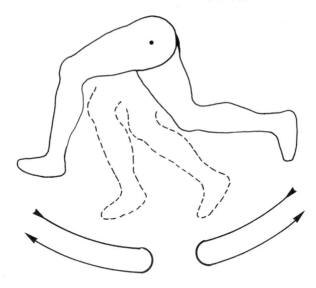

Figure 2.26 How the movement of the two legs actually swinging as in combination a of Figure 2.24 is "seen."

The perceptual result is the comic impression of a man hopping about as if he were doing gymnastics. At a certain point one has the impression that the two shoes never even overlap but, rather, that the tip of the rear shoe gives a little kick to the heel of the front one and then returns to its starting point. This impression is not changed even if a variation is introduced that ought to give additional support to the "walking" impression: if we make the man, while moving his legs, move forward at an appropriate velocity. We did this by having the apparatus advance on specially prepared rails and by adding a "floor" under the man's feet that remains in place with respect to the apparatus and the man.

The effect is even more comic if, instead of a man, we make an ostrich do this little dance (see Figure 2.27).

By appropriately varying the relative positions of the two legs— establishing, for example, a trajectory of the sort shown in part B of Figure 2.24—new "dance steps" may be obtained: for instance, rhythmic alternation of a short step and a long step schematically described in Figure 2.28a.

If a small white or colored disk is pasted on one of the two shoes (Figure 2.29), yet another amusing phenomenon occurs: the disk "jumps" from one shoe to the other while the legs continue to perform the same movements as before. Thus, the disk appears alternately on the back and the front shoes. This variation was added in the belief that

Figure 2.27

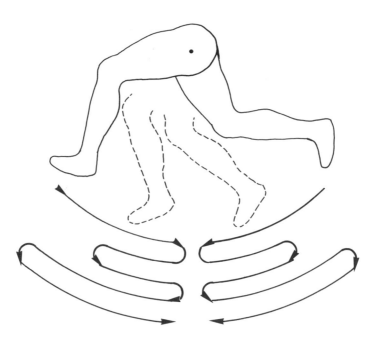

Figure 2.28 Phenomenal movements of the two legs oscillating as in Figure 2.24B. From the top to the bottom, the amplitude of the sequence of "steps" is represented.

Figure 2.29

it would be sufficient to make the feet phenomenally pass beyond the point of their encounter, thus making manifest their objective movement. Instead, although what they were doing was not familiar or common (as, for example, walking is), and therefore would not be expected, the feet continued to pass the disk back and forth—an extremely unusual thing, probably never before witnessed by most of the observers.

Ultimately, in order to make evident the actual and perfectly normal activity of the legs, it was necessary to change the color of a very large portion of one of them.

I have not conducted systematic research on these phenomena, investigating in detail the numerous variables that may be involved: frequency and amplitude of the oscillations, coloration, illumination, fixation point of visual attention, and so on. What has principally interested me in this context has been the fact that, in a situation where a particular "normal" perceptual impression is not only possible but to be expected, there occur instead, in an extremely compelling fashion, other perceptual responses that are unexpected because they are less familiar or even paradoxical.

Everyone to whom I have shown these situations has seen (with some individual variability as regards the optimal conditions of observation) the man or the ostrich leap in this very curious fashion, and not walk. In fact, this impression was so compelling that many of the observers, in order to be convinced that the legs did not jump back to their original end point at the moment of contact, but actually did pass one another, had to approach to within a few centimeters of the apparatus when it was well illuminated and operating at a very slow rate. And even so, as soon as they took two steps backward, the original kinetic organization returned. As curious as they may have found it, they could not resist the impression of the little leaps, even though they "knew" that in fact they were not occurring.

Once again, then, we find a situation in which past experience, "knowing," and subjective set are incapable of structuring the perceptual experience. Instead, the impression that occurs is *imposed* by the structure of the situation.

What are the perceptual laws that determine this particular solution to this situation? In his analysis of the factors that underlie the conservation of "phenomenal identity" in a moving object, Metzger (1934) observed that two objects in movement have a tendency to follow trajectories that do not cross one another, provided that in order to do so they are not obliged to alter some other important characteristic, such as color, form, or velocity. M. Bosinelli, R. Canestrari, and G. F. Minguzzi (1960) have shown that this tendency to avoid trajectories that intersect is even more pronounced in stroboscopic movement.

In the case of the little man who dances, the structural conditions (identity of color and form, and velocity of the two legs) do not require the crossing of the trajectories; this is required only by past experience and expectation. The result is a compelling impression of nonintersecting movements in spite of what past experience might lead one to expect.

3

GESTALT PSYCHOLOGY:
WHAT IT IS NOT

For a theory of any generality, there usually exists, in addition to its authentic, canonical form, a simplified version, more or less distorted, that is the result of oversimplifications of its basic assumptions, inappropriate generalizations of its concepts, and overemphasis of relatively unimportant details or hypotheses. Thus one can understand certain negative reactions to the theory as well as the inapplicability of its concepts in situations for which they were not intended or in which they make no sense.

With respect to gestalt theory there is a whole host of such misunderstandings and trivialization, not only among intelligent laymen who have only a general interest in scientific psychology but even among professional psychologists. Indeed, its most widespread image is the result of a combination of distorted commonplaces and stereotypic definitions current in more or less scientific discussions and passed from one general treatise to another, seeming to be a faithful representation of the theory if only because of the frequency of repetition. Few take the trouble to study closely what actually has been said by the theory's proponents.

It may be useful, then, to examine some of these misinterpretations that, considering their persistence and their diffusion, bear witness to a

---

Gaetano Kanizsa. 1978. "La teoria della gestalt: distorsioni e fraintendimenti." In *Psicologia della Gestalt e Psicologia Cognitivista*, ed. G. Kanizsa and P. Legrenzi, pp. 39-61. Bologna: Il Mulino.

secondhand acquaintance with the ideas, the reasoning, and the experimental work of gestalt theorists and researchers.

I shall discuss some of these points, selecting those that seem to me to illustrate the more misleading and systematic inaccuracies.

TRANSLATION OF "GESTALT"

There is a terminological problem that may seem insignificant at first sight but that has led to considerable confusion: there is no adequate translation in English (nor in French or Italian) of the German word "Gestalt." Unfortunately it has long been translated as "form," a word whose inadequacy has led to numerous ambiguities. "Gestalt" ought to be translated as "organized structure," as distinguished from "aggregate," "heap," or simple "summation." When it is appropriately translated, the accent is on the concept of "organization" and of a "whole" that is *orderly, rule-governed, nonrandom.* This concept is opposed to that of a merely *arbitrary, random,* and *unstructured* grouping. But in addition to its being used to describe the product of a process of organization, the term "gestalt" also indicates the structural properties of the process itself.

The term "organism" could be used, but it too is inadequate because, in its most frequent usage, it refers to a particular kind of gestalt (plant or animal). Similarly, the use of "form" is inappropriate because form is only one of the attributes of a gestalt.

GESTALT PSYCHOLOGY IS BASICALLY A PSYCHOLOGY OF PERCEPTION

There is no question that the phenomena of perception have been emphasized by gestaltists and have been the object of their best-known experiments. One-third of K. Koffka's *Principles of Gestalt Psychology* (1935) is devoted to an analysis of behavioral field–that is, to perceptual problems. But the other two-thirds is concerned with general theoretical questions, as well as with the problems of other areas of psychology, covering the entire gamut from learning to personality and social psychology. It must not be forgotten that Max Wertheimer's most important book is not on perception but on productive thinking (1920), and that two of the outstanding examples of gestalt research and theory also deal with this problem: K. Duncker's *On Problem-Solving* (1945) and W. Koehler's *Intelligenzprüfungen an Menschenaffen* (1921). Moreover, Koehler did not restrict himself to problems of perception and thinking. His contributions range from the philosophy of values to brain physiology and animal psychology, fields in each of which he sought to demonstrate the applicability of the ideas of gestalt theory. In addition, the principles of gestalt theory have been used by many to study a wide range of psychological issues: memory and learning (Wulf 1922; Zeigarnik 1927; Restorff 1933; Luchins 1942; Katona 1940), personality dynamics (Lewin 1935; Birenbaum 1930; Dembo 1931; Karsten 1928), social psychology (Lewin 1951; Asch 1952; Heider 1958; Brown 1936; Sherif and Sherif, 1969; Krech and Crutchfield 1948), psychology of expression and of art (Arnheim 1949; Metzger 1962) developmental psychology (Lewin 1931; Koffka 1928). No specific attempt to apply gestalt theory has been made in psycholinguistics and psychopathology.

If, then, gestalt theory is a very general system of psychological concepts that can be used in the study and understanding of virtually any aspect of experience and behavior, it remains to be explained how the erroneous idea has developed that it is limited almost exclusively to phenomena of perception. Perceptual, and especially visual, phenomena proved to be particularly suitable for demonstrating the action of gestalt principles and the fertility of gestalt methods and concepts. For these reasons the original experimental work was done in this area and, as a consequence, perception was strongly emphasized in the first general explications of the theory, partly because of the abundance of available visual demonstrations and partly because of their greater persuasive force.

It seems to me that, in addition to being more persuasive, these demonstrations have had such a "dazzling" effect that the coupling of gestalt and perception continues to be widespread.

GESTALT THEORY IS A REDUCTIONIST THEORY

One of the arguments frequently raised against gestalt theory is that it attempts to explain psychological phenomena in terms of physiological processes and according to principles that, in the final analysis, belong to physics. Thus, gestaltists have been accused of "physicalism" and of materialistic reductionism for having proposed the hypothesis of psychophysical isomorphism. In order to refute the assumption of atomistic and mechanistic theories in psychology, Koehler tried to identify in the realm of physics some examples of how structure may be a consequence not simply of special devices and constraints that channel forces to operate according to rigidly predetermined programs (as is the case with most man-made machines), but, rather, of dynamic self-distributed processes. His examples were drawn from those systems whose processes are regulated by field dynamics (gravitation, magnetism, electricity, thermal currents, chemical reactions). He maintained that the concept of a gestalt need not necessarily be restricted to the phenomenal and organic level, but may also be extended to the level of inorganic systems—that is, that one may speak of physical *gestalten*. This has been interpreted as an attempt to explain the superior by means of the inferior, to reduce mental phenomena to material phenomena. According to this view, gestalt theory is nothing more than a rather crude materialism that, in agreement with radical positivistic tradition, conceives of nature as the realm of quantity, where order is introduced only by chance, which is considered the ultimate universal explanatory principle.

Such an interpretation of psychophysical isomorphism would not be conceivable for anyone familiar with the writings of Wertheimer, Koehler, and Koffka, many of which contain powerful arguments against just this sort of reductionism. Koffka concludes his treatise with these words:

> If there is any polemical spirit in this book, it is not directed against persons, but against a strong cultural force in our present civilization which I have chosen to call positivism. If positivism can be regarded as an integrative philosophy, its integration rests on the dogma that all events are equally unintelligible, irrational, meaningless, and merely factual. Such an integration, however, seems to me equivalent to a complete disintegration (Koffka 1935, p. 684).

Koehler certainly wanted to relate the organization of psychological phenomena to natural laws, but he insisted that these laws are not simply of the probabilistic, mechanistic type. He tried to bridge the ancient gap between nature and mind, so strongly emphasized by Wilhelm Dilthey, who, in claiming a special status for psychology as "the science of the spirit" by virtue of the holistic nature of mental processes, revealed his conviction that the nature of physiological and physical processes was entirely atomistic and fortuitous. Koehler's research was intended to demonstrate that this claim did not take into account the fact that in the world of inanimate nature as well, one can observe the operation of principles of organization that are characteristic of psychological phenomena. In doing this he cleared the way for an interpretation of these phenomena that can be understood in terms of the natural sciences. Only if one means by "reductionism" an explanation of biological and physiological phenomena in accordance with the laws of the natural sciences can gestalt theory be properly labeled reductionist.

As for materialism, it is important to understand in what sense gestaltists refuse to be classified as materialists. Wertheimer clarifies the situation as follows:

> When one goes to the root of one's aversion to materialism and mechanism, does one then find the *material properties* of the elements which these systems combine? Frankly speaking, there are

psychological theories and many psychological textbooks which treat consistently of elements of *consciousness* and are nevertheless more materialistic, barren, lacking in meaning and significance than a living tree which possibly possesses nothing of consciousness. It cannot matter of what material the particles of the universe consist, what matters is the kind of whole, the significance of the whole (after Koffka 1935, p. 64).

And Koffka adds: "A physiological theory which allows to physiological processes more than mere summative combinations of excitations is less materialistic than a psychological theory which allows only sensations and blind associative bonds between them" (1935, p. 65).

When they speak of "materialism," then, gestaltists have in mind a definition of nature and its laws that is purely atomistic and probabilistic, a definition they do not share. Their conception of reality is monistic, and is a complete denial of the Cartesian dichotomy involving two autonomous substances and the consequent belief in two separate realms governed by different laws and commanding different levels of respect. In psychology the gestaltist's conception of reality finds its concrete expression in the hypothesis of psychophysical isomorphism. According to this hypothesis, the phenomenal or conscious world and the constellation of corresponding physiological processes are not two separate things that have a certain relationship; rather, they are two aspects of a single reality, aspects that are structurally identical—that is, isomorphic.

In evaluating gestalt psychology with regard to its scientific merits, one must not forget that the hypothesis of isomorphism is precisely that, a hypothesis. The principles of gestalt theory have been discovered and elaborated in the phenomenological realm; it is there that they may be confirmed or rejected and, thus, there that they have scientific value—a value they will continue to have even if it is demonstrated that Koehler's hypothesis is wrong and, therefore, that they are not directly applicable to physiological and physical processes.

GESTALT THEORY IS A NATIVIST THEORY

Since gestalt psychologists have dramatically recast the role of past experience in perception—to the point of having earned, somewhat unjustly, the label of anti-empiricists—it has been taken for granted that they must be considered nativists. If learning does not have a determinant influence on the unification and segregation of objects in the perceptual world, it is only logical that this organization must be due to innate mechanisms that automatically provide for the perception of depth, size, form, and so forth.

However, gestalt psychologists do not want to be considered nativists, at least not in the sense in which this word is commonly understood. They conceive heredity of function as in general being linked to the presence of particular anatomical structures or to specific histological conditions in the organism. In the case of perception, these hereditary elements are localized, according to gestalt theory, either in the central nervous system, even though in most cases we are not yet able to specify their nature, or in anatomic mechanisms of the oculomotor system, such as those that control accommodation, fixation, and convergence.

Let us consider the fixation reflex. If a luminous spot appears against a homogeneous background, ocular adjustments automatically place the image of the spot on the fovea. This occurs independently of the initial positions of the luminous spot and of the eyes. Koffka points out that a nativistic explanation even of such a simple event as this presupposes an extremely complex anatomical-physiological system of interconnections between the optic nerve and the motor system, whereas the independence of the final state from the initial one suggests a different type of explanation:

> This feature is common to a great number of physical events which occur without any such system of special connections as was assumed in the nativist theory of fixation movements. A swinging weight suspended by a string will eventually come to rest in the same position no matter in what direction nor how far it has been swung out because in this position the actual forces, gravitation on the one hand and the elasticity of the string on the other, are in perfect equilibrium (1935, p. 312).

Koehler often maintained that to pose the empiricist and nativist interpretations as alternatives—for example, with regard to the problem of the perceptual constancies—is to construct a spurious opposition, because the solution may be found in the dynamic self–regulation of the processes in a system: "We must attempt to discover a type of function that is structured and yet not merely imposed in a rigidly restrictive way by either hereditary or acquired processes" (1947, p. 117). In *The Task of Gestalt Psychology* (1969) Koehler further specified what he meant by clearly distinguishing between histological structures and the interactions that take place in them. The former have been transformed in the course of evolution, whereas the dynamic laws that govern the latter have remained invariant. The forces that affect an organism, and are no different from those in the inanimate world, have not undergone any qualitative changes in the course of evolution. The histological structures are the "topographic conditions" of the system, the "constraints" present in the organism. They never provoke action; they only modify it, preventing it from taking place freely. This does not mean that the forces that act in an organism do so according to laws different from those acting in inanimate nature, as the vitalists claim; rather, in living organisms the action of those forces is generally much more complex.

In any case, whether these assumptions are valid or not, the fact remains that gestaltists reject nativism in its integral form and propose instead a solution that is in accordance with their fundamental principles. The fact that one persists to classify them as nativists is clearly nothing more than a consequence of their vigorous anti-empiricism.

GESTALT THEORY REJECTS ANALYSIS

"The whole is greater than the sum of its parts." This proposition, which gestaltists owe to Christian von Ehrenfels, is one of the simplifying expressions most often heard in descriptions of the theory. It is, however, inaccurate. It would be more correct to say "the properties of the whole are not the result of a summation of those of the parts." A triangle is composed of three sides, but triangularity is not simply the result of adding together the three quantities of triangularity contained in each side. A side, in and of itself, has no triangularity at all in phenomenal terms, just as it has no hexagonality, nor any of the qualities characteristic of those polygons of which it might theoretically be a part.

From the above proposition and from its corollary, "The properties of a part depend on the whole in which it is included," gestaltists have drawn a number of methodological consequences regarding procedures of investigation that they consider legitimate in the study of psychological phenomena. During the period in which gestalt theory developed, psychology was basically elementaristic, a characteristic inherited from philosophical associationism. In connection with this elementarism there existed the belief that the study of the contents of consciousness and of behavior necessarily involved their initial decomposition into their most elemental form: pure sensations, elementary operations of will, reflexes, and so on. This attitude is understandable, since it was only natural that the founders of scientific psychology, most of whom had backgrounds in the natural sciences, should believe that the procedures that had proved so fruitful in physics, chemistry, and biology should also (when appropriately adapted to the particular characteristics of the new object of study) secure scientific dignity and rapid progress in the investigation of mental phenomena. Unfortunately the results did not confirm these expectations, and the type of analytical method that was adopted led psychology into a barren search for elements whose association never seemed to recapture the lively complexity of mental functions.

Among the critics of this situation were the gestaltists, whose position was distinguished for its vigorous attack on the doctrine of elementarism and on the form of analysis conducted with the classical psychophysical methods and with structuralist introspection. This criticism was sufficient for them to be classified as opponents of analysis in general and implicitly, since it is unthinkable that analysis should be abandoned in science, as proponents of some sort of direct mystical intuition of reality.

In fact the criticism expressed by the gestaltists was not aimed at analysis as such but, rather, at those particular instruments of analysis that had proved so inadequate in exploring the complexities of mental phenomena. These instruments were criticized not because they were analytic but, on the contrary, precisely because they were incapable of analysis. They gave the scientist the illusion of being analytic, but in fact merely distorted the processes they were supposed to analyze. The problems that the gestaltists raised were the "units of analysis" appropriate for exploring these phenomena and the correct methods for obtaining such natural units. In the field of perception they used the phenomenological method. The essential characteristics of this method are the return to genuine facts of immediate experience and the refusal to accept as data what in fact are nothing more than artificial products of the logical elaboration of these experimental data performed after the fact. Making use of this method, they demonstrated that the majority of the "elements" (particularly "sensations") that were believed to be the atoms of mental phenomena could be eliminated from the sphere of scientific concepts.

It is clearly false that the use of the phenomenological method implies a rejection of analysis as an instrument of scientific research in psychology. This method is essentially an analytic method in which phenomena are studied under the most appropriate conditions, so that they are not distorted or misrepresented. It is an attempt to distinguish natural, organic elements that are functionally meaningful parts of a more complex whole, rather than artificial fragments or irrelevant pieces. In phenomenological analysis, which consists in the unbiased, "naive" examination of conscious data as they are immediately experienced in perception or thought, the experimenter records and studies the transformations of the experience in a given situation by systematically varying the relevant factors, internal as well as external, that combine to produce that experience. In this way it is possible to determine the relative importance of the various factors, the limits and direction of their influence, and the laws governing their reciprocal functional interaction. Clearly, then, the phenomenological method is not simply a description of the data of consciousness, but a genuine form of analysis—not an analysis of the "essence" of phenomena, an enterprise that is beyond the grasp of research programs that want to remain within the arena of objective investigation, but, rather, an analysis of the conditions and the laws of their development, their persistence, and their interrelations.

There is another widespread prejudice that has contributed to the idea that gestalt psychology is anti-analytic: the prejudice that the phenomenological method implies, as a logical consequence, that "everything depends on everything else." The emphasis placed by gestaltists on the role of context effects and on the dependence of the parts on a whole does not in the least imply such an extreme consequence. On the contrary, gestaltists firmly reject this sort of formulation, which would effectively block any serious scientific investigation. To begin with, reality is composed not only of organic wholes but also of additive groupings. To consider the universe as a single whole or gestalt in which there is an absolute interdependence, such that it would be completely arbitrary to isolate any particular part for investigation, is a philosophical position that may have certain virtues as an abstract principle but has no value at the level of empirical research, where the opposite is consistently found to be true. The principle that "the parts depend on the whole" is valid within a gestalt, though with varying degrees of intensity, since there are both "strong" and "weak" *gestalten*. But a gestalt is a system that is more or less isolated from its surroundings and is, for all practical purposes, independent of other systems. The laws governing the segregation of one gestalt with respect to another are just as important as those that contribute to its unity— that is, the interdependencies of its internal parts. These are complementary aspects of a single reality, and it is misleading to ignore the one and focus only on the other. One of the tasks of phenomenological analysis consists in ascertaining the features and the extent of these relatively isolated unities, specifying the existence of potential functional relationships and measuring their intensity.

GESTALT THEORY IS A VITALIST THEORY

One of the most characteristic themes of gestalt psychology is a radical anti-mechanism. According to the gestaltists, the order that we see in nature cannot be the result of rigid constraints similar to man-made machines, as the mechanistic theories proposed by many biologists and philosophers maintain. Against such mechanistic interpretations of organic phenomena Hans Driesch and other vitalists had provided extremely convincing arguments. For example, when one of the parts of a machine is damaged, the other parts either jam or continue to operate without modification, even though this operation may no longer serve any function. There is no tendency to adapt to new conditions. Such adaptation, however, is precisely what happens in a living organism. It reacts to interferences with its functioning by means of self-regulating processes that are perfectly adapted to the disturbance and are capable of restoring the "meaningful" functioning of the organism.

Gestalt psychologists appreciate these anti-mechanistic arguments developed by the vitalists, and they have even provided additional arguments of their own. It is perhaps for this reason that some have sensed shades of vitalism in their position. However, they resolutely deny the vitalist label as well. In fact, they avoid the mechanism-vitalism dichotomy by offering a new solution, just as they did with respect to the empiricism versus nativism issue.

According to the vitalists, since organic phenomena cannot be explained by means of a model based on a machine that is not self-regulating, the explanation must involve the existence of an active principle that is peculiar to organic forms and does not exist in inanimate nature. In claiming this, however, they introduced into their description of nature a feature that gestaltists could not accept. To explain biological order by having recourse to an unknown secret and somewhat mystical agent is not to explain scientifically, but only to give a new name to the problem. What is needed, instead, is to develop an account that is compatible with the principles of the natural sciences. The gestaltist solution has its roots in Koehler's research on physical gestalten, thus avoiding any discontinuity with the realm of inorganic nature.

The vitalists' error, and that of many other theorists, is to assume that the world of physical phenomena is basically chaotic. In this view the processes that occur in inorganic nature take place in an orderly fashion only when they are rigidly channeled by special ad hoc devices that regulate even the most minute details of the events. Koehler has shown that the way in which machines operate is not characteristic of the world of physical phenomena. In fact, it is a very special case. It is easy to find in the physical world examples of systems that, unlike machines, have more than one degree of freedom and thus are capable of self regulation on the basis of their internal dynamics. The order that results in such cases is not the product of mechanical restraints but, rather, the natural result of organization. The belief that the physical world is of necessity at the mercy of disorder and chaos is the result of an unwarranted generalization from cases like those of solid-state mechanics, which are wrongly assumed to be typical. Once it is established that order and self-regulation are also characteristic of inanimate physical systems, there is no longer any need to have recourse to a special agent in order to explain their existence in organic nature. In this way one avoids introducing a dualism into nature that, as we have noted, is profoundly foreign to the gestaltist way of thinking.

GESTALT THEORY DENIES THE INFLUENCE OF MOTIVATIONAL FACTORS IN PERCEPTION

When transactionalism and the "new look" in perception were in vogue, many of the psychologists who shared a certain intolerance of what were held to be the characteristics of gestalt theory—an abstract mentalism and a rigid anti-environmentalism—proclaimed with great satisfaction: "Here is the experimental demonstration that Wertheimer's factors of figural organization are nothing but an abstraction and do not take into consideration the personality of the perceiver. They ignore the influence that needs, desires, values, defensiveness, etc. have on perception." This "new look" trend was followed by a backlash, and the more extreme claims were repudiated in large part by their authors. The idea remained, however, that gestalt psychology emphasizes only the role of the structural or autochthonous factors and ignores the effect of functional or motivational factors on perceptual organization. The fact is that the gestaltists, while not denying the influence of these factors, have reduced their importance. And, on the other hand, the authors of the "new look" attributed excessive importance to their experimental results, many of which were obtained under dubious methodological conditions.

What gestalt psychology does deny is that attention, intention, interest, attitude, and such can be considered the only, or even the most important, organizational factors in our perceptual experience. These factors have their place in the theory as ego forces, but this does not detract from the importance of the other forces in the field that have their origin in the stimuli. For the "new look" psychologists, however, perceived objects are the result of an autistic process in which the world is shaped according to the needs and expectations of the perceiver. The individual sees, on the basis of autistic and projective perceptual mechanisms, what he or she wants to see, and does not see, because of perceptual defense mechanisms, what is disturbing or anxiety-producing. A closer look at the evidence on which these strong claims are based reveals that the experimental conditions involved extremely impoverished or ambiguous stimuli. But observations in regard to this situation are frequent in the gestalt literature; and thus, if "not giving importance to the role of motivation in perception" means not making the excessive claims made by the "new look," then gestaltists may in fact be said to limit the importance of motivational factors. But if it means not adequately evaluating the effect of ego forces, this would rightly be denied by gestaltists.

This is the case as regards the primary processes of segmentation of the perceptual world into discrete and unified objects. If now the "valence" of the objects—that is, their "affordance," their being attractive or repulsive—is considered, then it must be admitted that few psychological theories have developed a conceptual system as rich as gestalt theory for explaining the dynamic relations between the ego, the world of objects, and behavior. In this case one certainly can speak of the decisive influence of motivational conditions on the characteristics of objects and, in general, on the behavioral environment. But it is their attractiveness or repulsiveness that is involved here, and not their segregation into phenomenal units, as objects that are distinct from one another.

> The hungry animal will be attracted by food, the same animal after a good meal will leave the food unheeded, again a close correlation between need and demand character. How delicious a beefsteak looks when we return from a long walk, and how cold we feel towards it after a sumptuous repast. It no longer looks the same, having lost its demand character (Koffka 1935, p. 355).

According to K. Lewin, the existence of a need can profoundly transform the affective character of an object, and this transformation in turn has an important effect on behavior:

> The dynamic situation, then, is this: I have a need which for the moment cannot be satisfied; then an object appears in my field which may serve to relieve that tension, and then this object becomes endowed with a demand character. . . . Dynamically speaking, this case is very complex, because of the role which the ego plays in it. At first, through a tension in one of its subsystems, it determines the field organization, and then its actions are codetermined by the object which it has endowed with the attractive (or repulsive) force" (Koffka 1935, p. 354).

It is likely that the claim contained in the title of this section is the result of not making a clear distinction between the problem of the formation of objects and that of their assumption of affective affordances.

GESTALT PSYCHOLOGY DENIES
THE INFLUENCE OF PAST EXPERIENCE

This is probably the most die-hard prejudice of all, and the authentic gestalt position on the problem of past experience is a continuous source of misunderstanding. Yet gestaltists have been quite explicit on this issue, so that the persistence of this prejudice must be attributed in great part to a superficial acquaintance with their work. Max Wertheimer, for example, after having specified several factors that determine the structuring of the perceptual world—proximity, similarity, common fate, closure, continuity of direction, and objective set—says explicitly:

> Another factor is that of past experience or habit. Its principle is that if AB and C but not BC have become habitual (or "associated"), there is then a tendency for ABC to appear as AB/C. Unlike the other principles with which we have been dealing, it is characteristic of this one that the contents A, B, C, are assumed to be independent of the constellation in which they appear. Their arrangement is in principle determined merely by extrinsic circumstances (e.g., drill). There can be no doubt that some of our apprehensions are determined in this way. Often arbitrary material can be arranged in arbitrary form and, after sufficient drill, made habitual (1923, p. 331).

W. Metzger points out:

> It is precisely on the basis of the principle of dependence-of-parts-on-wholes that it is *to be expected* that a perceived object, even when its external characteristics remain constant, *may* (though it need not) have different properties depending on whether certain experiences have occurred or not in connection with it; for example, depending on whether it, or another similar to it, has already been "encountered" or not (1954, p. 97).

It should be quite clear, then, that the claim that gestalt psychology denies the influence of past experience is false. The "empirical factor" is explicitly one of the factors of perceptual organization. However, gestaltists do not accept past experience as a universal explanatory principle, as do many empiricists. Indeed, their research has thoroughly demonstrated that past experience as such cannot be considered the only organizing force in the perceptual field. Koffka notes: "It will not be necessary to point out that this anti-empiricist attitude does not mean the denial of the enormous value of experience. Not *that* it makes use of experience causes our objection to empiricism, but *how* it makes use of it"(1935, p. 639).

In the face of such explicit statements as these, it remains to be understood how such an opinion about gestalt theory has developed and become widespread. Apart from lack of acquaintance with the theory, there must be something in the theory that accounts for, if not justifies, these persistent misunderstandings. Most likely they are the result of the gestaltists' strong anti-empiricist polemic and of the false belief, discussed above, that their thought is basically nativistic. It must be remembered that during the period in which gestalt research and theory regarding the interpretation of mental phenomena were being developed, the dominant positions in psychology were empiricist. As we have already noted, gestalt theorists opposed a purely empiricist explanation of human behavior in general and of mental phenomena in particular. They maintained, instead, that the structure, articulation, and formation of perceptual objects are due to the influence of autonomous organizational forces, and not only to the simple establishment of fortuitous associative bonds.

In light of this belief, the first research goal was that of demonstrating the existence and studying the effect of these organizational factors. In order to do this gestaltists had to use situations that would yield results unexplainable with a strictly empiricist theory; otherwise, when a given stimulus constellation is segmented into a certain set of distinct perceptual units, rather than another theoretically possible set, and the gestaltist claims that this segmentation occurs because of certain autochthonous factors of unification and segregation, the empiricist is always ready with the facile objection that the structuring is simply the result of familiarity with those units.

Thus, for purposes of demonstration it was necessary to find situations in which explanations based solely on the influence of past experience were inapplicable. With this in mind, it is easy to see why there were so many gestalt demonstrations in which the segmentation of the perceptual field occurs differently from what would be expected on the basis of the empirical factor alone. One can also see how, given the regularity with which experiments of this type occur in gestalt expositions (in which they actually had the positive function of demonstrating the validity of their claims), the impression may have been produced that the main point of these studies was of a negative character, an attempt to exclude past experience from the list of factors responsible for perceptual organization.

GESTALT THEORY EQUATES REGULARITY WITH SYMMETRY

I would like to comment briefly on one more very common misunderstanding regarding a fundamental concept of gestalt theory, one that has resulted in the utter misrepresentation of many of its claims. One of the most important principles of gestalt organization is the tendency toward *Prägnanz*—that is, the tendency of a process to realize the most regular, ordered, stable, balanced state possible in the given situation. This is also known as the principle of "good form." It is perhaps this latter formulation that has generated the ambiguity in which regularity tends to be understood as *geometric* regularity. It is not uncommon to hear someone say, "If the perceptual system always tends to reach the best possible form, to give rise to the most regular and simple configurations possible, why is it that we do not see a world populated with circles, triangles, squares, and other perfectly symmetrical figures?" Objections of this sort reveal a complete lack of understanding of the meaning of *Prägnanz*.

This concept derives from Koehler's statements regarding the "stationary processes"—that is, processes that occur at a fixed rate and are independent of time. All stationary and quasi-stationary processes evolve toward a final state in which their distribution contains a minimum energy capable of accomplishing work. Quasi-stationary processes (neural processes that are isomorphic to phenomenal structures are processes of this type) exhibit certain maximum and minimum properties—that is, the parameters of these processes must assume either the maximum or the minimum possible value. The qualitative aspect of such quantitative characteristics of natural processes is regularity and symmetry. Since in nature these changes are the product of irregularity and asymmetry, a system left to itself loses its asymmetry and becomes more regular little by little, as it approaches a time-independent state.

This line of reasoning would lead to the conclusion that the configurations of our perceptual world should always assume the most regular and symmetric forms possible: circles, squares, triangles, and so forth. But, as Koffka points out:

> The terms of this proposition are clear enough as long as the conditions under which the process occurs are simple. What will happen when the conditions are less simple? A very instructive example is presented by drops of water. Suspended in a medium of homogeneous density, they will be perfect spheres; lying on a solid support to which they have little adhesion, the spherical shape is slightly flattened; falling through the air they assume a new shape which, though less simple than the sphere, is still perfectly symmetrical and fulfils the condition that it offers the least resistance to the air through which it is passing, so that it can fall as fast as possible; in other words, the falling drop of water is perfectly streamlined; its symmetry corresponds again to a maximum-minimum principle. We see in this example how the shape of a stationary state becomes less and less simple the more complex are the conditions under which the equilibrium is established. Therefore, when the medium is complex, varying in its properties from point to point in a complex manner, then the ensuing stationary distribution will no longer be symmetrical or regular in the ordinary sense of the word (1935, p. 109).

This passage from Koffka should make it clear that the *Prägnanz* of a phenomenal configuration must not be taken to mean geometric regularity. The latter is a limiting case that occurs only under particularly favorable conditions. A figure has *Prägnanz* even when it is not symmetric, because *Prägnanz* also means stability, simplicity, cohesion, resistence to transformation. Regularity and symmetry, when they occur, are the maximum that can be obtained from the equilibrium of forces in a given situation.

The so-called optical-geometrical illusions are almost all examples of situations in which the maximum possible geometric regularity is not realized. Indeed, regularities that are objectively present in the distal stimulus are distorted in what is perceptually given and that is, thus, asymmetric or irregular.

Other examples of why the tendency to *Prägnanz* is not to be simplistically interpreted as a tendency to perfect symmetry, in all possible situations, can be found in Chapter 5.

FOR GESTALT THEORY PROBLEMS ARE RESOLVED BY MEANS OF "INSIGHT"

The introduction of the concept of insight is an important contribution of gestalt theory to the psychology of thinking. However, it has given rise to so many misinterpretations that it may also be considered as one of the main sources of misunderstanding of the theory. Insight, like the German word *Einsicht*, literally means "to see into." Koehler, Wertheimer, and K. Duncker used "insight" to describe a specific phase of productive thinking—that is, to emphasize what distinguishes an intelligent solution from one that has been reached by chance, by trial and error, without any real understanding of the problem. Insight, as they used it, indicates the "seeing into" a problematic situation that reveals its intrinsic structure, the understanding that occurs when the situation is reorganized in such a way as to become "transparent"—that is, when the essential features and the reciprocal relations are clearly and directly apprehended.

In a genuine case of productive thinking, an insight occurs each time that, among the available data of the problem, a relationship critical to the solution is grasped. In a complex problem, of course, there will not be only one such relationship to be discovered; there may be a series of relationships or even relations between relations. This means that even after certain relations have emerged and have been fully understood and "seen," the problem may remain unsolved because we cannot discover further critical relationships. Thus, insight is not simply what accompanies the final solution; in the course of a thought process, a certain number of partial insights usually occur, corresponding to the resolution of the various phases of the problem through the successive restructurings of the available data. Phenomenally, insight is accompanied by the experience of a sudden and quite gratifying feeling of enlightenment, called *aha Erlebniss* in German, which subjects express by exclaiming: "It's as if a veil had been lifted from my eyes!" "All of a sudden everthing became clear!"

While admitting that insight involves aspects that are characteristic of all truly productive thought, it must not be forgotten that *it is not an explanatory principle*, but has only phenomenological value. With insight we have not explained the process, but only described one of its aspects. This confusion, however, has occurred and has been supported by certain insufficiently rigorous and careful expressions used by gestalt authors, who at the beginning sometimes spoke of solutions being reached "by" or "through" insight. Although this interpretation has been repeatedly and firmly rejected (especially by Koffka 1935; Koehler 1959), the belief is still very widespread that insight is proposed as a causal agent in reaching solutions. However, gestalt theory maintains that intelligent solutions derive essentially from a restructuring or from successive restructurings of the problem situation, and gestalt research has attempted to establish the laws and precise causes of these restructuring processes. Insight is *not* one of these causes, nor is it a force that leads to restructuring; on the contrary, it is its consequence: through restructuring, the situation becomes transparent. Insight *accompanies*, but does not *produce*, the solution.

4

THE GESTALTIST'S ERROR AND OTHER EXPECTATION ERRORS

It has often been observed that a science of perception may be said to exist only when one begins to ask "why" and "how" our perceptual environment becomes articulated into objects that are distinct from one another, and why it consists of precisely *those* particular objects possessing just *those* characteristics. From the point of view of common sense, it is difficult to see the point of such questions. For the average person the world is made up of objects. We open our eyes and we find objects in front of us with all their characteristics—assuming, of course, that there is enough light. If anything, the problem is to understand the exact functioning of the sense organs that record this external reality, to determine their degree of precision and sensitivity, their rate of functioning, and so on. But these are questions that, in the light of our capacity to construct devises capable of as much as, and even more than, our own sense organs, do not appear to the average person to raise too many problems. The "person in the street" is probably convinced that scientists have already resolved these problems. And as for the fact that time after time just *those* objects with their appropriate characteristics are perceived, why should one expect to see anything else?

Whereas the attitude of common sense may involve ignoring the existence of questions about perception ("naive realist's error"), those

Gaetano Kanizsa. 1970. "Amodale Erganzung und 'Erwartungsfehler' des Gestaltpsychologen." *Psychologische Forschung* 33: 325–44.

scientists whose main interest is in perceptual phenomena see complicated problems in these apparently simple and obvious phenomena.
Even though it may be less naive, this attitude involves the risk that in
the observation and description of perceptual experience, some systematic errors will be committed. Such "mistakes" may be traced back to
a particular way of understanding the phrase "perceptual experience"
and of observing and describing this experience, as well as to particular
theoretical assumptions that may be more or less well-founded. The
best-known of these errors are the "stimulus error" and the "experience error".

THE STIMULUS ERROR

The "stimulus error" has been defined in several ways (E. G. Boring
1921; P. Bozzi 1972) but, without entering into too much detail, we may
say that, generally speaking, it consists in substituting the list of charac-

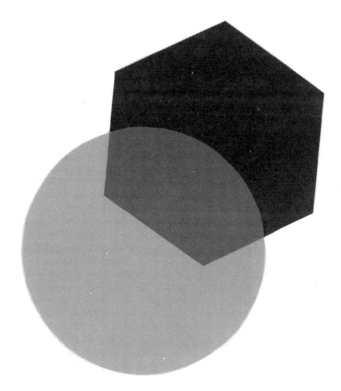

Figure 4.1 Physically: three juxtaposed opaque regions. Perceptually: a transparent disk
partially superimposed on an opaque hexagon. Replacing the latter description with the
former means making the stimulus error.

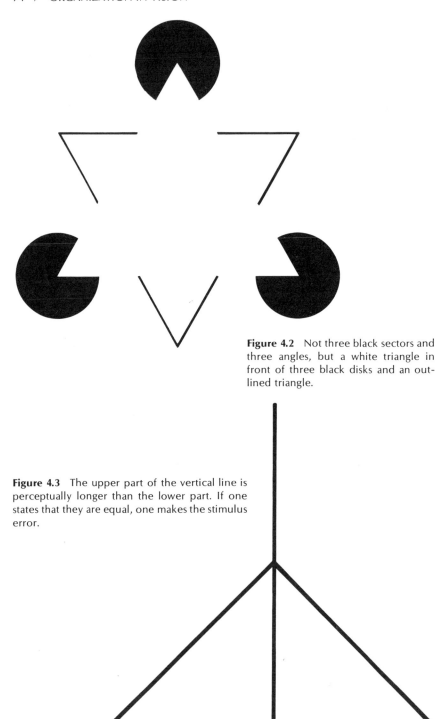

Figure 4.2 Not three black sectors and three angles, but a white triangle in front of three black disks and an outlined triangle.

Figure 4.3 The upper part of the vertical line is perceptually longer than the lower part. If one states that they are equal, one makes the stimulus error.

teristics of the distal stimulus, or source of stimulation, for the description of direct experience—that is, it consists in describing *what is known* about the stimulus rather than *what is seen.*

The stimulus error is committed, for example, when an optimal stroboscopic movement is described as "two lights that alternately go on and off," or when Figure 4.1 is described as "three irregular forms juxtaposed" without any mention of transparency, or when the observer, presented with a typical "phenomenal causality" situation, reports that "one of the two objects began to move after the other object had stopped moving." Similarly, one makes the stimulus error in describing Figure 4.2 as made up of "three black circular sectors and three angles," or in saying that "the upper part of the vertical line in Figure 4.3 is the same length as the lower part," or in asserting that a small square of gray cardboard "remains gray" when placed next to an intensely red surface, simply because it is known that in physical terms it cannot actually have changed color.

THE EXPERIENCE ERROR

The stimulus error, at least as it occurs in the above examples, is essentially quite similar to that made by "common sense" (which in such cases is likely to speak of "illusions" or of "deceptions of the senses"). But there is another error, more likely to be made by the scientist who is studying perception, which W. Koehler has labeled (perhaps unfortunately) the "experience error." This consists in attributing to the proximal stimulus characteristics that are proper only to immediate experience. When the perceptionist looks at an object in the external world, he knows that in fact his perception of the object is mediated by retinal processes. He may be led to describe the phenomenal object not on the basis of characteristics of the distal object, as in the stimulus error, but, rather, on the basis of what he knows about the proximal stimulus (the retinal image). But in doing this an intermediate, although necessary, phase of the perceptual process is substituted for the final outcome of the process. Is it appropriate to say that in Figure 4.4 we see "a circle of black points, because the corresponding retinal image is circular"? Absolutely not. In fact, the 12 physical points give rise to 12 distinct retinal processes, and there is no reason to speak of *one* retinal image—and even less reason to speak of a *circular* image. Although it is correct to consider the retinal process as a necessary intermediate factor in perception, we do not, as K. Koffka points out, see *the* proximal stimulus but, rather, *by means of* or *thanks to* that stimulus (Koffka 1935, p. 98).

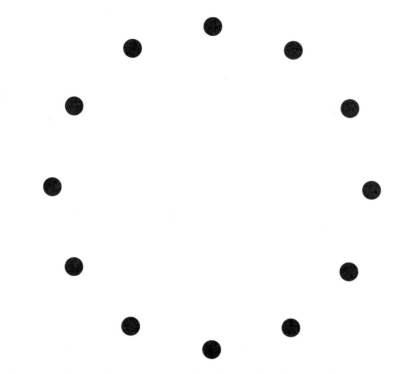

Figure 4.4 The retinal image is not circular; the circularity is the product of organization.

EXPECTATION ERRORS

In addition to these fairly well recognized errors (which are nonetheless sometimes quite difficult to avoid), it may be observed that any general theory of the perceptual process involves a tendency, in the observations and more especially in the description of the perceptual data, to make its own particular type of "error" due to the particular assumptions that any theoretical-interpretive system involves. Naturally it is much less easy to reach general agreement among interested psychologists on the definition, or even the existence, of such errors.

Along these lines, then, one may speak of an associationist's error. Indeed, associationism—and the atomism or elementarism that usually accompanies it—is always in danger of replacing the description of immediate experience with the description of elements that do not actually exist—that is, hypothetical elements, like sensations, that are required by the theory. This sort of error is made, for example, when one claims that "a line is composed (perceptually) of a series of points" or that "orange is composed of yellow and red sensations."

There is also an empiricist's error, which is a sort of programmatic blindness, inasmuch as a consistent empiricist theory often will not promote the examination of certain problems for which it already has prefabricated responses. For example: "We have *learned* to see the unity, structure, identity, constancy, movement, and affordance of objects in the phenomenal environment, gradually constructing them out of an initial, indeterminate chaos."

In addition, one may speak of the inferentialist's error, intending with this neologism to indicate the supporters of those theories of perception in which the intervention of conscious or unconscious judgmental processes is postulated. Included among these are the theories of Wilhelm Wundt and Hermann von Helmholtz, as well as the more recent ones of E. Brunswik, J. Bruner, and the transactionalists. The tendency in these cases to make such an error has as its source the conviction that direct experience *is actually not direct at all*, that it is instead the product of a judgment, an interpretation, an inference made on the basis of the "real" sensory data. An observer with this sort of theoretical framework may believe, thus, that the task is to describe not direct experience but, rather, what lies under or behind this experience, by liberating it from the deforming integrations and elaborations of his or her own interpretive activity. In other words, the inferentialist describes a sheet of paper lying on the table not as rectangular but as trapezoidal; a shadow is described as a dark spot, an object that is receding into the distance as one that is shrinking, and so on.

THE GESTALTIST'S ERROR

By considering other theories of perception, one might extend the list of "expectation errors," but I want to discuss here only the error that, by analogy with the above, I would like to call the gestaltist's error. I will give some examples to begin with. Several years ago a friend of mine, who then was just beginning his career as an experimental psychologist, asked me to observe the following situation, which both interested and puzzled him. Behind "cross" a in Figure 4.5, which was immobile and was composed of four circular sectors of 45 degrees each, he slowly rotated cross b, which had much narrower arms. Objectively the four relatively narrow arms of cross b were visible half the time, during which time they crossed the empty spaces between the arms of cross a; they were invisible while passing behind the wider arms of the immobile cross. What had attracted my friend's attention and surprised him was the fact that the movement of cross b was not, as he expected, a uniform and continuous rotation but, rather, a periodically jerky motion. When the four thin arms passed simultaneously behind the

a

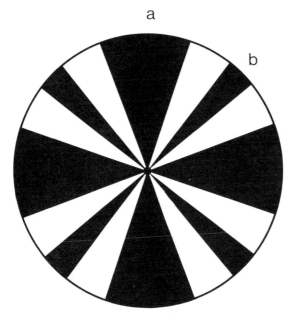

b

Figure 4.5 The cross with larger arms is immobile. The cross with thin arms rotates behind it at uniform velocity. Phenomenally one sees a jerky movement with pauses of immobility (Petter 1956).

wider arms, all movement suddenly ceased, only to resume after a period of complete immobility (corresponding to the duration of the passage behind the wide-armed cross).

On close examination my friend's surprise might appear somewhat unjustified. In fact, the phenomenal experience corresponds precisely to the conditions of stimulation. Half the time the physical conditions for the perception of motion are present and during the other half, when the thin arms are hidden behind the wide ones, these conditions are absent and it seems quite reasonable that no movement should be seen. If anything, it might appear that in such a situation one should be amazed if the opposite occurred. And yet his surprise is understandable because we regularly see objects "pass behind" other objects without an interruption in the continuity of their motion—that is, without noticing the sort of jerky motion that occurred in the case of the crosses. Movement that involves passing without stopping behind a screen, known as the "tunnel effect," has been studied by Max Wertheimer (1912), and more extensively by L. Burke (1952) and by G. Petter (1956), the friend in this example. This movement occurs in accordance with certain gestalt principles and depends on the presence of specific spatiotemporal conditions. The "jerky motion" violates the expectations created by the presence of the specific conditions of chromatic identity and uniformity of velocity and trajectory. It is for this reason that the surprise evoked may be referred to as a gestaltist's error.

Such an error is revealed in the form of surprise when faced with phenomena that do not conform to various interpretive principles characteristic of gestalt theory and that, thus, are unexpected to someone who is accustomed to reasoning too dogmatically in terms of that theory.

The errors in prediction that may be made when a principle of perceptual organization is applied without taking into account the "objective set" postulated by Wertheimer (1923) may also be included in this category. An example is shown in Figure 4.6. On the basis of the factor of proximity one would predict that the eight points in series "a" should be perceptually grouped 1-23-45-67-8, while the points in series "b" should be grouped 12-34-56-78. But if the points of series "b" are slowly displaced until they are arranged like those of series "a," they may maintain their original spontaneous perceptual grouping (series "b") for a certain period of time. This result is contrary to the expectation based on the principle of proximity.

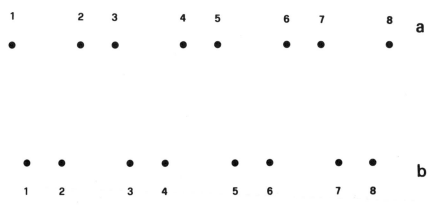

Figure 4.6 An instance of "objective set" according to Wertheimer (1923).

Another example is provided by the reaction that may occur in situations where the direction of movement of a line is perceptually determined by its frame of reference (Wallach 1935). Figure 4.7a is an illustration of this situation. When line *s* is moved into the direction indicated by arrow 1, and if its end points are visible, the perceived direction of its movement clearly corresponds to its real direction. However, if, as in Figure 4.7b an opaque screen with a circular hole is placed in front of the line's trajectory in such a way that for a certain period of time one can see the movement of the line without being able to see its end points, then the observer may be surprised to note that the *perceived* direction of movement does not always correspond to the *real* direction (indicated by arrow 1). Very often, in fact, the

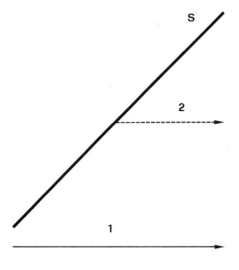

Figure 4.7a The phenomenal direction of movement of the oblique line *s* (arrow 2) corresponds to the real direction of its movement (arrow 1) (Wallach 1935).

Figure 4.7b Phenomenal direction and real direction do not coincide (Wallach 1935).

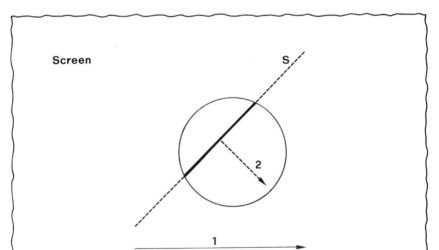

objective motion in the direction of arrow 1 is seen as a movement in the direction of arrow 2.

This initial surprise arises from the same reason that gives rise to the stimulus error: the conviction that the characteristics of the experience are completely determined by the distal stimulus. However, careful consideration of the characteristics of the proximal stimulus makes it clear that the motion of *s* in direction 1 gives rise to a change in the proximal stimulus that is *exactly the same* as the change that would

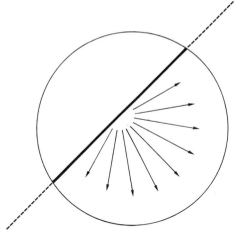

Figure 4.8 All objective movements in the arrow-marked directions give rise to the same proximal stimulus.

occur if *s* moved in direction 2. This being the case, the occurrence of both these perceptual experiences, given the same stimulus, no longer seems to present any problem. But a closer analysis of the situation reveals that the proximal stimulus produced by the motion of *s* in direction 1 corresponds not only to both of the directions described above, but also to a much greater number of real motions. That is, it corresponds to all the motions of *s* in the infinity of directions included in an angle of slightly less than 180 degrees (see Figure 4.8).

Now the problem becomes why, from among all the theoretically infinite number of directions that are possible in the above conditions, is only one (or at most two) of these directions perceived?

An account that has recourse to the proximal stimulus clearly involves the experience error—that is, trying to attribute to retinal processes characteristics that are actually peculiar to immediate experience.

The response proposed by H. Wallach (1935) avoids both the stimulus error and the experience error, and involves only well-grounded phenomenological principles. In the conditions of chromatic homogeneity of the entire length of the line and concealment of the line's end points, the perceived movement is based, according to Wallach, on the principle of minimal trajectories: the movement of the line as a whole, along a path perpendicular to itself, is the shortest movement possible, and it is the one that is perceived. In this case, then, the principle of perceptual organization accounts for the advantage that this direction has over the others in immediate experience.

Now, however, suppose a screen with an aperture like that shown in Figure 4.9 is placed in front of line *s*. If the line is moved in direction

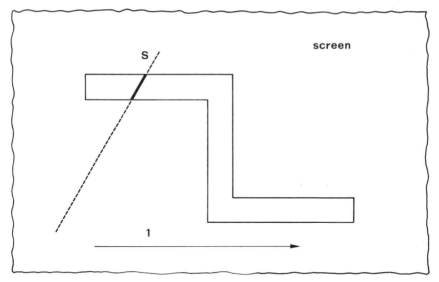

Figure 4.9 In what direction will the visible segment of line *s* move? (Wallach 1935).

1, one should be able to predict, on the basis of this principle, the perceived movement of the visible part of the line.

Following the above line of reasoning, we can reject the trajectory of the "real" motion (see Figure 4.10a) in order to avoid making the stimulus error, and instead apply the principle of minimal trajectories (see Figure 4.10b).

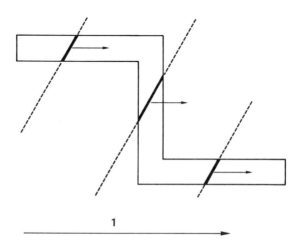

Figure 4.10a The arrows show the direction of real movement (the stimulus error).

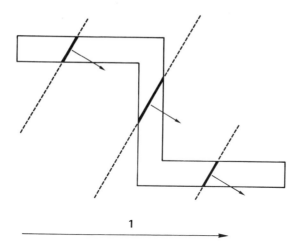

Figure 4.10b The direction to be expected on the basis of the principle of *minimal trajectories*, an instance of the principle of *proximity* (the gestaltist's error).

Neither of these trajectories occurs. Instead, the movement that is perceived in a compelling fashion is that shown in Figure 4.11. The surprise that may be felt when faced with this result is evidence of the gestaltist's error, which consists in the expectation that the movement shown in Figure 4.10b will be perceived. This expectation is based on a principle of organization erroneously believed to be applicable to any situation, regardless of the effects of a change in the frame of reference.

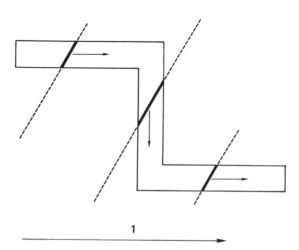

Figure 4.11 The direction that is realized perceptually (Wallach 1935).

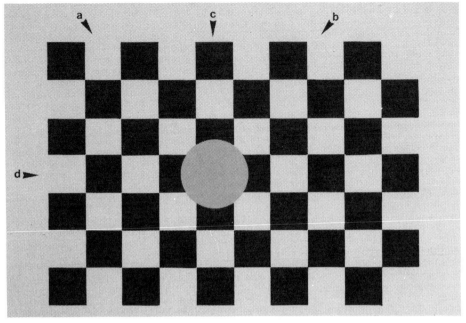

Figure 4.12 The black cross behind the disk does not conform to the overall structure of the checkerboard.

A situation in which the gestaltist's error occurs in a conspicuous way, it seems to me, is the following. Take a black-and-white checkerboard pattern and completely cover one of the white squares with a colored disk, thus partially covering each of the eight bordering squares, as shown in Figure 4.12.

Most observers maintain that in this situation they see a *black cross* partially covered by the colored disk. Similarly, if the colored disk is moved so that it entirely covers a black square and partly covers each of the eight adjoining squares, one sees a *white cross* partially covered by the disk (see Figure 4.13). One may wonder what is so unusual about these results, since the "amodal" completion that occurs in this case should be expected, given what happens when the two crosses are isolated (see Figures 4.14a and 4.14b).

Nevertheless, the perceptual experience of Figures 4.12 and 4.13 which surprised me when I saw it for the first time, also aroused some surprise among my colleagues when I showed it to them. This was especially true of those interested mainly in perceptual problems and who have a more or less gestaltist point of view. Whereas in Figures 4.14a and 4.14b the completion of the black cross and of the white cross behind the disk occurs *as expected,* the amodal completion that occurs in the case of the checkerboard is *unexpected* from the gestaltist point

Figure 4.13 The black square "required" by the global structure is not perceptually present behind the disk.

Figure 4.14a

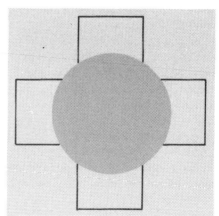

Figure 4.14b

of view, and thus arouses some surprise. What is expected is the completion of the "checkerboard"—that is, the global structure. In this structure the "cross" as such does not exist phenomenally. It comes into existence as an independent entity only after the superposition of the

Figure 4.15 The "law of the whole" does not impose upon the parts. Behind the disk there is a cross or a large square, but not the squares that are the elements of the regular array.

disk, which is to say that the cross in this case is entirely a product of the amodal completion.

The gestaltist's error here is revealed in the feeling of surprise that a perceptual organization may sometimes conform to *local* conditions, whereas according to the theory it ought to conform to the most general structure of the field. Indeed, it is commonplace to say that for gestalt theory "the law of the whole is imposed on that of the parts" or, conversely, "the destiny of the parts is determined by the global structure, by the context, and so on."* The checkerboard shown in Figure 4.12 requires the amodal presence of a white square behind the colored disk. The continuity of the two white diagonals (a and b) and of the horizontal and vertical series of alternating black and white squares

---

*It seems to me that calling attention to these situations may serve as a reminder that the mechanical application of any principle may well lead to erroneous conclusions. Thus, the gestalt point of view, like any other, when reduced to a few formulas or slogans becomes a caricature and can lead, as has been noted above with respect to the behaviorist position, to a sort of systematic blindness, inasmuch as instead of stimulating empirical research, it treats certain basic problems as resolved once and for all, without even examining them.

(c and d) requires this; that is, the global structure or network requires it. Since the global structure is a checkerboard, there "must" be a white square under the disk between the four black squares. And yet that white square—however indispensable or required it may be by the logic of the situation—can only be imagined or conceived mentally. It has no phenomenal reality. It would be incorrect to say that in its place there is a black square, since what lies amodally behind the disk is not a "square" but, rather, the central region of a black cross, the junction of the arms of the cross.

A similar predominance of the local structure over the completion required by the more global structure occurs not only in the case of the checkerboard but also in other situations characterized by a repetitive and regular structure. Some examples are shown in Figures 4.15–4.17.

Another situation in which the gestaltist's error may occur is that in which a relatively large frame of reference is in conflict with a relatively restricted one. From a purely theoretical point of view, one would expect that the larger frame of reference should determine the appearance, orientation, and destiny of all the parts or regions that it includes. Indeed, a tendency of this sort exists. Consider, for example, the importance of the principal (vertical and horizontal) axes of visual

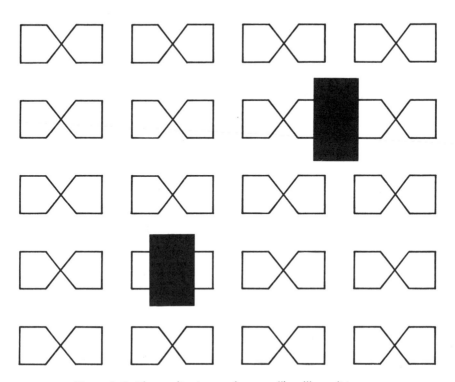

Figure 4.16 The totalization conforms to "local" conditions.

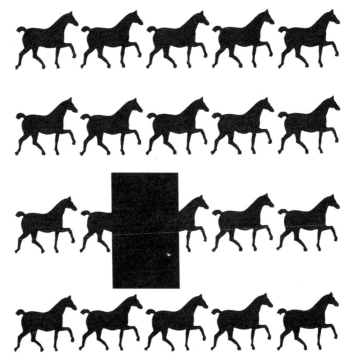

Figure 4.17 A "long" horse, seen against the suggestions of the larger context.

space. But often the relation between the principal frame of reference and other relatively subordinate frames is less simple, as is demonstrated in the situations examined by P. Bozzi (1969), in which the relatively near and the relatively distant frames of reference may act either cooperatively or in opposition.

In the example illustrated in Figure 4.18 (Kopfermann 1930), there is a case in which the *orientation* of a figure is relatively independent of the spatial coordinates of the surrounding system (provided in this case by the page). In fact, in 4.18–1 and 4.18–2 the enclosed figures are easily seen as a square and a "diamond," respectively, even though they are oriented with respect to the larger frame of reference (the page) exactly as 4.18–3 and 4.18–4 are (which are seen instead as a "diamond" and a square, respectively).

Even greater degrees of independence are possible. The point shown in Figure 4.19 is never spontaneously described as situated at the center of the large square but, rather, as not-at-the-center of the small square.

Such a close dependence on the immediately superordinate frame of reference is probably an important factor in the disintegration-of-rectilinearity effect studied by G. Giovanelli (1966). Some new examples of this effect are shown in Figure 4.20.

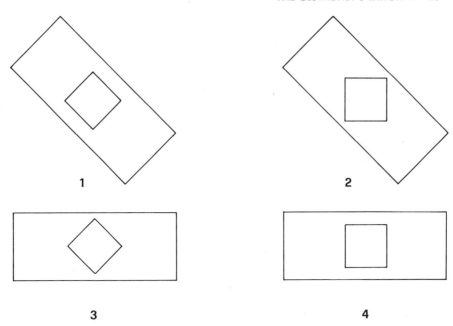

Figure 4.18   The appearance of a figure depends upon the orientation with respect to the nearest frame of reference (Kopfermann 1930).

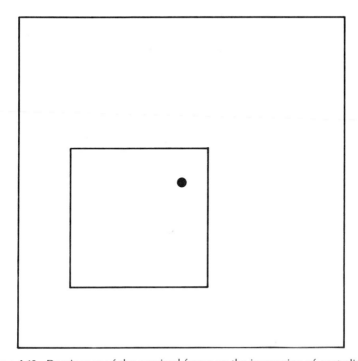

Figure 4.19   Dominance of the proximal frame on the impression of centrality.

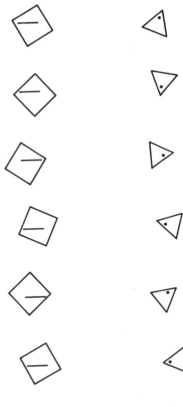
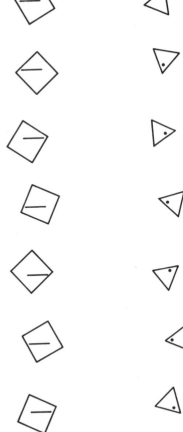

Figure 4.20 Each element is shifted by its frame of reference, and the rectilinearity is destroyed (Giovanelli 1966).

Figure 4.21 Distortion effect induced by the proximal frame of reference.

A striking example of the predominance of the local frame of reference, and thus the relative independence from the more distant one, is illustrated in Figure 4.21, another instance of the above-described opposition. The alignment of the eyes is not determined by the relatively large and principal frame of reference constituted by the face but, rather, by the relatively near framework of the mask, with distortion effects that are readily observed.

5

THE ROLE OF REGULARITY
IN PERCEPTUAL ORGANIZATION

The concept of *Prägnanz* or "goodness" is central in gestalt theory, but it is also the concept that has offered the most frequent and the best point of attack for critics. This is quite understandable because, while other principles of gestalt organization can be stated in a sufficiently clear and unequivocal way, and are therefore fit for experimental verification, the same cannot be said about the principle of *Prägnanz*.

It is possible to define and control in a sufficiently precise way the spatial and temporal distance, the closure or openness, the presence or absence of a "remainder." The definitions of similarity, continuity of direction, and common fate are less simple; however, they offer the possibility of developing satisfactory psychophysical measures and of comparing the structuring strength of these various factors by opposing them to each other, in order to establish their rank order. The definition of *Prägnanz*, on the other hand, is much less precise, and its action interferes with other factors while being difficult to control. Therefore the psychophysical measures of the other factors are reliable only under conditions of great simplicity. In fact, as soon as the situations studied reach a certain degree of complexity, the factor of *Prägnanz* begins to interfere. And, since it is not easy to express *Prägnanz* in quantitative

Gaetano Kanizsa. 1975. "The Role of Regularity in Perceptual Organization." In *Studies in Perception,* ed. G. B. Flores d'Arcais, pp. 48–66. Firenze: Martello-Giunti.

terms, recourse has often been made to intuitive judgment in order to determine, for example, whether two configurations have equivalent *Prägnanz*.

The degree of *Prägnanz* is usually considered equivalent to the degree of simplicity, regularity, stability, balance, order, harmony, homogeneity, and so on. But this definition allows for a great deal of ambiguity. The degree of simplicity is difficult to establish in an exact way, since there can be several criteria for describing this property and the selection of one criterion instead of another may lead to different results. If a purely quantitative point of view is adopted, it is possible to consider simplicity as being characterized by a minimum number of elements or parts. But apart from the difficulty in deciding what should be considered an "element" or "part," it is by no means certain that phenomenal simplicity follows such an elementary criterion. In several cases it is possible to increase simplicity by adding instead of removing some elements: this happens when a configuration "lacks" something—that is, when the phenomenal disturbance consists of a "gap." In other cases there may be some "extra" elements, and then the simplification takes place through the elimination of these elements. But if it is possible to obtain the same result by either increasing or decreasing the complexity of the stimulus, then clearly we have no unequivocal criterion for measuring simplicity.

This fundamental ambiguity of the notion of *Prägnanz* may explain the tendency common among psychologists to identify it with the notion of geometric regularity or, especially, symmetry, which can be mathematically defined and therefore permit exact quantitative measurement. Many of the studies that tried to develop a psychophysics of form adopted a criterion that was either mathematical or based on symmetry in order to define simplicity (Attneave 1955, 1959; Vurpillot 1959; Hochberg and Brooks 1960; Michels and Zusne 1965; Farné 1965).

This restricted view of the notion of figural "goodness" probably has been strengthened as well by gestalt psychologists' frequent utilization of examples in which the winning alternative among various possible organizations is a regular, symmetric, ordered structure. Among the classical exemplifications of the laws of perceptual organization, regular geometric figures are predominant: squares, triangles, circles, hexagons, sinusoids, cubes. The preference given to such examples has caused some misunderstanding, generating the easy objection: "If the perceptual system tends to realize the best possible form, then why don't we see a world populated by circles, triangles, squares, and other perfectly regular figures?" An objection of this type shows that a tendency exists to identify *Prägnanz* with geometric regularity, but it must be recognized that part of the responsibility is due to the emphasis placed by gestaltists on "regularity" in discussions about figural "goodness."

Fabio Metelli (1967; 1970), in his analysis of the conditions of phenomenal transparency, a study that transformed our conceptions about this matter, was the first to show clearly that having recourse to regularity as a determining factor of organization can be misleading, to the point of preventing the discovery of the real laws describing visual phenomena. The following observations may be considered a step toward a rethinking of the actual role played by the tendency to maximum regularity in the articulation of the visual world.

AMODAL COMPLETION

A first group of observations, in which the role of regularity appears rather limited, concerns situations of amodal completion. Figure 5.1a is perceived as "a square behind another square," and similarly Figures 5.1b and 5.1c are perceived as "a rectangle behind a square" and "a circle behind a square," respectively. It could be concluded that in all three cases the amodal completion takes place *in the direction of a regularization.*

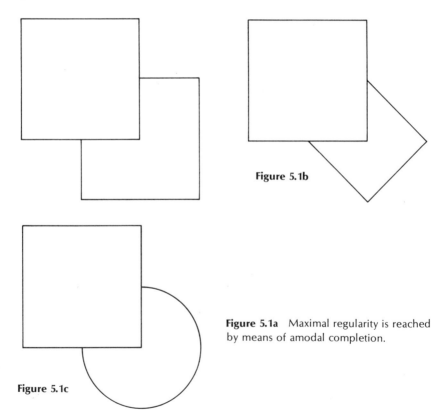

Figure 5.1b

Figure 5.1a Maximal regularity is reached by means of amodal completion.

Figure 5.1c

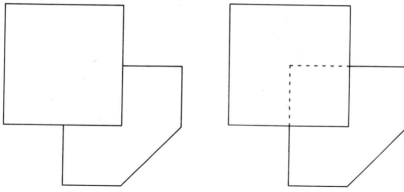

Figure 5.2a Among the possible completions, the most frequent (see Figure 5.2d) is not the one that corresponds to the most symmetrical figure.

Figure 5.2d

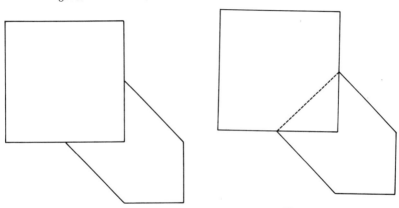

Figure 5.2b The most frequent completion is that shown in Figure 5.2e.

Figure 5.2e

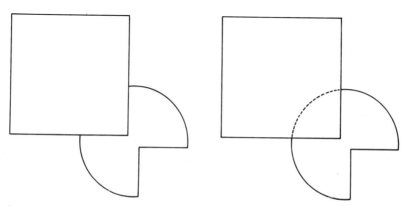

Figure 5.2c The most frequent completion is that shown in Figure 5.2f.

Figure 5.2f

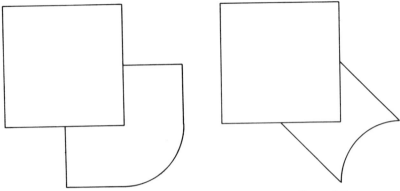

Figure 5.3a The symmetrical completion can be "thought," but is not realized perceptually.

Figure 5.3b

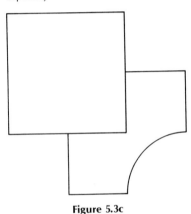

Figure 5.3c

But in Figures 5.2a–c it is demonstrated that regularization is probably only a by-product of the action of other, stronger factors. In fact, in these situations the completion occurs more often in such a way that less symmetrical figures are perceived (Figures 5.2d–f), instead of equally possible, perfectly symmetrical ones.

The "symmetrizing" completion becomes still more difficult when, as in Figures 5.3a, 5.3b, and 5.3c, the completion would have to be done with curved lines as continuations of straight lines.

From these first observations, which were confirmed in a quantitative study by P. G. Gabassi and L. Zanuttini (1978), it is clear that the tendency toward regularity does not always have a decisive influence on the perceptual result. The result of the amodal completion is decided by other factors. In the above cases the important factors seem to be the continuity of direction at the crossing point (Figures 5.1a, 5.1c, 5.2c, 5.3a, and 5.3c) and the minimal distance, when continuity of direction does not give rise to closed figures (Figures 5.1b, 5.2b, and 5.3b).On the contrary, a specific tendency to regularity does not seem to have an effect on the results. When, as in Figures 5.1a–5.1c, a regular and symmetric configuration is seen, it seems to be only a collateral effect of the action of factors that in themselves do not tend toward maximization of regularity.

This does not mean that regularity is not an important aspect of phenomenal reality: When the result of perceptual organization is regular, it seems to have a more immediate, stable, compelling character. In order words, the result appears to have a greater degree of *Prägnanz*.

EFFECT OF LOCAL CONDITIONS

In other situations regularity does not prevail, though in principle it should. This happens when a perceptual organization determined by local conditions prevails, thus causing an irregularity or a disruption within the regular structure of the wider field. This is exemplified by Figure 5.4, in which the two gray disks give rise to the perception of a totally white and a totally black cross, interrupting the regular alternation of white and black squares of the checkerboard. Several other situations, characterized by a local interruption of a repetitive and regular structure of the larger context, are referred to in Chapter 4.

Similarly, in Figure 5.5, which is a modification of a figure used by

Figure 5.4 Completion against maximal symmetry.

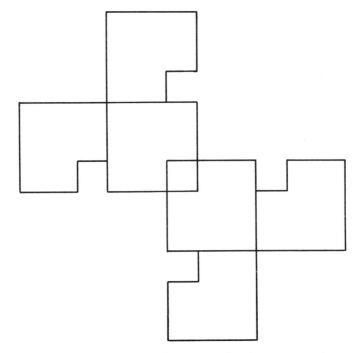

Figure 5.5 Not six L-shaped figures, but two overlapping squares at the center.

D. Dinnerstein and Michael Wertheimer (1957) for studying conditions of phenomenal superposition, the locally acting continuity of direction prevents, for most subjects, the perception of the "more logical" structure of juxtaposed forms, which characterizes the configuration.

TENDENCY TO MAXIMUM REGULARITY

One of the examples illustrating the law of "good" form is the following, due to F. Sander (1928). If A and B in Figure 5.6 moved toward each other until they are touching, as in C, at the moment of contact they suddenly change into two other partially superimposed figures, and it becomes almost impossible to see the configurations perceived earlier. In the new set, every line becomes a part of the whole that is structurally more congenial to it: The curved side of the quasi-hexagonal figure B attaches itself to the curved part of A, forming a circle, and the rectilinear segments join to form a regular hexagon. It may be thought, and it is often claimed, that this result prevails because two regular, symmetric, balanced figures are obtained, in place of the much less regular and less symmetric figures with which we started.

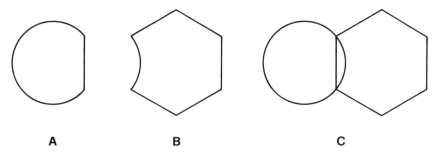

Figure 5.6 The configuration *c* is not formed by *a* + *b*, but by the overlapping of a circle and a hexagon. Structural coherence seems to prevail (Sander 1928).

However, at this point, in light of what we discovered about Figures 5.1a–c, we are compelled to ask whether the above result is really due to a tendency toward maximum regularity or whether the regularity of the resulting figures is perhaps only an accessory consequence of the action of some other, more influential factor. The relevant factor in this case could be continuity of direction, or a "tendency to convexity," which, as we will show later, is a possible structuring factor in other situations.

Some doubt about the reliability of the former explanation comes from the result obtained by moving A and B in Figure 5.7 together; each of them, although not perfectly regular, is constructed—unlike the corresponding A and B in Figure 5.6—with a certain degree of homogeneity, the first having only curved lines and the second only straight lines. In this case also, at the moment of contact an exchange of parts between the original configurations takes place; but in contrast with Figure 5.6, where two new figures appear, each constructed according to a principle of greater structural coherence, in this case the exchange has the opposite effect: in C two superimposed figures are seen as built of nonhomogeneous parts—that is, partly curvilinear and partly rectilinear. A possible factor in this case, besides the tendency to the continuity

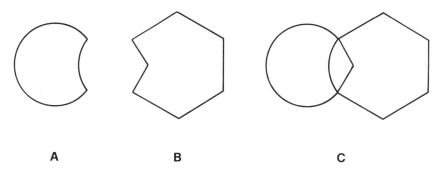

Figure 5.7 Structural coherence seems not to be working.

of direction, whose action seems undeniable, could be the "tendency to convexity," that is, a preference for forms with convex boundaries, avoiding as much as possible figures with concavities.

It may be objected that in the preceding example it was impossible to achieve a regular result, but let us consider Figures 5.8 and 5.9. Although each of them is constructed by juxtaposition of two regular, perfectly symmetrical figures, the privileged perceptual result is given by two much less regular figures having an inferior degree of symmetry. In this case also, each regular figure yields to the other the part that makes itself symmetrical and takes up the "wrong" part.

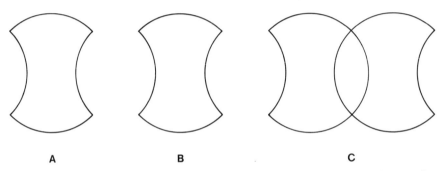

A   B   C

Figure 5.8 Not two symmetrical figures juxtaposed, but two overlapping less regular figures.

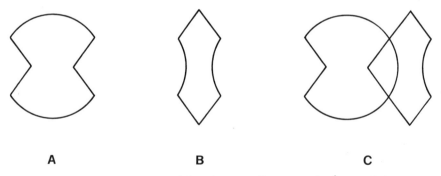

A   B   C

Figure 5.9 Continuity of direction prevails over maximal symmetry.

In B of Figure 5.10, it is almost impossible to see the five crosses represented in A, from whose juxtaposition it is constructed. The tendency toward continuity of direction gives rise to a central square, at the cost of the greater regularity and symmetry of the original configurations.

Following the scheme of Figure 5.6, W. Metzger (1975) constructed the figure reproduced as A of Figure 5.11. The regularity of the hexagon

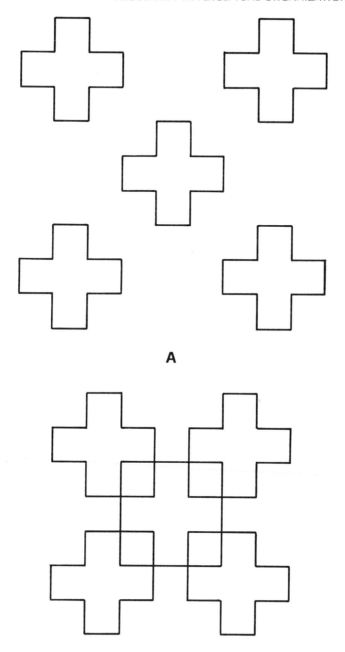

A

B

Figure 5.10 The disappearance of the five crosses does not increase symmetry.

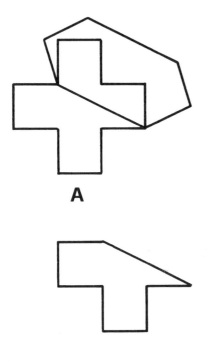

A

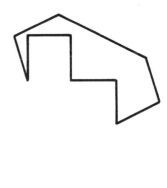

Figure 5.11 The configuration A articulates into two regular and symmetrical figures (Metzger 1975).

B

and of the cross would explain the compelling phenomenal result. Compared with these figures, the possible alternatives represented in B of Figure 5.11 are asymmetric, misshapen, and unordered.

But let us see whether the regularity of the final result is really necessary in order to obtain an articulation like that of A in Figure 5.11, instead of one like that of B in Figure 5.11. Figure 5.12a, which has been constructed so that the intersections of segments are similar to those of Figure 5.11, also is commonly seen as the two shapes of Figure 5.12b. These figures are no more regular than those of Figure 5.12c, but the latter are difficult to perceive.

There is no doubt that the regularity of the cross and of the hexagon give the first perceptual solution an elegance, a balance, an order, a sense of fullness that Figure 5.12a certainly lacks. But the fact that in both cases the perceptual scission takes place in a similar way suggests that regularity is in the first case only a result of perceptual articulation, and *not its cause.* Here, too, the real cause may be the tendency to build shapes that are, as much as possible, convex, with a minimum of concavities or indentations. Systematic research on this problem is necessary.

The same line of reasoning, based on the regularity of the resulting organization, has been applied by Metzger (1975) to explain phenom-

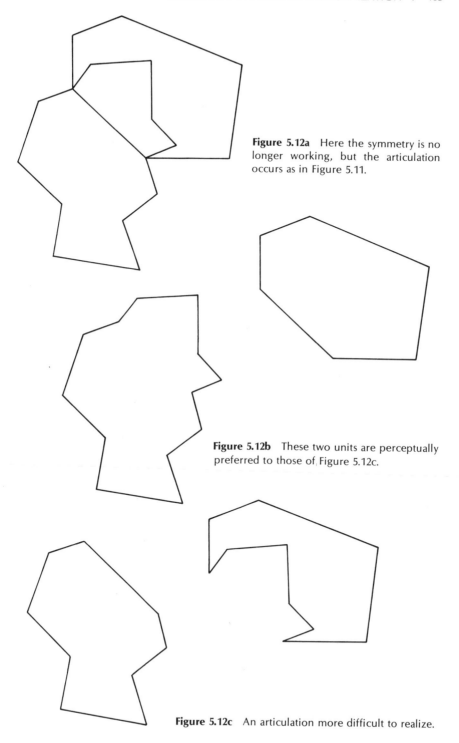

Figure 5.12a Here the symmetry is no longer working, but the articulation occurs as in Figure 5.11.

Figure 5.12b These two units are perceptually preferred to those of Figure 5.12c.

Figure 5.12c An articulation more difficult to realize.

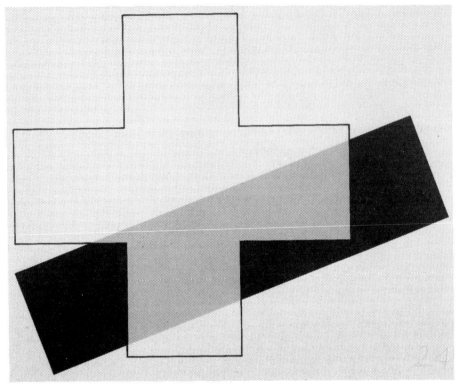

Figure 5.13 A partially transparent black bar on a white cross. Is transparency a consequence of the tendency to maximal regularity? (Metzger 1975).

enal transparency, as in the case of Figure 5.13, where without transparency the juxtaposition of five irregular shapes would be perceived. As noted above, Metelli (1967) showed that regularity of the resulting perceptual pattern is by no means a necessary condition for the perception of transparency. In fact, transparency is also perceived with totally irregular figures, as in Figure 5.14. Therefore, in the case of transparency as well, there are other factors responsible for its perception, although regularity of resulting organization has a positive influence on it.

Another standard situation for proving the existence and the strength of the tendency toward maximum regularity is represented by the reversible plane projection of a two-dimensional object, studied by H. Kopfermann (1930) and used by J. E. Hochberg and V. Brooks (1960) to obtain an objective measure of simplicity or goodness of a shape.

Figure 5.15a tends to be perceived predominantly as a transparent cube, or as a cube made of wire, while Figure 5.15b, although it also is a plane projection of a cube, is almost always perceived as a plane figure. It is also possible to perceive it in its three-dimensional version, but it is

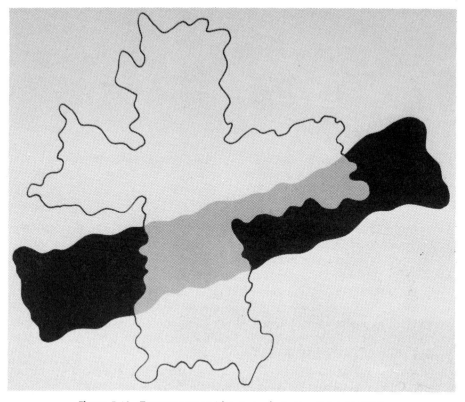

Figure 5.14   Transparency without regularization (Metelli 1967).

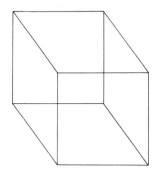

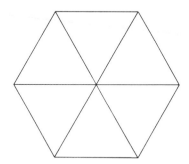

Figure 5.15a   The three-dimensional solution has a much more regular structure than the corresponding two-dimensional configuration (Kopfermann 1930).

Figure 5.15b   The two-dimensional configuration is already maximally regular. There is no necessity for three-dimensionality (Kopfermann 1930).

a rather difficult, and in any case an unstable, percept. The explanation might be sought in the fact that while Figure 5.15b, being regular and symmetric, is already a good shape when perceived as two-dimensional,

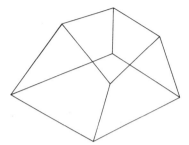 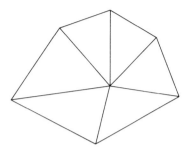

Figure 5.16a The three-dimensional version is not more regular than the two-dimensional one, but nevertheless prevails.

Figure 5.16b The two-dimensional version is preferred, even though it is not more regular.

Figure 5.15a "improves" greatly when perceived in three dimensions. The cube is a symmetric form delimited by six regular sides, while its plane projection lacks these distinctive features of regularity.

The argument is convincing, but it has a weak point; it applies only to projections of regular objects. Figure 5.16 also shows a very strong tendency to be perceived as three-dimensional, as a transparent solid body or as a wire model. Figure 5.16b lacks this tendency, although it is not impossible to see it as three-dimensional. But certainly it cannot be said that in the three-dimensional version (Figure 5.16a) it becomes much more regular than in the plane version. As a matter of fact, they are both very irregular and without a trace of symmetry. Similarly, Figure 5.16b is not much more regular when it is seen as a two-dimensional drawing than when it is seen as a body in the third dimension, and the latter perceptual solution is much more difficult to reach.

But if the explanation based on the improved regularity of the shape is correct in the case of the cube and of other regular solid bodies, it should also explain the perceptual result of situations like Figures 5.16a and 5.16b. Otherwise, factors acting in both cases have to be sought, and the increase of regularity in the first case should be considered only as a striking, but not as an essential, effect of phenomenal three-dimensionality. Apparently in this case also, continuity of direction plays a primary role.

TENDENCY TOWARD COMPLETION

When I studied the conditions that give rise to anomalous contours in the absence of an abrupt gradient in the stimulus, I thought I had found the cause of the phenomenon in the tendency toward completion of figures lacking some part (Kanizsa 1955a). I believe this is a

Figure 5.17 The regularity of the amodally completing figures is not a necessary condition for the formation of anomalous surfaces. (see Figure 5.18).

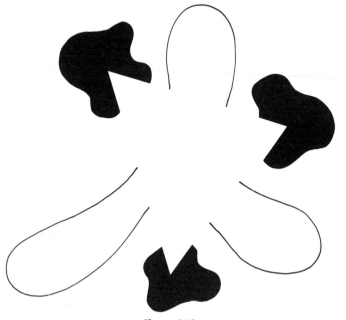

Figure 5.18

reasonable solution, but I think that I then gave an excessively restrictive meaning to the term "completion." This is shown by the configurations I selected in order to elucidate the phenomenon, which are almost always circles, triangles, squares, or crosses that lack a more or less extended part. In all these cases the figures achieve a structural improvement through completion. They acquire more regularity and symmetry and, thus, balance and stability. At present I am more prone to believe that—although a regular and balanced form, when reached, is particularly satisfactory and stable—the tendency to regularity is not in itself a very important factor for achieving anomalous boundaries. In fact, perfectly evident anomalous boundaries can be obtained by using completely irregular figures (see Figures 5.17 and 5.18). Therefore, in this case also, the main factor is not regularity as such, but the tendency to closure of open structures.

SYMMETRY

When the role of symmetry in perceptual organization is discussed, it is perfunctory to refer to the classic research of P. Bahnsen (1928), a pupil of E. Rubin who studied this factor in relation to figure-ground

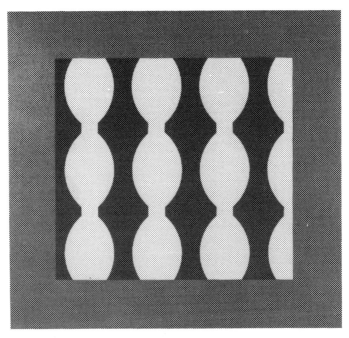

Figure 5.19 Both the black regions and the white region are symmetrical. The figure ground articulation is easily reversible, but convexity tends to prevail over symmetry.

organization. His black-and-white columns are reproduced in many textbooks dealing with visual perception.

Having observed that in the situations used by Bahnsen for his experiments, contour convexity, which always has a certain weight in figure-ground organization, had not been considered, I tried to construct some situations in which this factor is opposed to symmetry.

From the first observations made with this material, it appears that symmetry can at least be counterbalanced by preference for convex shape. In Figure 5.19, where convexity and symmetry are balanced, columns with more convex borders tend to prevail, although the model is easily reversible. In Figures 5.20a and 5.20b, where symmetry and convexity are opposed, symmetric columns are not more prevailing, as in Bahnsen's figures, although the opposition of the two factors causes a certain instability, with quick alternation between the two possible solutions. In a quantitative study (Kanizsa and Gerbino 1976) the following results were obtained:

	Area Seen as "figure"		
	Convex A symmetric	Symmetric	Alternating
Figure 5.20a	26*	8	6
Figure 5.20b	33**	3	4
Total	59**	11	10

* $p = .05$.
** $p = .001$.

The outcome is more unequivocal in Figures 5.21a and 5.21b, where the convexity of the less symmetrical regions is more accentuated, while contours of symmetrical regions are concave. In this case convexity prevails over symmetry. In the above-cited research (Kanizsa and Gerbino 1976), in 73 out of 80 cases the convex symmetric areas did not have an independent existence but, rather, fused to form a black or white ground.

CONCLUDING REMARKS

The preceding is not intended to be an analysis of figural "goodness," but only a discussion of its restrictive interpretation, according to which it would be equivalent to geometric regularity and symmetry. No one, of course, will admit having made such an identification, but it is implicitly contained in statements by both supporters and adversaries of gestalt theory. The former, when they want to give a visual illustration of the principle of good gestalt, seem unable to find any examples except

Figure 5.20a The white columns prevail over the symmetrical black columns.

regular geometrical figures. Therefore it could be said that although it may be doubtful that there is a tendency to maximum regularity in our perceptual system, it is probable that a "tendency toward the selection of a regular figure" exists on the part of gestalt psychologists when a perceptual law is being illustrated. The adversaries show that they have made the above identification when they seem to be convinced that in

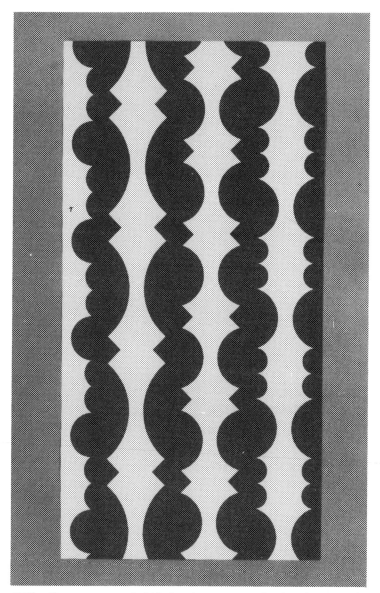

Figure 5.20b The not-symmetrical black columns are predominantly seen as figures.

order to disprove the statements of the gestaltists about *Prägnanz*, it is sufficient to call attention to the fact that the majority of objects in our phenomenal world do not have a regular and symmetric shape; in fact, according to their view, this sort of world would be natural for an organism with an autochthonous tendency to organize the sensory data into units of maximum regularity.

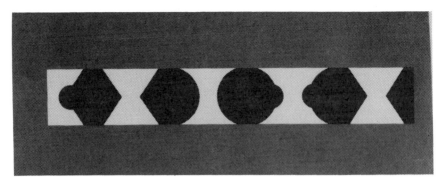

Figure 5.21a Convexity prevails over symmetry. (see Figure 5.21b).

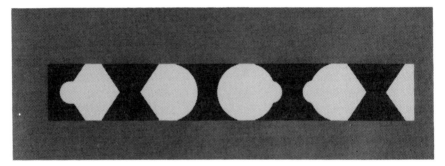

Figure 5.21b

The observations I have made require substantiation by precise experimental research. But even if they were confirmed completely by these empirical observations, and it had to be concluded that a specific tendency toward regularity either does not exist or has much less structuring strength than other factors, this would not mean that regularity and symmetry have no importance in the perceptual world. A regular result will still be more satisfactory, at least aesthetically, than a less regular one; and it could be shown that it is more stable and more resistant to deformation, and that it has a privileged status with respect to the processes of attention, memory, and thought.

6

THE POLARIZATION OF GAMMA MOVEMENT

THE PROBLEM

When a visual object is abruptly presented on a homogeneous background, its sudden appearance is accompanied by a movement phenomenon: an *expansion* of the object. A *contraction* movement is produced at the moment the object suddenly disappears from the visual field. Such movements, which have been observed by Hans Bethe, Ernst Mach, Karl Buehler, and Max Wertheimer, were labeled "gamma" movements by F. Kenkel (1913), who was the first to study them systematically in the course of his experimental analysis of Wertheimer's theory regarding the phi phenomenon.

K. Koffka attached great importance to gamma movements for theoretical reasons, considering them a potential point of departure for the explanation of visual processes according to an isomorphist hypothesis. He believed gamma movement to be the phenomenal correlate of the earliest phases of expansion, in the nervous tissue, of the psychophysical processes involved in figure perception. In other words, gamma movement corresponds, according to Koffka, to the phase in which the physiological gestalt is developing toward its final, stable state. In view of this theoretical importance, a detailed analysis of the gamma phenomenon was continued, despite its rather modest impor-

Gaetano Kanizsa. 1979. "The Polarization of Gamma Movement." *Italian Journal of Psychology* 6.

tance in everyday experience, by E. Lindemann (1922), P. Engel (1928), M. R. Harrower (1929), and E. Newman (1934).

The most significant results of these studies may be summarized as follows:

- Gamma movement is a sui generis phenomenon, not dependent on objective movement.
- It occurs in connection with the phenomenal appearance and disappearance in the visual field of a stimulus experienced as being a *figure*.
- The perception of gamma movement does not depend on tachistoscopic presentation, since it may occur even with nontachistoscopic presentation; rather, it is essentially a function of the "transition time" *(Übergangszeit)*—that is, of the time objectively taken by the stimulus to reach its maximum intensity. Optimal transition times are between 50 and 200 milliseconds.
- The basic phenomenal characteristic of gamma movement is the expansion of the figure upon presentation and its contraction upon disappearance.

The direction of movement of the figure, in configurations displaying a salient circular symmetry, generally is centrifugal/centripetal—that is, the expansion begins at the center of the figure when it is presented, whereas contraction takes place symmetrically from the periphery toward the center when it is removed. In the other cases the movement occurs mainly along the perceptually privileged axes or "lines of force" of the figure.

In the studies cited above, gamma movement was examined by using isolated visual objects that appear and disappear on a homogeneous background. What happens when the visual field is more structured? What is the effect on the occurrence of gamma movement, particularly on its direction, of the continuous presence of other visual objects in the field?

Observations on this matter appear in the studies cited above and in those of H. Lehmann (1939) and L. Knops (1947), who noticed that gamma movement may be modified somewhat if the appearance and disappearance of the figures occur in a field having some articulation.

In what follows I shall attempt a more systematic analysis of this relation between the gamma phenomenon and the structure of the visual field. The grounds for such a study lie not only in the desire to better understand a little-known aspect of the phenomenon but, more importantly, in the fact that a more systematic knowledge of the various types of apparent movement may cast some light on the problem of the perception of movement in general.

THE EXPERIMENT

Two projectors were used to present the stimuli. The first steadily displayed luminous figures on a translucent screen, while the second provided for the appearance and disappearance of other luminous figures, for which the particular direction of the gamma movement was to be determined.

The configurations to be projected were cut from a piece of cardboard in such a way that the resulting display was of luminous figures against the unilluminated background screen. The observations were made from the side of the screen opposite the projectors. Thus the images were seen "through" the translucent screen.

In a series of pilot experiments, in which I tested numerous situations, I ascertained that it is rather easy to produce changes in the direction of the gamma movement in a given figure by modifying, even slightly, the structure of the field in which it appears and disappears. I noticed, however, that the particular polarization of the movement that occurred was in each case the result of a large number of factors and that, in order to determine the regularities involved in its occurrence, it would be necessary to perform a systematic analysis of simpler situations, examining the influence of one factor at a time.

To do this I prepared a series of situations that would principally clarify the influence of the following factors:

- The distance between the continually displayed figure and the one that suddenly appears
- The relation between the sizes of the two figures
- The relation between the lengths of the contiguous sides of the two figures
- The spatial position of one figure with respect to the other.

The only nonhomogeneity in the visual field consisted of a permanently illuminated square (P) 3 centimeters on a side. The figures (A) that were abruptly added to the display by the second projectors were one or two rectangles or squares whose characteristics varied as follows:

- Length of the side of figure A that faces figure P
  La—the length of the side of A that faces P is *equal* to the length of P's sides (3 centimeters)
  Lb—the side of A that faces P is *shorter* (1 centimeter) than P
  Lc—the side of A that faces P is *longer* (5 centimeters) than P
- Width of A
  Wa—width of A is *less than half* (1 centimeter) the length of P

Wb—width of A is *equal* (3 centimeters) to the length of P
Wc—width of A is *greater* (5 centimeters) than the length of P

The nine figures obtained from the various combinations of these two factors are illustrated in Figure 6.1.

- Distance between A and P
  Da—one side of A is *in contact* with a side of P
  Db—A is separated from P by a distance (1 centimeter) that is *less than half* the length of one of P's sides
  Dc—A is separated from P by a distance (3 centimeters) *equal to* the length of one of P's sides
- Spatial position of A with respect to P
  Each figure (or pair of figures) A appeared at irregular intervals in the sequence of presentations four times: to the right of, to the left of, above, and below figure P.

Thus 219 situations were obtained. With them I prepared an irregular series in which every presentation differed from the preceding one in size, distance, number of A figures, or relative spatial positions of A and P.

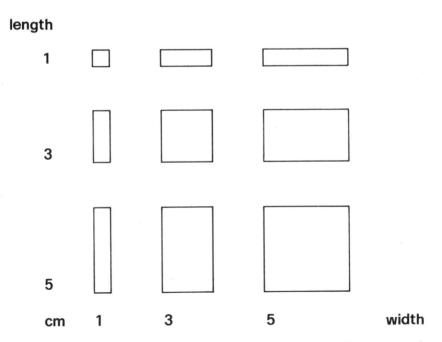

length

1   3   5

cm   1   3   5   **width**

Figure 6.1 The nine figures A that were suddenly flashed near the permanently illuminated square P.

The experiment was performed with 16 adult subjects. In each session only 20 or so observations were performed, all of which took less than an hour, so as to avoid possible effects of fatigue or boredom. Due to certain limitations of time, not all the subjects were able to complete the entire series of observations. Nevertheless, the number of subjects and the number of observations (never less than 76) performed by each are sufficiently large to guarantee the reliability of our results.

RESULTS

General Considerations

Frequency of Gamma Movement

The general results, presented in Table 6.1, are arranged according to frequency of polarized and nonpolarized gamma movement. This experiment confirms the fact that under adequate conditions gamma

TABLE 6.1

Frequency of Polarized and Unpolarized Gamma Movements

Polarized		*Unpolarized*	
AW	1,143	EXP	715
OTH	284	NOM	60
Total	1,427		775

AW = Movements polarized "away from the square P."
OTH = Movements polarized in a direction other than that of AW.
EXP = Simple gamma movement involving centrifugal expansion.
NOM = No movement.
Source: Kanizsa 1951, p. 238.

movement is quite compelling for most observers. In only 60 out of 2,202 presentations did the visual object appear instantaneously on the screen without displaying any form of movement. In all the other cases (97 percent) the figure possessed a special internal movement that was described as expansion, dilation, enlargement, growth, and lengthening. The disappearance phase was described as contraction, shrinkage, retreat, disappearance toward, and reentry.

Frequency of Polarization

A second general observation suggested by these results concerns the frequency with which the presence of a nonhomogeneity in the visual field—in our case a continuously exposed square—has a polariz-ing effect on the gamma movement. Here, too, under certain condi-tions, the effect is so strong that the phenomenon may be considered quite typical. For certain of the configurations, as we shall see later, frequencies approaching 100 percent are reached; but even consider-ing the results as a whole, in 65 percent of the cases the centrifugal expansion and centripetal contraction, which are characteristic of the two phases of gamma movement, produce movements that are clearly "oriented." The emerging figure appears to extend itself from a point or line situated on its periphery. Thus, the continually exposed figure constitutes a point of reference or anchor point that has a strong functional influence on the characteristics of any gamma movement in its vicinity. Changes in the visual field occur in relation to this figure.

Direction of Polarization

Considering for the moment only those cases in which polarized movement occurred, the effect of figure P shows a certain regularity, since in most cases (80 percent) the direction of the polarization is oriented "away from figure P." That is, the point of origin of the movement tends to be located on the side of figure A that faces figure P and the movement is described as a rapid growth or extension of A along an axis perpendicular to the side of P. The evolution of this movement is represented schematically in part A of Figure 6.2. In a few cases the movement occurs "radially" from the midpoint of the side of A that is closest to P (part B of Figure 6.2) or assumes an oblique direction along a diagonal of A (part C of Figure 6.2).

Figure 6.3 presents the types of unpolarized movements that I have classified as "expansion." As can be seen, they all involve development from a central point or a median axis. The latter may be vertical, horizontal, or even oblique, but it always passes through the geometric center of the figure.

Factors That Influence Polarization

The conclusions that have been drawn from these results with respect to the frequency and the direction of polarization are based on the values shown in Table 6.1, where the results of all the experimental situations are presented. The conclusions, thus, are correct in reference to the general trends of the phenomenon whose predominant tenden-cies they help to describe. But such general remarks necessarily ignore the weight of each particular factor in determining the final result. In order to bring to light the influence of each factor, then, the results will have to be regrouped and reanalyzed according to the experimental scheme, described earlier, for separating out their effects. To do this I have constructed Tables 6.2–6.6, in each of which the data have been

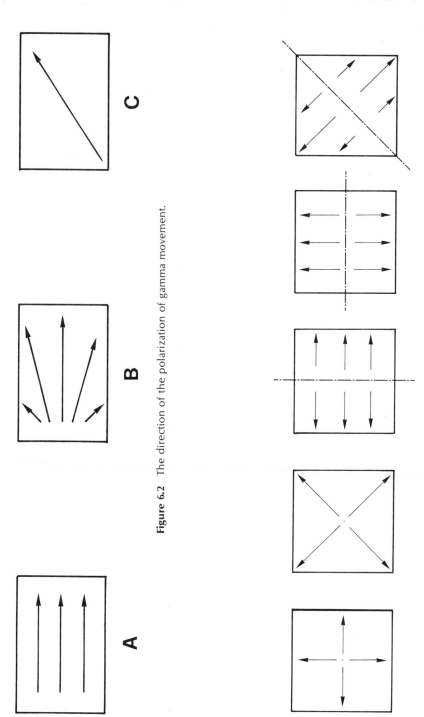

Figure 6.2 The direction of the polarization of gamma movement.

Figure 6.3 Types of unpolarized gamma movements.

TABLE 6.2

**Number and Percent of Polarized Movements
at Three Distances of Figure A from Figure P**

Distance	Observations	Polarized Movement	Percent Polarized Movements
Da	1,012	836	83
Db	589	372	63
Dc	601	219	36

Source: Kanizsa 1951, p. 238.

reorganized according to a particular combination of the relevant factors. So that the tables are easier to read, I have transformed the absolute values into percentages in the text that follows, so as to make the direction of each single variable's influence and the results of their combined influence immediately apparent.

Distance

The distance separating the figure that suddenly appears from the one that is continuously present has an important effect on the frequency with which polarization occurs. An examination of Table 6.2 reveals that the figures discussed under "Frequency of Gamma Movement" mask significant differences that exist between the various situations in regard to this distance. Whereas in situation Da, involving spatial contiguity of the objects, polarized gamma movement occurred in 83 percent of the cases, this percentage is only 63 percent in the figures projected at distance Db and drops to 36 percent in situation Dc, where a simple expansion movement again predominates. This trend is characteristic not only of the global results but also of each of the other experimental conditions, as can be seen in Table 6.3. For each width of figure A and each type of length of the contiguous side, the percentage of instances of polarized movement progressively decreases as we pass from distance Da to Db and thence to Dc. Thus, the functional dependence of gamma movement on the presence of a nonhomogeneity in the field decreases as the distance separating the figures increases until, finally, the tendency for the suddenly appearing figure to act as an independent entity prevails over the polarization.

TABLE 6.3

Percent of Polarized Movements for Three Widths and Three Lengths of Side of Figure A at Three Distances from Figure P

Length of Side	Width	Distance		
		Da	Db	Dc
	Wa	100	75	49
La	Wb	76	59	32
	Wc	80	57	40
	Wa	96	67	26
Lb	Wb	82	61	33
	Wc	70	62	48
	Wa	90	78	42
Lc	Wb	70	53	32
	Wc	62	46	25

Note: Test H Kruskal-Wallis
H = 47.52
α = .001.
Source: Kanizsa 1951, p. 243.

Length of the Side of A Facing P

The length of the side of figure A facing figure P also exerts an influence on the occurrence of polarized gamma movement, as can be seen in Table 6.4. When the two contiguous sides have the same length (situation La), polarized movement occurs with greater frequency than when these sides are of different lengths (situations Lb and Lc). These percentage differences are not high, but are in the same direction for all of the distances examined, even though statistical significance is reached only in the case of Da with respect to the difference between length Lc and lengths La and Lb. It is not hard to see that the reason for the greater effectiveness of situation La lies in the fact that the equal length of the two contiguous sides favors a closer phenomenal relationship between the figures.

The Width of Figure A

The width of A was measured along a perpendicular to the side of A facing figure P, and thus was equal to the length of the two sides of A that are parallel to this perpendicular. From Table 6.5, in which the

TABLE 6.4

Percent of Polarized Movements for Three Lengths of Side of Figure A at Three Distances from Figure P

Length of Side	Distance		
	Da	Db	Dc
La	85	65	40
Lb	83	63	34
Lc	73	58	33

Note: The Significance of differences is shown below:
At distance Da: La – Lb is not significant.
　　　　　　　 La – Lc, t = 3.303; p = .001.
　　　　　　　 Lb – Lc, t = 2.665; p = .01.
At distances Db and Dc the differences are not significant.
Source: Kanizsa 1951, p. 244.

TABLE 6.5

Percent of Polarized Movements for Three Widths of Side of Figure A at Three Distances from Figure P

Width of Side	Distance		
	Da	Db	Dc
Wa	97	73	40
Wb	76	58	32
Wc	73	55	37

Note: The significance of differences is shown below.
At distance Da: Wa – Wb, t = 8.638; p = .001.
　　　　　　　 Wa – Wc, t = 8.700; p = .001.
　　　　　　　 Wb – Wc is not significant.
At distance Db: Wa – Wb, t = 3.257; p = .01.
　　　　　　　 Wa – Wc, t = 3.459; p = .001.
　　　　　　　 Wb – Wc is not significant.
At distance Dc the differences are not significant.
Source: Kanizsa 1951, p. 245.

percentages of polarized movements obtained with the three experimental "widths" are shown, it appears that the frequency of polarization decreases (with different degrees of statistical significance) as the width of figure A increases.

Spatial Position

In arranging the sequence of situations, the relative locations of figures A and P were taken into account. The lateral position of A did not seem to create any appreciable differences in the frequency of polarization, whereas this frequency was slightly lower when A was situated below P. In Table 6.6 a single overall percentage, referred to as "lateral position," is given for the left and right positions.

As can be seen, the differences are small. However, they indicate, by their regularity, a superiority of the lateral positions relative to the two vertical positions in producing a tendency to polarization.

A Figural Factor

The following conclusions may be drawn from the above results. Gamma movement in a nonhomogeneous field is influenced by the distance of figure A from figure P, and to a lesser extent by the length of the side of A that faces P and by the width of A. Regarding these factors, the conditions most favorable to gamma movement are spatial contiguity, equal length of the facing sides of A and P, and a short width of A. The frequency of polarization decreases progressively as the distance between the figures increases, as the contiguous side of A increases in length, and as the width of A increases. Moreover, one would expect that the combined influence of these three factors, when all are acting in the same direction, would produce results that vary according to the intensity of each factor.

In order to examine this hypothesis, I have regrouped the data in each of the possible combinations of the three factors, thus yielding the

TABLE 6.6

Percent of Polarized Movements for Three Spatial Positions of Figure A with Respect to Figure P, at Three Distances from Figure P

Distance	Lateral	A Above P	A Below P
Da	86	80	78
Db	66	62	55
Dc	40	33	29
Total	68	64	58

Note: "Lateral" means that Figure A is to the right of or to the left of figure P.
Source: Kanizsa 1951, p. 250.

TABLE 6.7

Percent of Polarized Movements for Three Lengths and Three Widths of Side of Figure A at Distance Da

	Wa	Wb	Wc
La	100	76	80
Lb	96	82	70
Lc	90	70	62

Note: The significance of differences is shown below.
In column Wa between La and Lc, t = 2.793; p = .01.
            Wc between La and Lc, t = 2.842; p = .01.
In row   La between Wa and Wc, t = 5.685; p = .001.
            Lb between Wa and Wb, t = 3.038; p = .001.
            Lb between Wa and Wc, t = 4.575; p = .001.
            Lc between Wa and Wb, t = 3.006; p = .001.
            Lc between Wa and Wc, t = 4.171; p = .001.
Source: Kanizsa 1951, p. 246.

27 classes reported in tables 6.7–6.9. These results support the hypothesis most strongly when *all three* factors are changed in the same direction. Then the frequency of polarization decreases or increases according to the above-described rules, revealing a weakening or a strengthening of the functional relationship between the permanent figure and the one that suddenly appears on the screen. Thus, for example, we find 100 percent polarization in situation Da-La-Wa (upper left-hand cell in Table 6.7), 61 percent in situation Db-Lb-Wb (central cell in Table 6.8), and only 25 percent in situation Dc-Lc-Wc (lower right-hand cell in Table 6.9).

The same regularity, however, is not found in the percentage trends within each table—that is, when one takes into account the combined influence of length of side and width while holding distance constant. The frequencies ought to decrease regularly from left to right along each row and from top to bottom in each column. This trend is statistically significant only in Table 6.7, which corresponds to distance Da; there are more exceptions when the distance is greater. The analysis of these anomalies brings to light a factor that until now we have ignored, but that shows up in the irregularities contradicting our general rule.

What is involved is a figural factor that calls attention to the qualitative effects that occur along with the purely quantitative variations of the other factors. In fact, it is not possible to modify length of side and width without at the same time changing the global appearance of the figure, its form. For example, when the length of the side of A is equal to that of P, the progressive increase in A's width involves A's

TABLE 6.8

Percent of Polarized Movements for Three Lengths and Three Widths of Side of Figure A at Distance Db

	Wa	Wb	Wc
La	75	59	57
Lb	67	61	62
Lc	78	53	46

Note: The significance of differences is shown below.
In row La between Wa and Wb, t = 2.446; p = .02.
          between Wa and Wc, t = 2.087; p = .05.
     Lc between Wa and Wb, t = 2.616; p = .01.
          between Wa and Wc, t = 3.343; p = .001.
Source: Kanizsa 1951, p. 246.

TABLE 6.9

Percent of Polarized Movements for Three Lengths and Three Widths of Side of Figure A at Distance Dc

	Wa	Wb	Wc
La	49	32	40
Lb	26	33	48
Lc	42	32	25

Source: Kanizsa 1951, p. 246.

transformation from an upright rectangle into a square and then into a rectangle lying on its side. But when the side of A facing P is shorter than that of P, the same quantitative variations of the width lead to the transformation of figure A from a square into a longer and longer rectangle. Now, aside from their geometrical differences, a square is different from a rectangle by virtue of its special perceptual character involving its greater symmetry and equilibrium. Also, rectangles differ perceptually from one another according to their various degrees of slenderness, elegance, verticality, or horizontality. Rectangles that are extremely long and narrow may even lose their phenomenal character of being rectangles and be seen as strips or bands.

If a qualitative factor of this sort does influence the polarization of gamma movement, one would expect an increase in the frequency of polarization when the figural factor acts in the same direction as the quantitative factors, and a decrease when their directions are opposite.

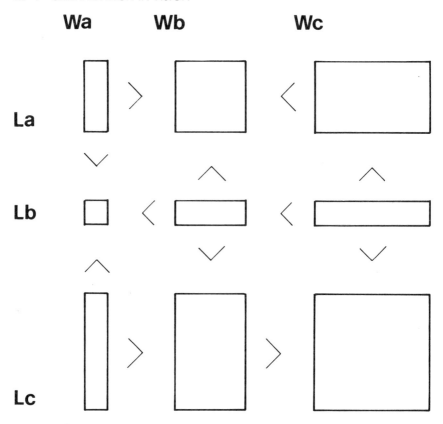

Figure 6.4 $>$ = relative frequency of polarized gamma movement in situations where the only relevant factor is the figural factor.

In order to check this hypothesis, I arranged the nine versions of figure A according to the schema followed in constructing the tables (Figure 6.4).

If it is assumed that the tendency to polarization is directly proportional to the degree of slenderness of figure A, then Tables 6.7–6.9 immediately become clearer. In this case the frequency of polarization should not decrease from left to right in each row and from top to bottom in each column; rather, it should be distributed as shown in Figure 6.4 by the inequality signs. This is precisely what happens in Table 6.9 and, with some exceptions, in Tables 6.7 and 6.8.

The exceptions cease to be such when account is taken of the fact that, in addition to the figural factor, length of side and width are involved. Showing that no contradictions remain in the results when the direction of the two quantitative factors is the same as that of the figural factor is sufficient for the results to be seen as well-ordered. The anomalies, then, may be understood as the outcome of contrasting factors. This is easy to demonstrate. If in Figure 6.4 we indicate by means of another inequality sign the relations between the various percentages that would be expected on the basis of the influence exerted by the factors length and width, we obtain the schema shown in Figure 6.5. Here it is easy to see the situations in which the figural and quantitative factors act in the same direction and those in which their action is opposite.

In Tables 6.7–6.9 it can be seen that only in the cases of opposition do divergences from the schema of Figure 6.4 appear. These divergences are, thus, plausibly accounted for, and no longer anomalous. In

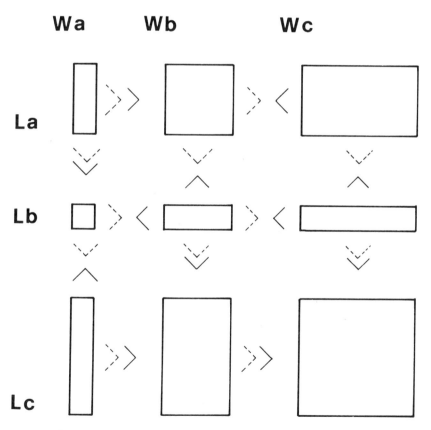

Figure 6.5 $\rangle$ = relative frequency of polarized gamma movement on the basis of the figural factor.

$\rangle$ = relative frequency of gamma movement on the basis of "width" or "length of side."

$\rangle\rangle$ = figural factor and quantitative factor acting in the same direction.

$\rangle\langle$ = figural factor and quantitative factor acting in the opposite direction.

those cases where the influence of length or of width coincides with that of the figural factor (inequality signs pointing in the same direction), there is not a single exception.

An additional piece of evidence in favor of this interpretation lies in the absolute regularity of the distance factor's influence. Variations in distance lead to no modifications of the figural aspect, and so the results of such variations are constantly manifest without undergoing perturbations due to factors having opposite effects.

FUNCTION OF EYE MOVEMENTS

It has often been maintained, in the course of the long debate on the essence and causes of apparent movements, that they are due to changes in viewing direction that are provoked by the particular stimulus conditions in which these experiments are performed. The popularity of such an interpretation is understandable, since without having recourse to new hypothetical processes, it accounts for the phenomenon in terms of already known factors that are relatively easily adapted to experimental study. Among the better-known supporters of this point of view have been F. Hillebrand (1922) and V. Benussi (1925).

The opposite hypothesis, which denies any substantial dependence of this kinetic effect on eye movements or on orientation reflexes, has been proposed by Max Wertheimer (1912), who supports his position with some decisive experimental evidence. He has controlled for any possible eye movements with the use of afterimages, and has demonstrated that apparent movements can occur in two or more directions simultaneously.

This issue is also important in regard to the gamma phenomenon, since reflex eye movements, caused by the sudden appearance of figure A, could be considered important factors in the occurrence of polarization. In an attempt to investigate this experimentally, I have used both of Wertheimer's procedures.

To be sure that the eye does not move during the occurrence of the gamma phenomenon, I produced an especially clear and persistent afterimage by fixating an incandescent metallic object and then monocularly fixating the continuously present square P in such a way that the afterimage fell just inside the square (Figure 6.6). Every little eye movement was immediately revealed by a corresponding movement of the afterimage. In this way I and other observers were able to determine that polarized gamma movement occurred in figures A, maintaining all of its characteristics of clear polarization, vividness, and velocity, despite the absence of any eye movements.

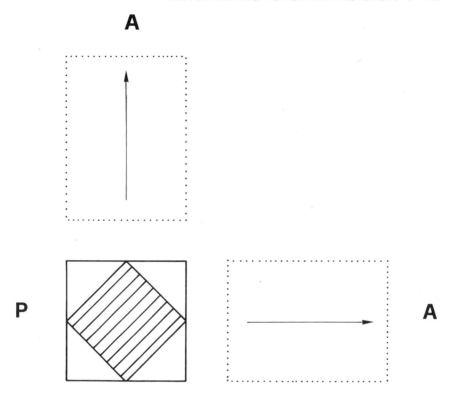

Figure 6.6 A = figures that display polarized gamma movements.
P = continuously present square.
Inside P is the afterimage of a incandescent metallic square.

Even more convincing are the results obtained with the use of an apparatus that produces polarized gamma movements that develop in several different directions simultaneously. In the examples shown in Figure 6.7, and Figure 6.8 the various figures A simultaneously execute movement oriented in the directions indicated by the arrows. It is impossible to account for these apparent movements by means of concomitant eye movements simultaneously occurring in different and even opposite directions.

It is possible that in more natural observation conditions, eye movements caused by the orientation reflexes of the ocular bulbs have some function in determining the direction of the movement. But this function can only be accessory in the above experiments, which clearly demonstrate that polarized gamma movements occur unaltered under circumstances that absolutely exclude any essential participation of eye movements.

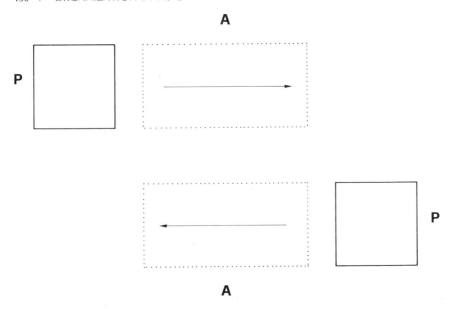

Figure 6.7 Figures A simultaneously execute movements in the directions indicated by the arrows. (see Figure 6.8).

EFFECT OF SERIAL PRESENTATIONS

In the present study the effect of certain objective conditions that might influence the gamma phenomenon, such as the intensity relations between the figures or their chromatic relationship, has not been examined. Such an investigation would have required as much work as has just been presented.

For much the same reason I have not undertaken a systematic study of the influence exerted by subjective factors, such as concentration of attention and the various types of set or attitude that subjects may be induced to assume with regard to the experimental task. It seems likely that certain attitudes, which the subject may assume, and to a certain extent control, might well favor or inhibit the occurrence of some aspects of the phenomenon, even to the point, within given limits, of substantially modifying it. Such an influence has been found to operate on perceptual impressions in a number of analogous situations.

Of greater interest, I believe, is the problem of subjective set as seen from another point of view. It is possible, for example, to produce a set without specifically proposing any particular attitude to the subject—that is, without constraining the person to adopt consciously, perhaps with considerable effort, a certain *Einstellung*.

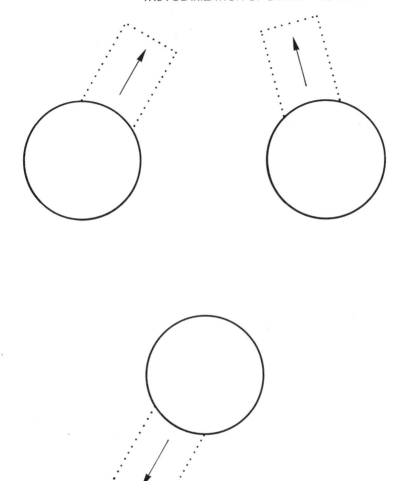

Figure 6.8

K. Gottschaldt (1929) and Wertheimer (1912) have demonstrated that it is possible to obtain substantially different perceptual impressions of a given stimulus by appropriately modifying the succession of stimuli that make up the series of which it is a part. In this way one can sometimes produce a certain phenomenon under circumstances that normally would not be adequate, or produce one with quite different characteristics. This sort of set, which is not intentional on the part of the subject but is produced by certain characteristics of the total stimulus situation, may be referred to as "objective set."

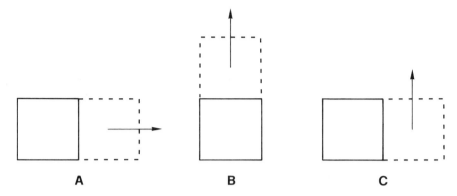

Figure 6.9 *Einstellung* effect.

In our case, for example, the movement of figure A can be made to assume a direction that under normal circumstances it would not take. This can be done by preceding the presentation of A with a long and rapid series of stimuli that clearly exhibit movement in that direction. That is, whenever a series of polarized gamma movements is observed to occur in a given direction for a sufficiently long period of time, it is relatively easy to obtain polarization in the same direction for a figure A that, without the preceding series of presentations, would have been seen as moving in a different direction. For example, in situation A of Figure 6.9 the movement of figure A normally assumes the direction indicated by the arrow. If, however, this situation is preceded several times by configuration B, in which the movement is polarized upward, then the first few presentations of situation A will yield a movement with this same vertical component (configuration C).

In these cases the visual field itself seems to be polarized in some sense—that is, it is as if a certain functional disposition were induced that influences the succeeding presentations.

I have not systematically studied the quantitative aspects of the phenomenon, such as the minimum amount of time required to produce it, the rhythm of the preceding series, or the duration of the effect. The last, however, is not very long and the effect is soon overwhelmed by the other, normally dominant factors.

DISCUSSION

The results that have been presented and analyzed demonstrate, first of all, that the occurrence of the gamma phenomenon in a structured visual field differs considerably from that in a completely homogeneous field.

The structure of the field influences mainly the direction of the movement. A simple centrifugal expansion movement may be transformed into a movement oriented in a single direction. This polarization invests the phenomenon with an important new characteristic: whereas in the first case the visual object that appears exhibits simply an expansion or growth, in the second situation a clearer movement appears. It begins at a given point and covers a specific distance.

In view of these characteristics, polarized gamma movement may be located, from a phenomenal point of view, in an intermediate position between gamma movement and beta movement. It shares with the former the character of movement that is internal to the appearing figure but, as in the beta phenomenon, the movement is polarized in direction and has an aspect of "coming from" somewhere else.

There is, in addition, a strong similarity between polarized gamma movement and "partial movement" (Singularteilbewegung), which is one of the qualitatively distinct phenomena that, as the temporal interval between the two lights is progressively reduced, lies between optimal stroboscopic movement (involving an impression of figural identity) and simultaneity. Wertheimer (1912) describes it in the following manner: "One of the two objects is motionless, the other performs a partial movement [Singularbewegung]."

Polarized gamma and Singularbewegung are quite similar from an objective point of view. The essential difference consists in the fact that in the stroboscopic situation—involving the successive presentation of two stimuli, a and b—when b is presented, a is no longer present as an active stimulus, whereas in the polarized gamma movement situation, a continues to be visible when b is presented. Thus, there is no possibility that an impression of identity will be generated—that is, that a single object moves from position a to position b. However, as noted above, the second visual object is dominated by a movement that might be described as a more vigorous gamma movement with a clearly oriented

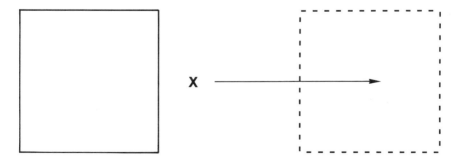

Figure 6.10 Complete analogy with singular partial movement: the point of origin of the gamma movement is located outside the figure.

direction. Moreover, there are numerous protocols in which the point of origin of the movement is located outside of the figure (Figure 6.10). In these cases the analogy with singular partial movement is complete.

One conclusion that may be drawn from the above is that the characteristics of polarized gamma movement reveal the existence of a functional connection between the gamma effect and the perception of movement caused by static stimuli presented in rapid succession. From gamma movement, through polarized gamma, singular partial, and dual partial movements to optimal stroboscopic movement there is a continuity. On the basis of an elementary fact shared by all, they are progressively differentiated by the influence of new conditions.

The basic element that makes possible the perception of each of the other movements is, on the present hypothesis, the gamma effect—that is, the fact that the simple introduction of a discontinuity (a visual object) into the visual field gives rise to a process that develops and extends and whose corresponding phenomenal impression is movement.

On this account the other forms of apparent movement are the result of the dynamic interaction of other processes occurring at the same time in the field and obeying laws established by experimental studies (M. Wertheimer 1912; A. Korte 1915; G. Zapparoli and F. Ferradini 1963; L. Aarons 1964; P. Kolers 1972).

In this light, polarized gamma movement, inasmuch as it seems to constitute a bridge between the simple centrifugal expansion of figures introduced abruptly into a homogeneous visual field and the more complex phenomena of apparent movement due to intermittent stimulation of several retinal points, takes on considerable theoretical interest.

7

MARGINS AND COLOR

MODE OF APPEARANCE OF COLOR

Although they are still found in introductory psychology manuals because they have a certain didactic value, the various geometric systems of representing the color space (Wundt's sphere, Ebbinghaus' double pyramid, Nickerson's cylinder, Munsell's solid) are no longer considered adequate descriptions of chromatic phenomena. Indeed, such representations deal only with chromatic *sensations*—that is, with color impressions "as such," in their pure form, leaving aside the various contexts in which they are experienced. A chromatic impression can vary along three dimensions: hue, brightness, and saturation. These correspond to three well-defined characteristics of the physical stimulus, which is composed of luminous radiation falling on the photosensitive retinal surface: wavelength or frequency, intensity or amplitude, and spectral composition or purity. In a color diagram all these impressions are unambiguously located on the basis of the values that may be assumed by the three fundamental physical variables. These variables are considered to constitute a sufficient description of any color.

In reality we never perceive pure chromatic qualities, except in extremely artificial situations, such as when we observe spectral hues in the laboratory. Instead, we always experience colors in relation to a particular perceptual structure. They are colors *of* something, and are integrated with the other phenomenal aspects of the visual world. D.

Gaetano Kanizsa. 1960. "Randform und Erscheinungsweise von Oberflaechen." *Psychologische Beiträge* 5: 93–101.

Katz (1911; 1935), in his systematic research on the spatial and temporal attributes of colors, clearly demonstrated that the traditional view of the attributes of color sensations would have to be reformulated, taking into account the "modes of appearance" of colors. The classification of modes of appearance proposed by Katz is still largely accepted, even though numerous attempts at further specification and logical clarification have been made.

The fundamental distinction is that between "surface color," "film color," and "volume color." Surface color is the mode of appearance characteristic of most of the objects in our everyday experience. In this case the color appears to be an integral part of the surface of objects, part of the objects themselves even to the point of possessing their form and texture. It is always localized in space at a well-defined distance from the observer; it appears to be compact, solid, material. Not all the colors that we experience as belonging to objects are surface colors, but all surface colors belong to objects.

Film color, unlike surface color, does not possess a well-defined position in the third dimension. It has a less substantial appearance; it is less dense and more soft, spongy, velvety. It is perfectly uniform, without texture or nonhomogeneity. Typical film colors are those seen in a spectroscope, subjective ocular gray, the color of a cloudless sky, fog, smoke, the color of afterimages, or the color of a surface observed through a reduction screen (from which comes the terms "aperture color" and "reduced color").

Whereas a surface color "offers resistance" to the observer's gaze, forcing a halt at the external surface of an object, a film color has less compactness or hardness, and thus yields the impression that to a certain extent one can visually penetrate inside it. This characteristic of having a certain depth has led to the name "film color." Indeed, faced with a color of this sort, one has the impression of a colored, translucent "layer," a sort of membrane or soft, gelatinous film.

Volume color, or bulky color, phenomenally fills a three-dimensional region in space. It is usually the color of a gas or a liquid, or of a transparent piece of ice, of crystal, or of Plexiglas. In order to produce this impression of chromatic voluminosity, a certain degree of transparency is required. Gaze must not only "penetrate" into the chromatic substance, as in the case of film color, but must also pass completely through it so as to be able to detect objects behind it.

FUNCTIONS OF THE MICROSTRUCTURE AND THE MARGINAL GRADIENT

It is sometimes possible, by means of relatively small variations in the stimulus conditions, to make a color pass from one mode of appearance to another. A condition that seems to be necessary for the transformation of a surface color into a film color is the elimination of the microstructure, those minute nonhomogeneities responsible for the texture of a surface. Katz's reduction screen method is based essentially on this principle.

> The surface color impression normally given by an object can easily be supplanted by the impression film color if a screen, containing a single aperture, is so placed before the object as to conceal it completely, except for the part appearing through the aperture, and at the same time to prevent the recognition of any surface structure in the object (Katz 1935, p. 10).

This characteristic of eliminating or strongly reducing the nonhomogeneities in the stimulus is also present in the other procedures (monocular vision, nonsharp accommodation, fusion color resulting from the rotation of Maxwell disks) that, according to Katz, are capable of producing intermediate stages between surface color and film color. W. Metzger (1930), with his research on the phenomenology of the *Ganzfeld*, extended the generality of Katz's claim. He showed that in order for an observer to perceive a surface, the stimulus must possess a certain degree of complexity. When, as in Metzger's experimental *Ganzfeld* situation, the stimulus at the retinal level is as elementary as possible—that is, composed of radiation that is perfectly homogeneous across the entire receptive surface—the observer does not perceive a surface that is homogeneous in color and brightness, corresponding to the real, physical surface from which the luminous radiation arrives.

Instead, an entirely different experience occurs: the observer is immersed in a mist of light that extends indefinitely in all directions. It is only as the intensity of the illumination is increased that the observer begins to distinguish the minute nonhomogeneities in the special reflecting surface; gradually the mist recedes, condenses, and gradually assumes the appearance of a solid surface located at a definite distance from the observer and separated from the observer by empty space. The perception of color concentrated on a surface with empty space in front of it is, thus, the result of a process of differentiation from a more elementary perceptual organization. If the perceptual field is to have any articulation, the stimulus cannot be completely homogeneous. Some discontinuities must be present in the light; in the above situation these were produced by the different coefficients of reflection of the minuscule regions corresponding to the texture or microstructure of the physical surface. This is perfectly understandable if perception is conceived of as a dynamic event, produced by real forces in a determinate equilibrium, since a force clearly requires a nonhomogeneity.

J. J. Gibson, J. Purdy, and L. Lawrence (1955), using the optical tunnel technique, found that the physical correlate of a visual surface is a distribution in which the order of the stimuli varies in a cyclical and alternating fashion.

However, the absence of microstructure does not always give rise to the perception of film color. Homogeneity in the stimulus is then a necessary, but not sufficient, condition. The color of a visual object (for example, the wall of a house), located at a distance such that its texture is not distinguishable, may nevertheless have the solid appearance of a surface color. The factor that in these cases determines the mode of appearance of the color is not the nonhomogeneity in the microstructure, but another type of nonhomogeneity: that represented by the contours of the colored area.

A phenomenal margin normally corresponds to the border between two regions in the visual field that yield radiant stimuli of differing intensities or wavelengths. The line along which the change in the stimulus occurs is the site of segregation forces that tend to keep the two regions separate. The intensity of these forces depends on the nature of the transition from one region to the other—that is, it depends on the type of marginal gradient between them. When the gradient is abrupt or steep, involving a "leap" or a sudden change in the stimulus, the separation between the two visual regions is quite well-defined and sharp phenomenal margins appear. When, however, the gradient between the two regions is uniform, strong phenomenal contours are not formed; instead, there is a gradual transition in brightness or tonality between the two regions.

In the former case a stable and precise visual organization is produced, whereas in the latter the structure of the field is indefinite and unstable as regards the separation of the visual regions. What is interesting here is that this characteristic of indefiniteness in the *spatial* organization is transmitted to the phenomenal *colors* of the respective surfaces. Thus, the mode of appearance of these colors is intimately related to the marginal gradient between the two regions of the field. If the gradient is sharp, the color has the solid aspect of a surface color; but as the gradient becomes less steep, the chromatic substance, which is no longer organized in a solid structure, tends to dissolve, to spread out, and to become unstable and indefinite in location.

The strict causal relationship between type of marginal gradient and mode of appearance of chromatic impressions was described by E. Hering (1920) in his observations on the "shadow phenomenon" and was exhaustively analyzed by L. Kardos (1934). The experimental study of Kardos showed that the brightness gradient along the borders of the shadow plays a central role in the formation of shadow impressions.

While Hering and Kardos projected real shadows in their research, G. A. Fry (1931) and R. B. Macleod (1947) reached the same conclusions by using a different technique. Employing appropriately constructed rotating disks, they were able to create what Macleod called an "artificial penumbra"—a uniform shading of the brightness from one region to the other. This led to a change in the phenomenal character of the entire enclosed area. When the margin is sharp, the color has a solid, surfacelike aspect. Little by little, as the slope of the gradient becomes less steep, the color becomes softer and more airy, gradually passing from a filmlike appearance to that of a volume.

It is possible to show the effect of a marginal gradient on the mode of appearance of a chromatic zone in the visual field in an even simpler and more direct way than that used by Kardos, Fry, and Macleod—that is, in a way that does not involve the rather complicated procedures of shadow projection or rotating disks (whose color has a rather special phenomenal nature that is not entirely equivalent to that of a surface).

The color of the homogeneous black disk in Figure 7.1a clearly has the aspect of a surface. If, as in Figure 7.1b the sharp contour of the disk is eliminated by introducing a band of marginal shading, the mode of appearance of the disk's entire surface is transformed. The observer has a strong impression that the two disks are objectively different, that they have been painted with different coloring materials. The texture of the chromatic substance in the disk with sharp margins is compact, smooth, and solid, whereas that in the disk with fuzzy margins is soft and doughy. The latter has a certain thickness, and there seems to be a layer of dust or of mist extended across it. This effect disappears as soon as the "fuzzy" disk is covered by a page having a circular aperture with a diameter slightly smaller than that of the disk so that the fuzzy region is

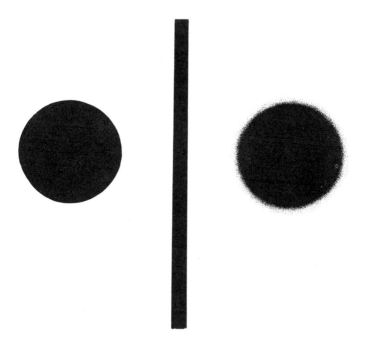

Figure 7.1a Surface color.

Figure 7.1b With the introduction of a uniform marginal gradient, the color becomes softer and "doughy."

occluded. The color then becomes more dense, reacquires the aspect of being a solid surface, and thus becomes identical to the comparison disk.

The same result is obtained when a white or colored disk is substituted for the black disk. The necessary and sufficient condition for effecting the passage from one mode of appearance to another lies entirely in the presence or absence of a uniform gradient of stimulation between the involved regions.

This phenomenon seems to me to demonstrate quite clearly how a local perceptual characteristic need not be a function only of the local stimulus, but may be determined by more global structural characteristics of the field.

Another translocal effect produced by the introduction of a uniform marginal gradient is the transformation of the attributes of the relevant visual regions that are, strictly speaking, "chromatic." The two regions that are in contact also undergo, on passing from one mode of appearance to another, noticeable changes in brightness and in saturation. This demonstrates once again that these chromatic qualities cannot be accounted for with an oversimplified function that relates the qualities to variations along the physical dimensions of the luminous radiation; instead, the perceptual impression, for a given constellation of values of the impression, varies as a function of the mode of appearance—that is, as a function of the structural characteristics of the spatial organization in which these values are incorporated. As for brightness, the fundamental observation to be made is that the difference between the brightnesses of the two areas tends to diminish as the margin separating them approaches a uniform gradient, as opposed to a sudden discontinuity or a sharp contour. A gray figure on a light background becomes, under these circumstances, not only filmlike but also brighter in color, whereas against a dark background the figure becomes phenomenally *darker*. Brightness transformations, similar to those undergone by the figures, are also undergone by the backgrounds.

How can these assimilation processes be explained in terms of the "slope" of the excitation gradients? A tentative interpretation may be proposed on the basis of the following considerations. A phenomenal margin corresponds to the border between the two regions that are stimulated with light of differing intensities; the line along which the discontinuity between the two processes is established is the site of segregating forces that tend to keep the two zones of excitation separate, thereby hindering their interaction. As established by S. Liebmann's research (1927), when the difference in intensity between two regions is reduced and their brightnesses are made to coincide, the marginal tension is canceled and there is no longer a sharp line of demarcation: perceptually the figural margins are attenuated. It is reasonable to suppose that, inversely, if—while holding constant the difference in intensity of stimulus between the two regions—the sharp margin is removed and replaced by a zone of gradual transition of intensity, then processes of reciprocal interaction will be established between the two zones and, phenomenally, their respective brightnesses will tend to become more similar.

INFLUENCE OF FORM OF MARGIN ON THE MODE OF APPEARANCE OF SURFACES

The above observations indicate that chromatic qualities should not be considered merely as the *material* on the basis of which perceptual space is organized; instead, one must also take into account the effect of spatial organization on the perception of the chromatic aspects. That is, space and color are not distinct elements but, rather, are interdependent aspects of a unitary process of perceptual organization. In this regard it seems to me that the following observations on the relationship between the *form* of a surface's margin and its mode of appearance are of considerable interest.

E. Rubin (1921), in his analysis of the relationship between a figure and its contour, concluded that there is a phenomenal and functional primacy of the figure over the contour. He also found figure and contour to be relatively independent of each other.

> Such relative independence between contour and figure may be observed by looking at an ordinary stamp. At first sight one would probably observe that a stamp is quadrangular, and yet its contour is full of indentations. To be sure, once one's attention is directed to this fact he will observe that he had not taken the indentations into account, but having said this he will then admit that in fact the contour has a characteristic that is not directly connected with the phenomenal form of the stamp's surface. What is involved here is a quite general fact, namely that certain characteristics of contours are seen as aspects only of the contour itself and these may play only a very minor role in determining the phenomenal form of the global surface. The figure is, so to speak, too massive and solid to be influenced by a trifle like nonhomogeneities, regular or not, in the contour (Rubin 1921, p. 136).

Rubin's observation is no doubt accurate, but it seems to me to be valid only insofar as it regards the relative independence of the *form* of a surface from the microstructure of its contour. Such independence, however, does not seem to exist if one considers not the form, but the *mode of appearance* of the surface.

In fact, with this in mind, if the figure with the serrated edges in

Figure 7.2 Influence of the *form* of the margin on the mode of appearance of color.

Figure 7.2 is compared with the corresponding figure with rectilinear contours, it is clear that their colors differ somewhat in brightness and in saturation, but even more striking is the difference in their mode of appearance. As in the situation in which the contour consists of a uniform marginal gradient, the chromatic substance becomes thinner, taking on a less dense and solid appearance. The observers whom I have asked to compare the two surfaces report having the impression that they are made of two slightly different materials; surfaces with serrated edges suggest something like blotting paper, chamois cloth, or flannel.

Thus it appears that certain characteristics of the contour, while not substantially modifying—as Rubin observed—the form of the surface they contain, do have some effect on the organization of the chromatic substance. In the situation of Figure 7.2 the "indeterminateness" or "indecision" of a broken contour, one that continually changes direction, seems to transmit to the region contained within it the indeterminateness that is characteristic of the film color mode of appearance.

Some support for this hypothesis is offered by the following observation. The print in the two newspaper clippings in Figure 7.3 is the same. My subjects, however, have reported the impression that the print in the serrated clipping is slightly larger and, more important, that the characters are more widely spaced. This observation also suggests that replacing a rectilinear margin with one that is rather minutely serrated favors the impression of a loss in the compactness and density of the surface.

Figure 7.3 Which characters are more widely spaced?

8

SOME OBSERVATIONS ON COLOR ASSIMILATION

CONTRAST AND ASSIMILATION

The phenomenon of simultaneous contrast involves modifications of chromatic (hue and saturation) and achromatic (brightness and whiteness) attributes that occur in the perception of two colored surfaces when they are spatially contiguous. Although the effect is reciprocal, its intensity varies according to the relative sizes of the surfaces involved in such a way that the influence of the larger surface is proportionally greater. For this reason it used to be common to speak (though somewhat loosely) of "inducing" and of "induced" surfaces, meaning by the latter the region that undergoes the greater modification of its chromatic qualities as a result of its proximity to the other surface. Thus, in order to obtain a strong contrast effect, it is useful to choose an inducing region that is larger than the induced and to have the former surround the latter. In fact, in the classic demonstrations of this phenomenon, a colored square is usually presented with a smaller, gray square or disk at its center. Under these conditions the smaller, central figure acquires to a certain extent the complementary hue of the larger, "inducing" square that surrounds it.

There are, however, certain situations in which, instead of induced color *contrast*, the opposite phenomenon occurs: the *assimilation* of color and brightness.

Gaetano Kanizsa. 1954. "Alcune Osservazioni sull' Effetto Musatti." *Archivio di Psicologia Neurologia e Psichiatria* 15: 265–71.

The necessary condition for the occurrence of this effect—discovered in 1874 by V. Bezold and thoroughly studied by Cesare Musatti (1953) and by H. Helson (1963)—involves the degree of "compactness" of the inducing surface. That is, assimilation instead of contrast takes place when the inducing surface is "dispersed" (in the form of thin lines, small disks, fragments— into the induced surface.

The explanation of this phenomenon may be found in the general hypothesis that Musatti proposed regarding the relation between the contrast and the constancy of colors. According to this account, the basic phenomenon, in the action that two contiguous surfaces exert on each other, is one not of contrast but of assimilation. In most cases assimilation occurs between the components of the total radiation that are experienced as the ambient light. Phenomena of color and brightness contrast that occur between object colors are, in Musatti's account, a residual effect of assimilation. There are, however, other conditions, among which that of "dispersion" seems to be the most effective, in which the assimilation is between object colors; and in this case one would expect a greater nonhomogeneity in the perceived ambient light. In fact, this expectation is not fulfilled in the experience of those who observe such situations. They experience a chromatic assimilation of the surfaces but perceive no difference with respect to their illumination.

Some observations that I have made in the course of an attempt to determine more precisely the conditions involved in "dispersion" may help to clarify these issues.

EXPERIMENTS WITH A SHADOWED REGION

The fact that first caught my attention was that, when faced with situations in which the assimilation effect occurs, not all observers see the stimuli in the same way. Rather, they fall into two groups.

The first and more numerous group is composed of people who are not familiar with the problems and principles of color perception. Their response to situations represented, for example, by patterns A and B of Figure 8.1 (A is a gray background within which are dispersed some patches of white; B is a gray background with black patches) is to affirm without any hesitation that the gray in B is "blacker" than that in A (which is described as "whiter").

If, however, the same patterns are shown to a painter or to someone who for some other reason is accustomed to judging colors, the response is likely to be different, and in any case is not expressed with as much certainty. Painters generally tend to distinguish between chromatic value and degree of brightness or, as they put it, degree of

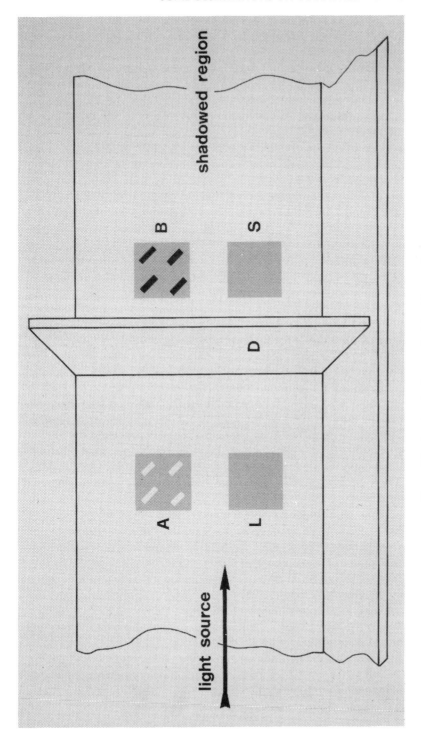

Figure 8.1 A = gray background with white patches.
B = gray background with black patches.
L = gray rectangle in direct sunlight.
S = gray rectangle in shadow.

"brilliance." They say that the gray in pattern A is whiter but at the same time "duller," whereas the gray in B is more "brilliant," "alive," or "insistent."

In these modes of describing color that are employed by artists and color experts, one can see the beginnings of a distinction between the chromatic characteristics of objects and the nature of the illumination in which they are found, a distinction that seems to be completely ignored by the layman.

The observation of this difference in perceptual behavior suggested to me a simple experiment that would demonstrate the existence of a double order of visual impressions that enter into the perception of a surface composed of regions of differing brightness.

Making use of D. Katz's experimental apparatus for studying the constancies, two patterns like those shown in A and B of Figure 8.1 were prepared. Pattern A was placed in a position where it received direct sunlight from a nearby window, while B was placed in the shadow of a screen. Then two additional rectangles were cut from the same gray paper that was used to make A and B, and were placed as shown in Figure 8.1, one of them (L) next to A in the direct sunlight, and the other (S) next to B in the shadowed area. In comparing the four rectangles, the majority of observers noted that the gray in pattern A is similar to that of S, and that B is similar to L.

In other words (since objectively, with regard to albedo, the four grays are identical) a gray surface with *white* inducing patches (A) is seen as similar to the same surface (without the patches) *in a shadow,* and similarly a gray surface with black inducing patches (B) is seen as similar to the same gray (without those patches) *in the light.*

These results demonstrate that there is really no contradiction between the two modes of judging colors used by laymen and by experts. They simply differ in the weight that they give to complementary aspects of the same phenomenon. In an achromatic surface two features may be distinguished phenomenally: the *whiteness* (which can vary along a continuum that goes from white through the series of intermediate grays to black) and the *brightness* (which varies between the two extremes of darkness and light). Whiteness is a more or less permanent characteristic of an object and corresponds to its reflectance or albedo; brightness corresponds to the varying intensity of light by which it may be illuminated. Both of these phenomenal aspects, which correspond to the two objective variables just described, are, however, a function of a single variable of the stimulus: the quantity of light reflected by the object that falls on the retina. Thus, their combination in all probability constitutes an invariant, such that for a given change of whiteness, there is a corresponding appropriate change in brightness, and vice versa. If, then, two surfaces that *objectively* have the same albedo and are located in identical illumination (under normal circumstances they would appear to have the same whiteness and brightness) differ *phenomenally* with respect to one of these characteristics (as happens in the situation studied by Musatti, in which there is a diffusion of the color from one area toward the area immediately surrounding it), then these two surfaces must also differ with respect to the other characteristic. For example, if one of the two surfaces appears to be whiter, it will nevertheless also seem to be darker (that is, less illuminated), and conversely, if it appears blacker, it will also seem lighter (that is, illuminated more intensely).

And this is exactly what our two categories of subjects say, except that the laymen notice primarily the color of the object's surface (these subjects talk about differences in whiteness and pass over—as we all do most of the time, when we look at the objects around us—the aspect that corresponds to their illumination), whereas for the artists and experts the aspect involving the illumination of the object is more important (and they speak of grays that are "blacker but more bright or brilliant" and of grays that are "whiter but darker").

In this regard it should be remembered that in the constancy phenomena (those of size and shape as well as of color), two distinct modes of observation have been noted (by D. Katz, R. H. Henneman, J. J. Gibson, and J. Beck among others): one is natural, spontaneous, global, and aimed at seeing objects (favorable to constancy), while the other is more analytic, artificial, and in general can be described as looking at the visual field "through a painter's eyes," with the intention of distinguishing the various aspects of a given percept (an attitude that greatly reduces the phenomena of constancy). The existence of these two types of perceptual sets may help to account for the variability of the impressions of assimilation noted by Musatti in some of his experiments.

THE EFFECT OF GRADUAL MARGINAL GRADIENTS

There is a way to render more evident the phenomenal separation between object color and ambient illumination: by increasing the incidence of positive chromatic interaction between the surfaces in contact. This effect may be achieved by reducing the steepness of the gradient between the two surfaces along their common border. By introducing, in place of sharp marginal gradients (corresponding to abrupt changes in the level of stimulation), a more gradual gradient of change, a shaded region, the processes of assimilation are favored (see Chapter 7).

As shown in Figure 8.2, the presence of these gradual gradients of change not only intensifies the assimilation effect, but also clarifies the way in which the change in whiteness is accompanied by a complemen-

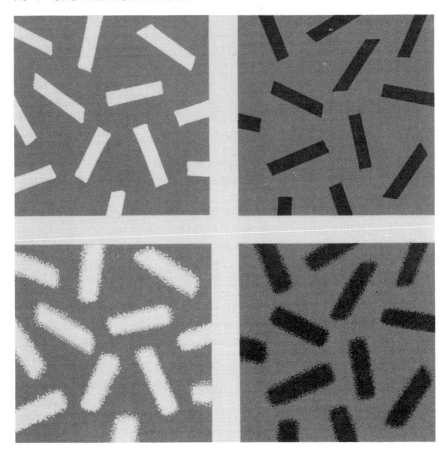

Figure 8.2

tary change in the phenomenal illumination or brightness. In zones A_1 and B_1, for example, the gray has lost some of its compactness and become somewhat softer and more insubstantial. It is as if a faint haze or shadow has been extended across it. Analogous but more intense effects may be obtained by using the "chromatic" series of colors.

A PARADOX

Numerous theories have been proposed to explain the phenomena of color vision, a situation that clearly demonstrates the intricacy and difficulty of the problems in this area. Their complexity becomes evident if, for example, we compare, the perceptual impressions that occur in assimilation and those in the classic contrast situations.

If patterns A and B of Figure 8.3 are presented to a subject (who is not a painter or an expert in problems of vision), and the subject is asked to describe the difference between the two interior, gray squares, in most cases the response is that A is "blacker" and B is "whiter."

If, then, patterns C and D of Figure 8.3 are presented to the same subject, the likely response is that the background gray in C looks "lighter" than that in D, which is described as "darker."

Although it remains to be explained why the responses are different in the two situations, until now everything has gone more or less as expected on the basis of what we know of the phenomena of contrast and of assimilation: When the inducing surface surrounds a compact induced surface, the latter is modified so as to increase the difference between the two (contrast); when, however, the inducing area is composed of several small patches distributed within the induced area,

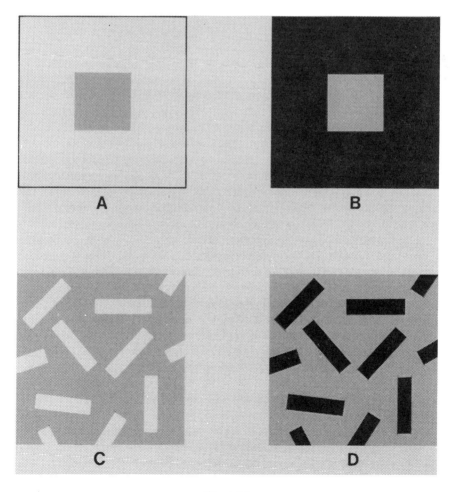

Figure 8.3

the chromatic transformation of the latter reduces the difference between the two (assimilation).

But the results that are obtained if the experiment is continued as described below are unexpected, and present, by virtue of their contradictory nature, a rather embarrassing problem.

Now, show the same subject all four of the patterns in Figure 8.3 (A, B, C, D), and ask whether the gray square in C is more like that of A or that of B, and which of the two is more similar to D.

The naive observer will, without noticing the contradiction, judge A to be similar to C. and B similar to D. This leaves us with the paradoxical result that although A = C and B = D, nevertheless A is darker than B and C is *lighter* than D—and not C darker than D, as one would logically expect on the basis of the preceding equality relations. The same thing happens when, instead of using black, white, and gray figures, one employs the chromatic series of colors in the interacting areas.

Faced with these results, one may wonder whether there really are two distinct and opposite phenomena (contrast and assimilation), or whether perhaps it is not simply a matter of the same process giving rise to different illusory impressions in the two situations. Aside from the fact that calling a perception "illusory" does not make much sense, and is above all a way of eliminating a problem without resolving it, the problem remains of determining the nature of the hypothetical single process: is it the process of assimilation or that of contrast? The fact is that in the two situations, the impressions are qualitatively very different; and the paradoxical results, obtained by comparing the situations, simply demonstrate how sensitive chromatic phenomena are to structural changes in the perceptual whole in which they are observed.

It seems to me that the paradox arises from the fact that in making use of the equality and inequality relations in a way that is formally correct, as we have here, it is implicitly assumed that when a given term is successively compared with a number of other terms, it remains the same. While that may be true from a purely logical or physical point of view, it is not true in the case of perceptual phenomena. For when a perceptual element enters into a different structure, as it does in the operation of comparison, it does not remain unchanged, and thus cannot be considered identical to what it is in a different global structure.

When laboratory experiments are performed with chromatic displays, it is extremely difficult to compare directly the phenomena of contrast and assimilation. One is in the curious situation that in order to obtain the two effects, they have to be isolated from each other. If one attempts to observe them at the same time, they interact in such a way that it is no longer possible to decide with certainty which one is occurring.

9

PHENOMENAL TRANSPARENCY

THE CONDITIONS

Seeing an object "through" a transparent surface is a common experience, and may be rather simply described in terms of a physical property of the surface—that is, the surface allows at least some of the light that strikes it to pass through.

In the case of a colorless sheet of glass that is not too thick and has very low indexes of absorption, reflection, and refraction, almost all of the light rays pass through without undergoing any appreciable change in direction or chromatic composition. In this case the level of transparency is essentially perfect, and approaches that of the atmosphere.

The situation becomes more complicated, but still remains explicable in terms of the principles of optics, when the thickness of the glass is increased, and more particularly when its permeability varies, as it does with changes in the chemical composition of the glass such that only radiation within a certain range of wavelengths can pass through. This is the case, for example, with colored glasses.

It is considerably less simple to find an adequate explanation of the phenomenon of transparency from a psychophysical point of view. Since the light rays coming from the transparent surface, as well as those reflected from the object situated behind it, strike the same area on the retina, thus giving rise to only *one* receptor excitation process, percep-

Gaetano Kanizsa. 1955. "Condizioni ed Effetti della Trasparenza Fenomenica." *Rivista di Psicologia* 49: 3–18.

Figure 9.1 Physical transparency is not a *sufficient* condition for phenomenal transparency. The rectangle is opaque, and the triangle is physically transparent; in this arrangement there is no phenomenal transparency.

tual transparency poses the problem of how a single sensory process can give rise in experience to *two* perceptual objects.

A considerable amount of discussion and experimentation have been devoted to this problem and, as with so many issues in the field of visual perception, the views of the two "great men" of the visual sciences—E. Hering and Hermann von Helmholtz—do not agree. The most important studies on this subject were done by W. Fuchs (1923), B. Tudor-Hart (1928), H. Kopfermann (1930), G. Moore Heider (1933), and, more recently, by Fabio Metelli (1967; 1970; 1974a). The problem received a new and more productive formulation in these latter studies in that they were directed not at how transparency is possible from a physiological point of view but, rather, at what the conditions are in

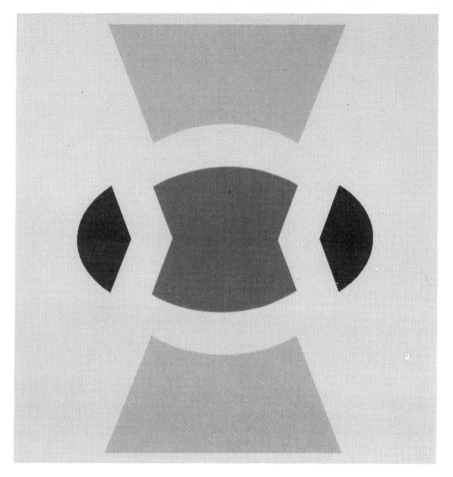

Figure 9.2a Five opaque areas.

which two chromatic surfaces are seen "one behind the other" along the same line of sight.

In fact, the attempt to pursue the problem of transparency in terms of two points situated on the same line of sight has been unfortunate. Transparency is a feature that visual objects assume only to the extent that they are surfaces having certain extensions and belonging to visual arrays with certain structures. To pose the problem with reference to two individual points is inappropriate because in such a situation, transparency, understood as the simultaneous perception along a single line of sight of two distinct points, never occurs. This can be readily demonstrated by isolating in any of a number of ways (for example, by concentration of attention or, better, by means of a reduction screen) a small area of a transparent surface. The impression is always that of a

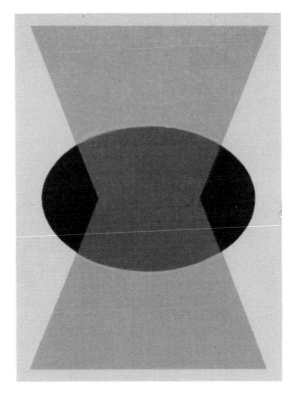

Figure 9.2b Physical transparency is not a *necessary* condition for phenomenal transparency. The juxtaposition of the five completely opaque areas of Figure 9.2a gives a distinct impression of transparency.

spot of color of an entirely homogeneous hue that corresponds to the combined effect (fusion) of the light rays arriving from the two superposed surfaces.

And yet that same small area of surface *can* be seen as two distinct surfaces located at different distances from the eye, and its color *can* be separated into two chromatic components seen as belonging respectively to these two surfaces, one of which is transparent, as soon as that area belongs to a larger figural structure whose total spatial and chromatic organization "requires" the presence of transparency.

An examination of the situations in which the visual field is so structured as to require the transparency of some of its surfaces makes clear the fact that physical transparency is not in and of itself a *sufficient* condition for the experience of perceptual transparency, since physically transparent surfaces are in some cases not seen as such. Situations of this type, in which real, physical transparency is not perceived, are

Figure 9.3a Topological condition: each one of the two areas to be unified in the transparent surface must be in contact with the homologous area and with *only one of the two other areas.*

readily producible. On the other hand, physical transparency is not a *necessary* condition for the occurrence of a strong visual impression of transparency. Indeed, it is quite simple to arrange things so that an entirely opaque surface will be experienced as obviously transparent. An example of the former of these situations occurs when a physically transparent surface and the surface lying behind it are arranged so as to form perfectly congruent images on the retina, or when the transparent surface is smaller and seen in front of the other (see Figure 9.1).

The fact that physical transparency is not a necessary condition is shown in Figure 9.2b where the juxtaposition of five completely opaque areas (Figure 9.2a) gives a distinct impression of transparency.

If phenomenal transparency is, thus, neither simply, nor even necessarily, a function of physical transparency, what are the conditions of its occurrence? The conditions are of three types: topological, figural, and chromatic. In order to have the impression of transparency we need, first of all, four areas in the visual field. Two of these areas have to be unified in a single visual object—that is, the object that has to appear transparent and, thus, to be located in front. This condition obviously implies that these two areas have some of their contours in

Figure 9.3b The topological condition is not satisfied; therefore there is no transparency. (See Figures 9.3c, 9.3d, 9.3e).

Figure 9.3c

Figure 9.3d

Figure 9.3e

Figure 9.4 Figural conditions are not favorable to the impression of transparency. (See Figure 9.5).

common. Furthermore, the other two areas must also be in contact in order to constitute a bicolor region—that is, the region that has to appear opaque and thus to be located behind, and seen through, the first one.

The topological principle can be defined as follows: Each one of the two areas to be unified in the transparent surface must be in contact with the homologous area and *with only one of the two other areas* (see Figure 9.3a). Every time that the shared contour of the two unified areas comes into contact with both of the two other areas, the impression of transparency disappears (see Figures 9.3b–9.3e).

This topological condition, although necessary, is not sufficient. It must be accompanied by other conditions that we may call "figural"— that is, those conditions that allow the two areas to be perceived as a single figure or a single object. When these figural conditions are absent, or when they tend to form a "duo" figure instead of an "unum" figure, there is no impression of transparency, even if the topological condition is respected (see Figures 9.4 and 9.5). In other words, when the figural and topological conditions come into conflict, the topological condition dominates (Figure 9.6).

Among the factors that facilitate unification, one of the most

Figure 9.5

important is continuity of direction (Figure 9.3a and 9.7). However, there is some leeway in the continuity condition, In particular, the line dividing the two transparent areas can change direction sharply at the point where division of the two opaque areas begins (Figure 9.8).

Stratification of the areas on different planes also has been proposed as a condition of transparency (Kanizsa 1955b; Metelli 1974a). Indeed, there is no transparency without stratification, since by definition transparency consists in the simultaneous perception of two surfaces, one behind another. However, it is not clear whether stratification is a cause or an effect of the transparency impression, though it is likely an effect.

Chromatic conditions are very relevant for the perception of transparency. This aspect of the phenomenon was considered in the pioneering research of G. Moore Heider (1933), but impressive progress in this direction is due to Metelli (1970) and 1974b, who was able to build an elegant formal model of the chromatic relations necessary for the perception of transparency.

In order to state the chromatic conditions of transparency, Metelli starts from a paradigmatic situation, a figure (Figure 9.9) with four regions labeled A, P, Q. B. The lowercase letters a, p, q, b symbolize the

Figure 9.6 Topological and figural conditions are in conflict; there is no impression of transparency.

Figure 9.7 Topological and figural conditions combine to cause an impression of transparency.

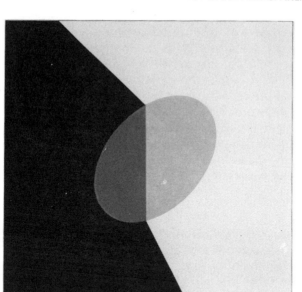

Figure 9.8 Continuity of direction is not a necessary condition of phenomenal transparency.

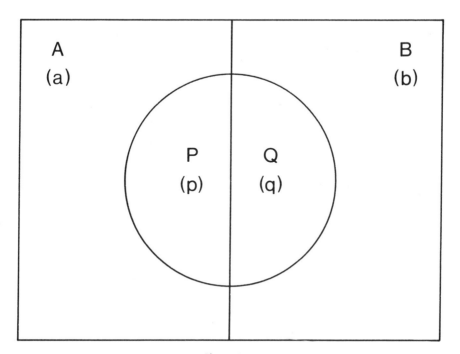

Figure 9.9

measures of reflectance of each region. The propositions for the quantitative theory of the chromatic conditions of transparency are the description of transparency as a phenomenal scission; G. Moore Heider's theory, according to which scission colors are such that, mixed together, they reproduce the stimulus color; Talbot's law, which allows prediction of the reflectance of the fusion color, when the component colors and their proportions are known.

Then, since the chromatic scission can be considered as the inverse of the chromatic fusion, Talbot's equation, read in the inverse direction, represents the quantitative law of transparency. Using the symbols of Figure 9.9 the equation is

$$p = \alpha a + (1 - \alpha)t \tag{1}$$

where t is the reflectance (only indirectly measurable) of the transparent layer, while α and $(1 - \alpha)$ are the proportions of the stimulus color p in the scission layers a and t.

Because there are two unknowns, the equation is indeterminate. But only the left part of Figure 9.9 has been used; the right half allows the writing of an analogous equation:

$$q = \alpha_1 b + (1 - \alpha_1)t_1 \tag{2}$$

When $\alpha = \alpha^1$ and $t = t^1$—that is, when the transparent layer is homogeneous in transparency and color—we have a system of two equations in two unknowns, whose solution is

$$\alpha = \frac{p - q}{a - b} \tag{3}$$

$$t = \frac{aq - bp}{(a + q) - (b + p)} \tag{4}$$

The meaning of t has already been clarified. As for α, it is enough to consider that with an increase of α there is an increase in the quantity of color going to the layer seen through the transparent layer (that is, its visibility) and the quantity of color going to the transparent layer (that is, its opacity) decreases. Therefore, α is a coefficient of transparency.

Keeping in mind that α can vary only between 0 and 1 (otherwise one of the two layers would receive a negative quantity of color, which is absurd), from equation (3) two necessary conditions of transparency can be deduced: the difference in brightness between p and q has to be less than the difference in brightness between a and b; and if p is brighter than q, then a has to be brighter than b. From the same equation a series of inequalities can be deduced, allowing prediction of the color of the transparent layer.

CHROMATIC EFFECTS OF TRANSPARENCY

Now we can turn our attention to the effects produced by the phenomenon of transparency. Some are of considerable interest in connection with a more general theory of color perception, and as such are often used to sustain particular theoretical positions.

First of all, the chromatic scission of the "shared" region, or region of superposition of the two surfaces, constitutes a clear case of "double presence" in which two distinct features in concrete psychological experience correspond to a single sensory process.

"Double presence" can also occur in the absence of transparency—for example, in the figure-ground phenomenon. The ground "continues under" or "passes behind" the figure. It is "present," even though invisible, behind the figure. The same region of stimulation is, thus, twice present in experience; this is not simply due to the characteristics of the region itself but, rather, to factors that lie outside it (or, more strictly speaking, factors that belong to the *relation* between the shared region and those that border on it).

In the case of transparency, the double presence is more striking perceptually because the two components into which the shared region separates are both "visible," one behind the other.

Another example of double presence that comes to mind in this regard is the separation of the illuminated from the illuminating—that is, the set of phenomena known as the constancies of color and brightness. In these situations as well there is a single sensory process, which corresponds to the light reflected from the object, giving rise to two perceptual "facts" in visual experience: the color or brightness of the object itself and the color or brightness of the illumination. Moreover, one might speak of a special sort of transparency here: the object as seen "through" the illuminated atmosphere.

Cesare Musatti (1953), whose theory of color perception offers a unified solution to the problems of constancy, assimilation, and contrast, attaches a great deal of importance to the separation of "object color" and "ambient light." Having postulated a general tendency toward assimilation that operates on the components of the ambient light, he shows how the phenomena of contrast and constancy can be understood as residual effects of this more basic process of assimilation. In his discussion of these phenomena, he points out that situations involving transparency are special cases that may be accounted for by using this same theoretical framework.

Figure 9.10a differs from Figure 9.2b with respect to a single, but important, detail; whereas the oval and the region of superposition are black and gray, respectively, the rest of the configuration is simply outlined and its interior is of precisely the same color as the background.

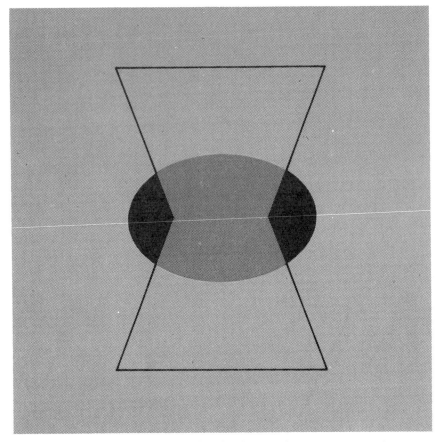

Figure 9.10a The area that is simply outlined undergoes chromatic scission with transparency effects. (See Figure 9.10b).

All the subjects to whom I have shown this figure have reported a clear impression of transparency, even clearer than that seen in Figure 9.2b. They describe an "hourglass" made of glass or transparent celluloid placed askew over the black oval. Similarly, in Figure 9.11 the black irregular figures are partially covered by a glassy rectangular surface.

What is remarkable here is that the chromatic scission occurs not only in the neutral "shared" region but also in the area that is simply outlined. This area, as a consequence of the separation into two surfaces—the transparent surface and the figure lying behind it— undergoes a brightness transformation that differentiates it phenomenally from the rest of the background. Nevertheless, the two are identical with respect to the quantity and quality of reflected light.

The direction in which the shift of brightness occurs is determined

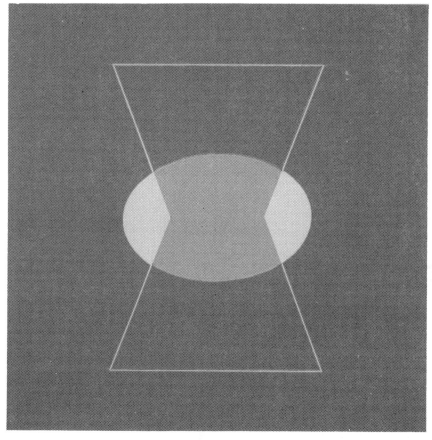

Figure 9.10b

by the chromatic relationship between the overlapping figures. The figure above the black oval of Figure 9.10a or the rectangle above the black figures of Figure 9.11 become lighter than the background, while the one above the white oval of Figure 9.10b becomes darker.

The changes in brightness that occur in the outlined region might simply be considered as a case of simultaneous contrast. Consider, however, the results obtained from the display illustrated in Figure 9.12. Two quite distinct figural organizations are possible, to each of which corresponds a different color for a certain region of the figure. The organization that usually prevails, especially when the figure is observed through the gray rectangular frame, is a gray background on which there are some black circles partly covered by a thin film or transparent veil slightly lighter than the background. Note that in this case the border of the transparent surface has not been traced, even

Figure 9.11 The vertical rectangle is also transparent in the regions that are the same color as the background.

Figure 9.12 The brightness of a region depends upon figural organization.

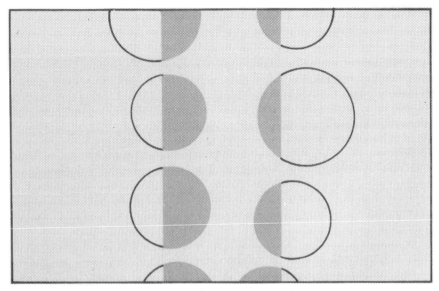

Figure 9.13a Is the grayish tonality of the central region the result of assimilation or of transparency?

though phenomenally it is clearly present and constitutes a precise line of demarcation between the areas of differing apparent brightness (see Chapter 12).

A second perceptual organization, which may occur spontaneously or may require some voluntary set (and which, in any case, is facilitated by the removal of the rectangular frame), involves quite a different structuring of the configuration: on a black background there is a dark gray rectangle, and above this (or in front of it) a light gray rectangle with holes in it. Through these holes one can see part of the black background as well as part of the dark gray rectangle, which is seen as amodally complete, without any sign of transparency.

In this case there is no apparent difference in brightness of regions that are objectively the same, as in the previous organization. The large gray rectangle with circular holes in it now appears perfectly homogeneous in color and in brightness, and there is no trace of the "anomalous contours" that separated an interior region (corresponding to the transparent film) from the slightly darker remainder of the larger rectangle.

The results of this experiment are interesting in that they demonstrate how different chromatic experiences may result from different perceptual organizations of a given configuration.

It does not seem, thus, to be a question of contrast but, rather, of brightness transformations based on an organization of the field involving a transparent surface.

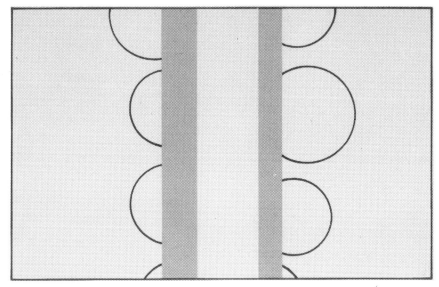

Figure 9.13b Without transparency there is no brightness transformation.

Another alternative explanation of these phenomena involves the process of assimilation, described by Fuchs as a virtual diffusion or irradiation of the chromatic processes beyond the area of stimulation.

The results of the experiment just described, however, are opposed to this interpretation as well, since the elimination of the effect on the basis of a figural reorganization means that it is due neither to contrast nor to assimilation caused by chromatic diffusion.

Moreover, the results of the experiment shown in Figure 9.13a are also inconsistent with an assimilation account of these brightness phenomena. In Figure 9.13a the dark central veil might be thought to be the result of assimilation brought about by the darkened parts of the white circles. If, however, the configuration is modified as shown in Figure 9.13b, so as to remove the conditions for the perception of transparency but, at the same time, leaves unchanged those that could bring about assimilation, the central transparent veil disappears, and with it the grayish tonality of that region (which in Figure 9.13b has the same brightness as the rest of the field).

Here, also, what is important in determining the chromatic "mode of appearance" of the critical region is its spatial relation to the other regions—that is, the mode of appearance of a given area is connected to the role it plays in the broader structure of which it is a part.

In other words, the brightness transformation phenomena illustrated here should be considered a consequence of the phenomenal presence of transparency, and not its cause.

10

STRUCTURAL FACTORS IN BRIGHTNESS CONTRAST

BRIGHTNESS INDUCTION: A RELATIONAL PHENOMENON

A large number of experiments, from those of C. Hess and H. Pretori (1894) to the more recent studies of E. G. Heinemann (1955) and of L. Hurvich and D. Jameson (1966), have supported the fact that simultaneous brightness contrast in a particular ("test") region depends in a systematic way upon the luminance and the size of the contiguous "induction" region. As for the corresponding physiological mechanism, modern electrophysiological research (F. Ratliff, H. K. Hartline, and W. H. Miller 1963) seems to support E. Hering's theory, which attributes the phenomenon of contrast to lateral inhibition processes taking place at a peripheral level of the nervous system.

However, in addition to this physiological work, there are many observations that do not support the hypothesis that there is a simple relation between phenomenal contrast and quantitative variables such as the intensity and spatial distribution of the stimulus. These observations suggest that there are structural factors involved, factors that were once referred to as "central" and now are called "cognitive."

The best-known of these observations is that of W. Benary (1924). In Figure 10.1, the gray triangle that lies on the black cross undergoes a

Gaetano Kanizsa. 1975. "Some New Demonstrations of the Role of Structural Factors in Brightness Contrast." In *Gestalttheorie in der Modernen Psychologie*, ed. S. Ertel, L. Kemmler, and M. Stadler, pp. 219–26. Darmstadt: Steinkopff.

Figure 10.1 The Benary cross. The contrast effects are the opposite of those to be expected on the basis of a summation theory. The gray triangle outside the black cross appears darker than the gray triangle on the cross.

contrast effect in relation to the cross, while the triangle that lies on the white background contrasts with that background. Thus, the direction of the simultaneous brightness contrast is determined in this case by the specific relation of phenomenal belongingness *(Zugehörigkeit)*—that is, by the relation of the "induced" surface to the contiguous surfaces, and not simply by the extension of these surfaces.

As W. Metzger (1931) has very convincingly demonstrated, the investigations of W. H. Mikesell and M. Bentley (1930) and of J. G. Jenkins (1930) fully confirm Benary's results.

Another example of how the conditions affecting belongingness determine whether or not contrast occurs has been given by W. Wolff (1933). In his experiment two small, gray squares of equal brightness

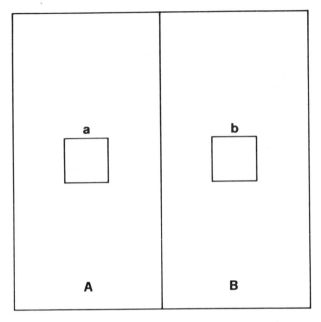

Figure 10.2 The experiment of Wolff (1933). *A* is a dark gray surface, *B* is a light gray surface, *a* and *b* are two small test fields of equal luminance.

were suspended at a given distance in front of a visual field that was divided into two parts, one of which was dark gray and the other light gray (Figure 10.2). When the two small squares were seen as localized at their objective distance from the background, they were seen as equally bright. That is, they did not undergo any noticeable contrast effect in relation to their respective backgrounds. If, however, they were seen as resting directly on the background surface, they underwent a contrast effect such that one was seen as somewhat brighter and the other as darker.

Since the retinal stimulation was the same in both cases, it must be concluded that the decisive factor in the determination of whether contrast occurs is that of belongingness. Another variable that can affect contrast is the perceived figure-ground relationship. This was demonstrated by W. Wolff (1934) with the display shown in Figures 10.3a and 10.3b. Physically, the "figures" in Figure 10.3a have the same luminance (that is, the light reflected from them is equal in intensity) as the ground in Figure 10.3b, and vice versa. Phenomenally, however, the figures in Figure 10.3a are lighter than the ground in Figure 10.3b, and the figures in Figure 10.3b are darker than the ground in Figure 10.3a. Thus, in this situation the "figures" undergo a greater contrast effect than the ground does.

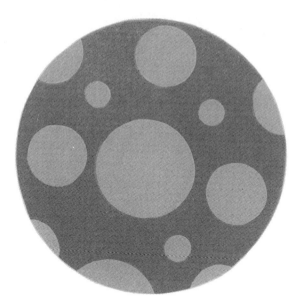

Figure 10.3a

This fact has been reconfirmed by S. Coren (1969). Using the ambiguous pattern in Figure 10.4 he found that a given region of the visual field undergoes a greater contrast effect when it is perceived as a

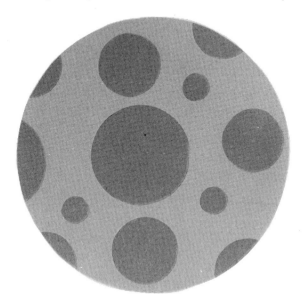

Figure 10.3b   The display of Wolff (1934) (from Metzger 1975).

Figure 10.4 The women-rabbit figure of Coren (1969). In this orientation the central patch is seen as a gray rabbit on a black background; if the display is rotated 180 degrees, the same test patch is seen as gray space between two black women's faces.

figure than when it is perceived as a ground. He reached the same conclusions by varying the figural characteristics of a region with stereoscopic cues.

PHENOMENAL BELONGINGNESS

In the examples that follow, the dependence of brightness induction on figure-ground conditions and on the factor of belongingness seems to me to be quite evident. Note, for example, the difference between Figures 10.5a and 10.5b. Whereas in the former the horizontal strip is homogeneous in brightness, in the latter two quite distinct levels of brightness appear as a function of the change in "belongingness" of the central zone. The same is true for the remarkable brightness transformation that occurs in the central disk in Figure 10.6a when its belongingness relations are modified as in Figure 10.6b.

That such differences in the intensity of induction effects do not depend mainly on spatial variables or on luminance as such but, rather, as in the case of Benary's cross, on belongingness, can be seen from the example shown in Figure 10.7, in which all three of the central white regions are surrounded, from a purely retinal point of view, by black regions, and in which the spatial and luminance conditions are identi-

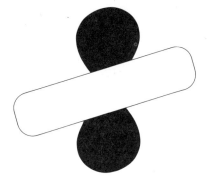

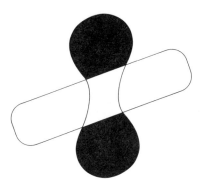

Figure 10.5a The white horizontal strip is in front of the black figure. In this condition of relative independence, the influence of brightness induction is rather weak.

Figure 10.5b The central zone "belongs" to the black figure and, as a result, undergoes a strong brightness induction effect.

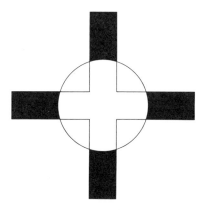

Figure 10.6a The white disk "lies in front of" the black cross.

Figure 10.6b The region that "belongs" to the cross undergoes brightness induction from its darker extremities.

cal. Yet their respective brightnesses vary as a function of their differences in phenomenal belongingness. The central white region belongs to the vertical rectangle and undergoes brightness induction from its dark extremities; the two lateral white regions do not, however, belong to the corresponding black regions; rather, they lie in front of them.

The observation of Figure 10.8a leads to the same conclusions. The central part, although surrounded on four sides by identical black patches, is composed of zones of differing phenomenal brightness. As for the role played by organizational factors in the type of contrast that occurs, it is quite instructive to compare Figures 10.8a and 10.8b. The

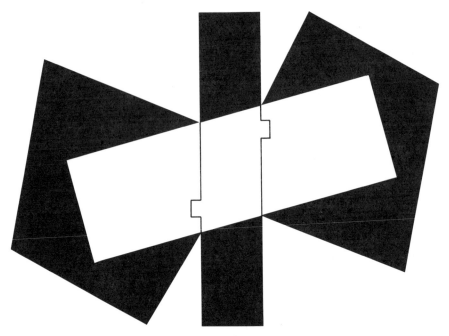

Figure 10.7 The amount and type of induction do not depend only on the area of the inducing region. Here the same luminance conditions hold for all three central white regions, but their structural statuses are different, and as a result their degrees of brightness are different.

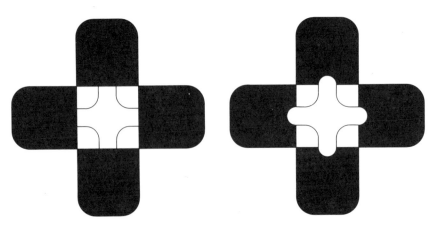

Figure 10.8a The five regions into which the central white square is divided are submitted to the same "amount" of induction, but appear to have different brightnesses.

Figure 10.8b The white cross undergoes contrast in relation to the black regions.

cross in Figure 10.8b appears to be brighter than that in Figure 10.8a as a consequence of the different phenomenal stratification. As in Benary's display, the cross in Figure 10.8b lies on black fields and undergoes a contrast effect in relation to them, whereas the cross in Figure 10.8a lies on a white background and thus appears darker.

Since Wilhelm Wundt's time it has been known that the presence of lines or contours has an effect on contrast phenomena (P. Berman and H. Leibowitz 1965). The effects that we have examined thus far could conceivably be attributed to the influence of this variable. But the display shown in Figure 10.9 demonstrates that this is not the only factor involved. Although the entire surface is homogeneously covered with black disks, the square central region is clearly distinguishable in brightness from the remainder of the field, even though it is delimited in large part only by "contours without gradient"—that is, by contours for which there is no corresponding nonhomogeneity in the stimulus. The same is true for Figure 10.10, which is simply the "photographic negative" of Figure 10.9. Here also the central region is much darker than the rest, even though conditions are present that normally would yield equal contrast over the entire dark surface.

In this case as well the phenomenon seems to depend on the different role assumed by the central region, for structural reasons, with respect to the rest of the field. The stratification that takes place in Figure 10.9, as a consequence of the amodal completion of some black

Figure 10.9 The central "anomalous" square is whiter than the ground.

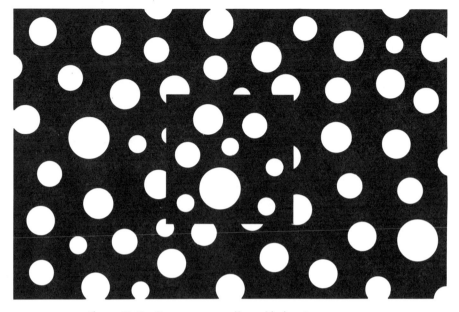

Figure 10.10 Contrast as an effect of belongingness.

disks, occurs in such a way that the central part assumes the role of "figure" and thus undergoes contrast in relation to the black regions on which it lies. The reverse is true in Figure 10.10.

This account receives further confirmation from Figures 10.11 and 10.12. In these displays, too, there is a separation of the central region from the remainder of the field. But this time the amodal completion of the disks favors a different stratification: the central zone tends to be localized behind the surrounding surface and is seen as a figure rather than as a ground.

The fact that transformations in brightness of an area of the visual field depend on structural factors—that is, figure-ground organization—is clearly shown by the formation of an anomalous surface (see Chapter 12). Some researchers have tried to explain the phenomenon of anomalous surfaces by proposing contrast as the cause (see W. Brigner and M. Gallagher 1974). But, as I have shown in Chapter 12, it is just the opposite. The brightness transformation is an effect, rather than a cause, of the generation of an anomalous surface. We arrive at the same conclusion if we examine some displays in Chapter 9. In Figure 9.12, the apparent brightness of an area undergoes relevant transformations without any change in the intensity of the light reflected, but only as a function of the change in phenomenal state. It is the transformation of the figural organization that brings about a chromatic transformation.

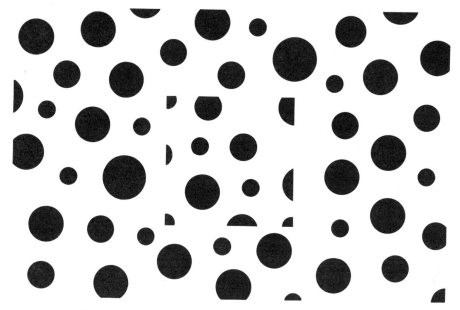

Figure 10.11 The central region, seen as ground, looks darker.

Figure 10.12 The region seen as ground is brighter.

Figure 10.13a   **Figure 10.13b** Paradoxical differentiation in phenomenal brightness.

A century of observation and experimental research has shown that chromatic and brightness contrasts are very complex phenomena, as are chromatic and brightness assimilation, constancy, and the transformation of color from one mode of appearance to another. One thing is certain: these phenomena are *relational.* I think that this comes out clearly not only in the examples given in this chapter but also from those in chapters 7, 8, and 9. To reinforce the point, take the following example, in my opinion one that is particularly puzzling. If, in the zone internal to a black ring (Figure 10.13a) we draw a thin black line, the two zones created by this division take on different degrees of brightness (Figure 10.13b). Since the conditions for brightness contrast are identical for the two zones, the differentiation in phenomenal brightness is paradoxical. The only possible explanation is in terms of structural features. The introduction of a boundary line creates two areas with different phenomenal statuses: this apparently is sufficient to give to them different chromatic aspects.

11

PHENOMENAL SHRINKAGE AND EXPANSION OF VISUAL SURFACES

THE PHENOMENON

In Figure 11.1a the square in the middle, partly covered by the black strip, seems to most observers to be narrower than the two uncovered squares, so that this central square appears to be a rectangle. Figure 11.1b demonstrates that this contraction may occur not only in regions seen as "figure" but also in those seen as "ground," since even the empty space covered by the strip is narrower than that, to the right and equal in size, that is not covered.

I have proposed elsewhere (Kanizsa 1972a) that these visual phenomena are especially interesting because of the insights they yield about the nature of visual space in general. Visual space is not a static geometrical scheme, nor is it a simple transposition, on the perceptual level, of the topographical arrangement of the retinal stimulus. Rather, it should be considered the result of an extremely dynamic event, as demonstrated, for example, by W. Metzger (1930) in his research on the *Ganzfeld*. In his studies the amplitude and the articulation of phenomenal space were strictly determined by the energy distribution originating from the proximal stimulus. When this stimulus is homogeneous and of low intensity, visual space "shrinks" or contracts, and tends to

Gaetano Kanizsa. 1975. "Amodal Completion and Phenomenal Shrinkage of Visual Surfaces. *Italian Journal of Psychology* 2: 187–95.

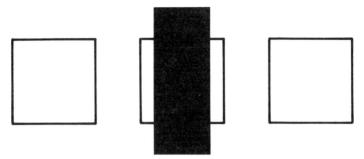

Figure 11.1a Which square is narrower?

Figure 11.1b Phenomenal "shrinkage" of amodal space.

assume the least possible size, given the forces that are active at the moment. The resulting visual organization thus obeys a "minimum principle" (Koffka 1935).

Another example of this dependency of phenomenal size on energy levels in the visual stimulus is the well-known phenomenon in which empty spaces appear to be notably shorter than filled spaces that are objectively equal in length (see Figure 11.2).

Similar observations on apparent size in visual space may be made regarding all those situations in which the intensity of the external stimulus is quite low (tachistoscopic observation, reduced illumination, afterimages, blind spot, hemianopsia). In these situations the organization of the stimulus is for the most part accomplished "internally."

Another situation in which the organizational power of the exter-

Figure 11.2 The empty space is shorter than the filled space.

nal stimulus is reduced to a minimum is that of "amodal completion." A visual object that is completed behind another has at its disposition a reduced quantity of energy, because the energy that is produced in the area where the superposition occurs is entirely consumed by the processes involved in constructing the covering object. On the basis of a "Minimum principle," this situation should result in a shrinkage of the phenomenal size of the covered area. This hypothesis receives support from the observation of Figures 11.1a and 11.1b.

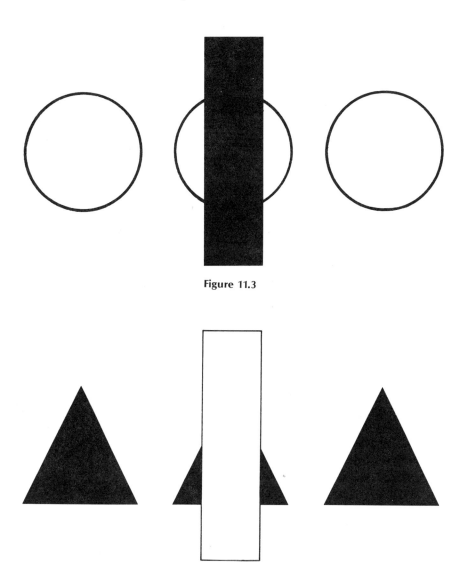

Figure 11.3

Figure 11.4

Figure 11.5

Additional situations in which amodal completion probably contributes to the apparent shrinkage of an object that is partly covered by another are shown in Figures 11.3–11.5.

In order to determine both the extent of this phenomenal shrinkage (in situations where amodal completion occurs) and its dependence on the size and type of area completed, two experiments have been performed.

RELATION BETWEEN EXTENT OF SHRINKAGE AND SIZE OF AREA COMPLETED AMODALLY

Method

The display used in the first experiment is shown in Figure 11.6. The first pattern consisted of a square, 50 millimeters on a side, partially covered by a black rectangle 40 millimeters wide and 150 millimeters high. The second and third patterns were identical to the first, except that the black rectangle was, respectively, 30 millimeters and 20 millimeters wide. Each of these three (standard) patterns was compared with a series of 15 quadrilaterals, equal in height (50 millimeters) to the square but different from one another in width. The series of 15 quadrilaterals was constructed using increments of 1 millimeter from the narrowest (43 millimeters) to the widest (57 millimeters). Each of the three standard patterns was drawn to the right of each of the comparison quadrilaterals on a gray card 20 centimeters by 30 centimeters. The resulting 45 displays were individually presented in a frontal parallel plane 180 centimeters from the subject.

The order of presentation of the three series of 15 displays was identical. First a display (standard pattern plus comparison quadrilateral) was presented in which the comparison figure was clearly nar-

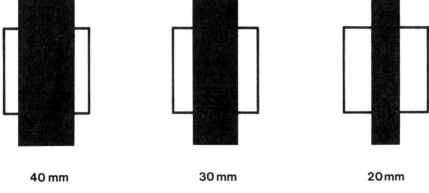

| 40 mm | 30 mm | 20mm |

Figure 11.6 Shrinkage increases with the extent of amodal completion.

rower than the square in the standard pattern. This was followed by a display in which the comparison figure was clearly wider. Then the other comparison quadrilaterals were randomly alternated. With each presentation the subject was asked to indicate which of the two quadrilaterals in the display (the uncovered comparison quadrilateral to the left or the partially covered standard to the right) was wider. Judgments of equality were not accepted. Twenty-five adult subjects were used in each of the three experimental series.

The judgments obtained for each of the three standard patterns were ordered from that relative to the narrowest comparison quadrilateral to that relative to the widest. In the process the judgments were divided into two classes: those of "left" (that is, "the wider figure is the one on the left" or "the comparison quadrilateral is wider than the standard pattern") and those of "right" (that is, "the wider figure is the one on the right" or "the comparison quadrilateral is narrower than the standard pattern"). From these distributions of judgments an estimate can be made for each subject on the extent of spatial deformation (shrinkage, in the present case) that is undergone by the squares in the standard patterns. This estimate consists in the difference, expressed in millimeters, between the width of the comparison quadrilateral that represents the "point of subjective equivalence" (PSE) and the width (always 50 millimeters in this experiment) of the standard pattern. When there is a clear separation between the two classes of judgments ("left" and "right"), the PSE is represented by the midpoint between the width of the narrowest comparison quadrilateral that was judged to be wider than its corresponding standard pattern and the width of the widest comparison quadrilateral judged narrower. In those cases, on the other hand, in which the two classes of judgments were overlapping, the PSE was calculated according to the formula proposed by E. B. Titchener

(1905) for the determination of difference thresholds. (The arithmetic mean of the widest comparison figure judged narrower than the standard pattern and the narrowest comparison figure judged to be wider is calculated.)

Since the standard pattern was always located on the right side of the display, thus allowing the possibility of a systematic position error, an appropriate control group was run. Each of 25 subjects in this group saw another series of 15 displays that were identical in all respects to those described above except that the standard pattern, still on the right, consisted simply of a square 50 millimeters on a side with no black rectangle partially covering it. In this situation, of course, amodal completion does not occur.

TABLE 11.1

Mean Values of PSEs for Four Groups in the First Experiment (values in millimeters)

Group	Number of Subjects	Mean PSE	Difference from Standard	Difference from Control	Percent Difference
A1	25	48.16	−1.84	−2.48	4.89
A2	25	49.04	− .96	−1.60	3.15
A3	25	49.56	− .44	−1.08	2.13
Control	25	50.64	+ .64	0	

A1   = standard pattern with black strip 40 mm × 150 mm.
A2   = standard pattern with black strip 30 mm × 150 mm.
A3   = standard pattern with black strip 20 mm × 150 mm.
Control = standard pattern without black strip.
N.S.   = not significant.

Significance of Differences

	t	
A1 – A2	1.52	N.S.
A2 – A3	.98	N.S.
A1 – A3	2.72	$p < .01$
A1 – C	5.35	$p < .001$
A2 – C	3.33	$p < .01$
A3 – C	2.67	$p < .01$

Source: Kanizsa 1975b, p. 192.

Results

Table 11.1 reports the mean PSE for the four groups and the mean values for the PSEs obtained in each situation. From these results the following can be seen:

● The "square" in the standard pattern undergoes a phenomenal shrinkage in all three experimental situations.

● The phenomenal shrinkage seen by the experimental groups is significantly (p < .01) larger than the spatial deformation (in the opposite direction) undergone by the standard pattern in the control group.

● The extent of the shrinkage increases regularly as the width of the black strip increases, reaching almost 5 percent with the 40-millimeter strip.

EFFECT OF AMODAL COMPLETION IN SOME COMMON FIGURE-GROUND SITUATIONS

The regularity of the relation between the extent of shrinkage and the width of the superimposed strip supports the hypothesis, proposed above, that the phenomenon of shrinkage is the result of conditions created by amodal completion. To test this hypothesis further, the conditions for the occurrence of amodal completion must be reduced as much as possible while the relation between the sizes of the black and white regions remains unchanged (with respect to the first experiment). To accomplish this, a second experiment was performed, using the patterns reproduced in Figure 11.7.

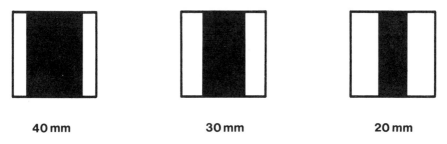

| 40 mm | 30 mm | 20 mm |

Figure 11.7 The displays of the second experiment.

As can be seen, these patterns have been derived from those used in the first experiment by reducing the height of the black strip to 50 millimeters, so that its upper and lower extremities coincide with those of the square. What is perceived with these latter patterns is, however, quite different. Whereas in the patterns shown in Figure 11.6, we tend to see a figure (a square) that is completed amodally behind another figure, the patterns in Figure 11.7 are typical figure-ground situations in which the figural character of the white region is less accented. In fact, superposition may not be perceived if, for example, the pattern is seen as resulting from the juxtaposition of two white rectangles and a black one.

TABLE 11.2

Mean Values of PSEs for Four Groups in the Second Experiment (values in millimeters)

	Number of Subjects	Mean PSE	Difference from Standard	Difference from Control	Percent Difference
B1	25	48.42	– 1.58	– 2.22	4.38
B2	25	49.22	– .78	– 1.42	2.80
B3	25	50.10	+ .10	+ .63	1.24
Control	25	50.64	+ .64	0	

B1 = standard pattern with black strip 40 mm × 50 mm.
B2 = standard pattern with black strip 30 mm × 50 mm.
B3 = standard pattern with black strip 20 mm × 50 mm.
Control = standard pattern without black strip.
N.S. = not significant.

Significance of Differences

	t	
B1 – B2	1.62	N.S.
B2 – B3	2.31	$p < .05$
B1 – B3	3.01	$p < .001$
B1 – C	4.81	$p < .001$
B2 – C	3.77	$p < .001$
B3 – C	1.59	N.S.

Source: Kanizsa 1975b, p. 194.

This experiment was performed with another group of 25 subjects. The procedure and data elaboration were identical to those of the first experiment. The results, shown in Table 11.2, display the same trend, with a slight decrease in the extent of the shrinkage, as in the first experiment.

Such unexpected results demonstrate that if the hypothesis that the shrinkage depends on the occurrence of amodal completion is correct, such completion is no less effective in figure-ground situations than in those where one figure is completed behind another, with a more compelling stratification. G. Tampieri (1978), using a very sensitive experimental method, was able to show that the shrinkage effect is due really to the action of an amodal completion. Indeed, when we are able to create the impression that the zone in question is not seen as "figure" but as "ground" viewed through a hole in a square, the dimensions of such a square do not undergo modification.

A confirmation of the energetic model proposed here in relation to the width of the visual field can be found in an experiment by W. Gerbino (1975). He discovered that when a transparent object is

Figure 11.8 The black trapezium adjacent to the rectangle is phenomenally larger than the other three trapeziums.

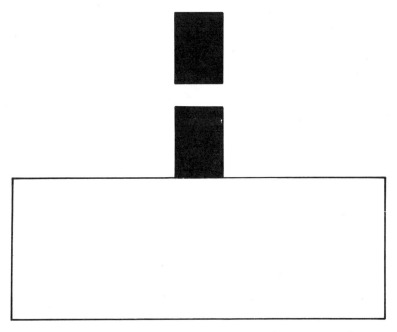

Figure 11.9 The display of the experiment of Kanizsa and Luccio 1978. The rectangle adjacent to the larger surface is overestimated. The expansion effect is about 8 percent.

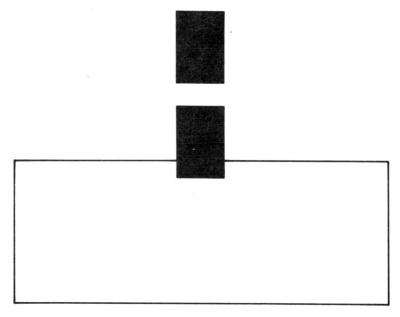

Figure 11.10 The display of the control experiment of Micali, Giurissevich and Seriani 1978. Without amodal completion there is no significant overestimation of the rectangle that is near to the larger surface.

superimposed on an opaque zone, the perceptual sizes of both depend on the degree of transparency. On the basis of two independent measurements, he arrived at the following conclusions: the size of an object seen behind a transparent one is a direct function of the degree of transparency; the size of a transparent object is an inverse function of its degree of transparency.

PHENOMENAL EXPANSION AS A CONSEQUENCE OF AMODAL COMPLETION

Amodal completion may cause not only a shrinkage but, under appropriate conditions, also an expansion of a surface. In Figure 11.8, the black trapezium adjacent to the rectangle appears larger than the other three trapeziums. In an experiment carried out with R. Luccio (Kanizsa and Luccio 1978), using the same method described earlier in this chapter, under "Relation Between Extent of Shrinkage and Size of Area Completed Amodally," we found that the expansion effect is about 8 percent (see Figure 11.9).

In a control experiment, carried out with displays like those in Figure 11.10, G. Micali, O. Giurissevich, and M. Seriani (1978) confirmed that the expansion is due solely to the amodal completion and not, for example, to an assimilation effect resulting from the nearness to the largest figure (Delbeuf's illusion). Indeed, in their experimental conditions they did not find any significant overestimation of the rectangle that is near to the larger surface.

In sum, the following facts must be considered. First, shrinkage by amodal completion always affects the space between two modally visible surfaces adjacent to an overlapping surface (Figure 11.1a). Second, under conditions of amodal completion visible surfaces undergo expansion (Figure 11.9). There may well exist a relationship between these two phenomena. In this case the actual shrinkage of the amodally completing part may be even larger than the 5 percent figure found in the first experiment. For this reason this relationship deserves further study.

12

ANOMALOUS CONTOURS AND SURFACES

Recently there has been some interest, both experimental and theoretical, in the problem of contours that appear in the visual field even in the absence of abrupt gradients in stimulation (brightness, hue, or saturation) that normally give rise to perceptual contours.* Some new phenomena related to the existence of such "contours without gradients" have been discovered (M. Farne 1968; N. Pastore 1971; D. Varin 1971; R. L. Gregory 1972; S. Coren 1972; M. Sambin 1974) and new explanations have been proposed (M. Stadler and J. Dieker 1969; S. Coren 1972; R. L. Gregory 1972; A. Ginsburg 1975; S. Ullman 1976).

Gaetano Kanizsa. 1971. "Contours Without Gradients or Cognitive Contours. *Italian Journal of Psychology* 1: 93–112.

*Such contours have been called by various names. In order to emphasize the fact that they have no counterpart in the stimulus, some have referred to them as "illusory" or "subjective" (F. Schumann, S. Coren). From a phenomenological point of view, this is not a felicitous way of labeling them, since there is no experiential difference between these contours and those that correspond to real discontinuities in the stimulus (and that are therefore considered "objective"). Nevertheless, we are forced to recognize that these phenomena are universally labeled as "subjective contours." For the same reason it no longer seems to me suitable to use the term "quasi-perceptive," which I proposed in 1955. R. L. Gregory has called them "cognitive" contours, but this term implies an explanatory theory that I do not share. The most acceptable proposal seems to me that of R. B. Lawson and W. L. Gulick, who have referred to them as "anomalous" contours. In fact, since they occur in the absence of the normal conditions for contour perception, they cannot be explained according to the usual models of visual processes, and thus they may be called "anomalous." I propose to call them contours "without gradients," a term that, although it has only a descriptive value and is thus neutral from a theoretical point of view, makes the nature of the anomaly of such phenomenal contours more specific.

Figure 12.1a Phenomenal description: a white triangle having margins without gradients on three black disks and on a white triangle with a black border.

Since reference is often made in this recent work to an earlier study of mine (Kanizsa 1955a), I would like to join the discussion by examining these proposals and then describing some new observations on the subject.

After reexamining an observation of F. Schumann's (1904) that had been virtually ignored for many years, I constructed a series of visual patterns in which the phenomenon of contours without gradients was very compelling, and showed, contrary to what Schumann had thought, that it is possible to obtain curvilinear as well as straight contours without gradients (Figures 12.1a, 12.1b, 12.2, 12.3).

The analysis of a number of situations of this type led me to define their common phenomenal characteristics as follows:

• In a particular region of the visual field, transformations of brightness and/or of "mode of appearance" or *Erscheinungsweise*

Figure 12.1b Black triangle without gradients on white disks and on a black triangle with a white border.

(Katz) occur that phenomenally distinguish that region from the contiguous region, even though the stimulus from both areas is the same.

• Phenomenally the region undergoes a displacement in the third dimension and is seen as situated "in front of" or "over" the rest of the field.

• The region possesses a more or less clear border that separates it from the contiguous areas, even though there is no quantitative or qualitative change in the stimulus that might justify the presence of such a border.

• When the conditions are optimal, all the above interconnected phenomenal aspects (chromatic transformation, displacement in the third dimension or stratification in different planes, presence of the border) are extremely compelling and acquire a *modal* character that distinguishes them from the perception of merely "virtual" lines.

Figure 12.2 White square without gradients on a black cross and on a white square with a black border.

That is, they are phenomenally present with the usual characteristics of visual modality. On the other hand, one may speak of "amodal presence" when a structure is present in perception but does not have the phenomenal characteristics of a sensory modality, as in the case of Figure 12.4, where the black disk is completed in just this amodal way behind the gray square.

As for the singling out of the factors that determine the formation of these contours without gradients, I noted that there is one condition that is always present: the existence of parts that require completion that will transform them into more stable, more regular, and more simple figures.

Thus Figure 12.1a might be described as consisting of three angles and three black circular sectors. Some subjects, with a strongly analytic set, have given a geometric description of this sort as an initial response. But the phenomenal result that imposes itself on the great majority of

Figure 12.3 Even curvilinear contours without gradients are possible.

observers is three black disks and a triangle with a black border, partially covered by a white triangle.

The second perceptual organization possesses obvious advantages, with respect to the first, from the point of view of simplicity and stability: the three angles become one triangle—a more stable and balanced figure—and the three circular sectors acquire "completeness" and "regularity" by becoming three disks. But for this improvement in overall organization to occur, the white area in the center must be seen as an opaque triangular surface superimposed over a black figure that is in turn superimposed on the background. And since a surface does not exist without borders, the phenomenal emergence of borders (in the absence of gradients in the stimulus) should be considered a direct

Figure 12.4 Amodal completion of the black disk.

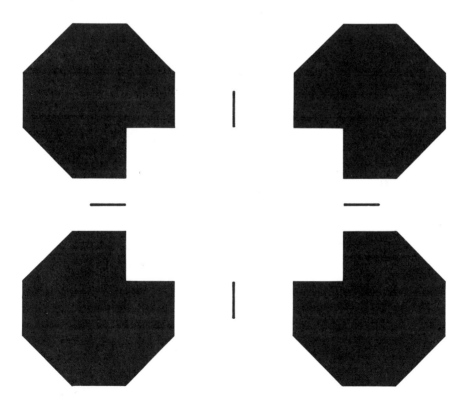

Figure 12.5 A white rectangle having contours without gradients on a black cross and on four black octagons.

Figure 12.6 Figure 12.5 has been modified so that each black element has become self-sufficient. There no longer being a tendency to completion, the formation of an interposed surface without gradients does not take place.

consequence of the above-described stratification. This stratification is produced by processes of amodal completion required by some figural elements of the overall configuration. The same may be said for the situations in Figures 12.1b, 12.2, and 12.3.

If the above assertions are correct, one should be able to demonstrate that, other things being equal, the phenomenon will not occur if completion—which, according to the hypothesis, is the critical and necessary factor—is lacking. It seems to me that a quite convincing confirmation might be given by the following examples.

Let us consider the different perceptual responses to Figures 12.5 and to 12.6. In the former Figure 12.5 one sees, as a rule, a stratified organization: an opaque white rectangle that partially covers a cross and four black octagons. In Figure 12.6 there are four crosses in a white field and four white rhombuses, each with a diagonal. While in the first case the white background splits and is stratified, with the consequent formation of contours without gradients, in the second case the

Figure 12.7 This figure is related to Figure 12.1a in the same way that Figure 12.6 is related to Figure 12.5.

background remains unitary and is not crossed by contours. One can certainly imagine lines that would delimit a rectangular area in the center of the background, but such lines do not have the *modal* character of the contours of the corresponding rectangle in Figure 12.5.

The reason for the difference in results would appear to lie in the diverse figural character of the black elements in the two patterns. The crosses are in themselves balanced and self-sufficient structures with no need of completion. The margins, thus, belong to them and not to the background, which continues without any contours of its own under the figures. Instead, in Figure 12.5 the black forms are phenomenally "incomplete," and only when they are seen as regular octagons do they acquire a much greater degree of stability and of compactness. In this case the internal angular borders do not belong to the black forms but, rather, to a white surface, which, being situated in front of the octagons that lie on the background, must therefore be detached from the background. This white area thus appears to be divided from the background by means of its own borders.

An analogous example is illustrated by Figure 12.7 which is derived from Figure 12.1a in the same way that Figure 12.6 is derived from Figure 12.5. Here one may also use the same line of reasoning: in place of incomplete structures there are self-sufficient figures that show no tendency to completion and, thus, the formation of an opaque surface with its own margins positioned above the black figures does not occur.

BRIGHTNESS MODIFICATIONS:
A CAUSE OF A CONSEQUENCE OF ANOMALOUS SURFACES?

An alternative explanation remains to be examined. It has been seen that the anomalous surface looks quite different from its background, even though the stimulus from both is identical. These differences involve the degree of apparent brightness and the mode of appearance (Erscheinungsweise). For example, in Figure 12.1a the triangle localized in front appears to be brighter than the triangle it partially covers and than the remaining white background. The same may be said for the corresponding parts of Figure 12.1b if one substitutes "darker" for "brighter."

One may wonder whether this difference in brightness should be considered a consequence of the fact that the anomalous surface is organized as a figure or whether it should be considered a causal factor of the figure-ground organization. If one accepts the second alternative, the phenomenon of contours without gradients may be considered an indirect consequence of brightness contrasts. In this case the differentiation and separation from the background would be due primarily to brightness contrast. W. Brigner and M. Gallagher (1974), and L. Spillman (1975), also present this thesis. However, without excluding the possible participation of chromatic induction processes in this phenomenon, certain facts may be cited in opposition to this explanation.

First, in comparing Figure 12.5 with Figure 12.6, and Figure 12.1a with Figure 12.7, it is clear that, under the same conditions of brightness contrast, the stratification occurs only in the presence of certain structural requirements—that is, only when it is necessary for the amodal completion of the incomplete parts of the field. One could, it is true, object that in Figures 12.6 and 12.7 there has been a decrease in the inducing, black areas with respect to the corresponding areas of Figures 12.5 and 12.1a. But one should note, then, the result obtained in Figure 12.8, where the crosses of Figure 12.6 have been reduced to half their original size. In this case too there is scission of the background

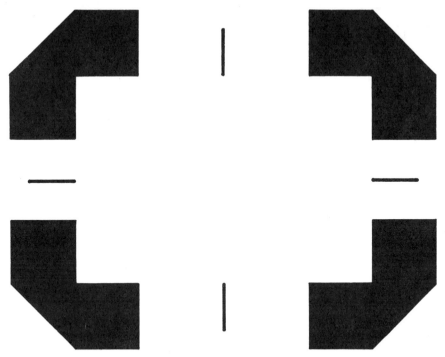

Figure 12.8 Contours without gradients do not depend on brightness contrast. In this figure the crosses of Figure 12.6 are half their original size, yet the contours still occur.

Figure 12.9 The transverse bar is brighter than the white regions surrounded by the black figures.

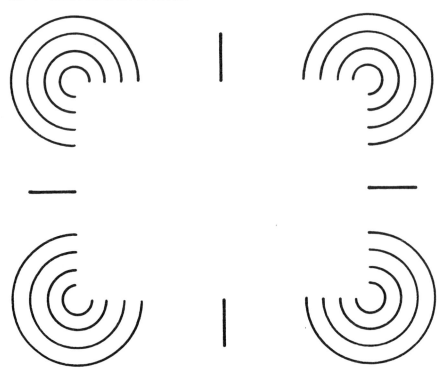

Figure 12.10 The interposed rectangle is no less bright than the one obtained by using black disks (from Varin 1971).

and the formation of contours without gradients. Since in this case the black figures are no longer self-sufficient, as the crosses are, but tend to be seen as incomplete hexagons, the conclusion seems inevitable that it is precisely in order to aid their amodal completion that the perception of an opaque rectangular surface is necessary. In Figure 12.6, on the other hand, such a rectangular area would serve no function.

Second, in Figure 12.9 an opaque white bar having visible contours even in the places along its borders where there is no discontinuity in the stimulus partially covers some black and white figures that are completed behind the bar. Note that the perceived brightness of the bar is greater even than that of the white regions that are surrounded by the black figures, which regions ought, by virtue of their position, to undergo a stronger brightness induction. Even in this case, then, the changes in brightness of the critical area do not follow the usual laws of simultaneous contrast. Thus, it does not seem appropriate to assign contrast a primary causal role in the phenomenon of contours without gradients.

Third, another fact that does not fit well into the contrast hypothe-

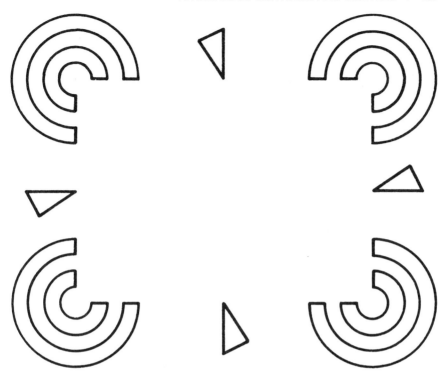

Figure 12.11 Without a decrease in the quantity of black, the contours without gradients nonetheless have disappeared.

sis has been emphasized by D. Varin (1971). By modifying the situations examined up to this point as shown in Figure 12.10—that is, by drastically reducing the amount of black—the effect is not diminished. In fact, it is augmented: 84 percent of Varin's subjects saw the rectangle induced by the "rings" as brighter when compared with an analogous rectangle induced by black "disks." Figure 12.11 demonstrates that here as well the important factor is the completion, and not the brightness induction; the effect disappears when some very small changes are made, even though the changes entail an increase, not a decrease, in the area covered by black inducing lines.

Another important piece of evidence that contrast is not a necessary condition for the formation of a contour without gradients is illustrated in Figure 12.12, where all of the striped area is subject to the same contrast-inducing conditions, yet the figure is crossed by a perceptually clear line.

That the principal causal factor of the scission of the homogeneous background into two planes is not contrast as such but, more important, the tendency to completion, is also clearly visible in the comparison of

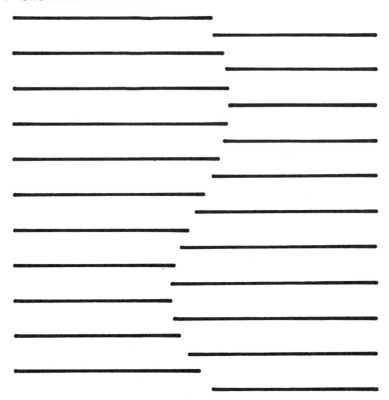

Figure 12.12 A clearly visible contour without gradients, without differences in brightness due to contrast.

Figures 12.13a and 12.13b where the perceptual effect is quite different even though only very small changes have been made in the inducing areas. The same can be said for Figure 12.14, in which we have three brighter anomalous surfaces, while the region between the two superior black disks does not increase its brightness in comparison with the ground, although the conditions of luminance are identical. These examples seem to demonstrate that the part of the background that is destined to split, and the form that this part will take, depend exclusively on the type of completion required by the configuration.

In conclusion, the modifications of brightness are *not the cause*, but a *consequence*, of the particular spatial configuration that the perceptual field is forced to assume because of the conditions at a given moment. The same conclusion has been reached by D. Bradley and S. Dumais (1975), and by D. Bradley and S. Petry (1977), who have used ambiguous configurations, and by Sambin (1978).

This conclusion leaves open the possibility that some factors other than contrast are "prior to" the brightness effects. For example, much

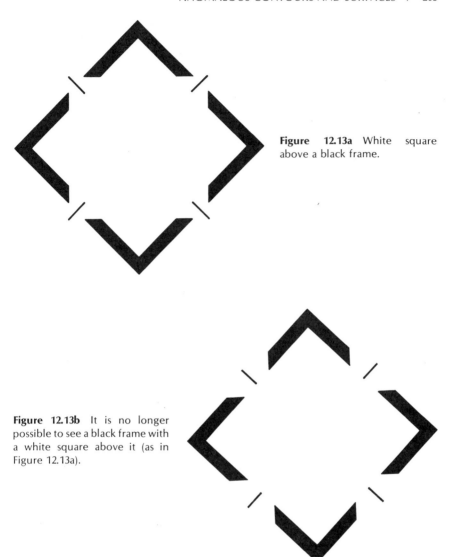

Figure 12.13a White square above a black frame.

Figure 12.13b It is no longer possible to see a black frame with a white square above it (as in Figure 12.13a).

more fundamental than the modification of brightness may be the changes that have to do with another aspect of the critical area: its "mode of appearance." The part of the background that, due to the amodal completion of other figures, becomes an autonomous, opaque surface, endowed with its own borders and displaced into a different plane from that of the rest of the background, acquires an "object" character—that is, an aspect of greater density and solidity. It has a characteristic surface color. This aspect of the problem deserves further study.

Figure 12.14 Brightness contrast is a consequence, not a cause, of the formation of anomalous surfaces.

ANOMALOUS CONTOURS IN STEREOPSIS

A compelling instance of visual contours in the absence of a corresponding abrupt brightness gradient in the stimulus is given in the stereoscopic situations discovered by B. Julesz (1960; 1964) and particularly used to study the formation of such contours by T. Shipley (1965) and by R. B. Lawson and W. L. Gulick (1967). Since in these cases the stereoscopic perception is obtained by means of a stereogram that contains only dots instead of lines and that, because of this, does not reveal any contours when observed monocularly, S. Coren (1972) has advanced the hypothesis that both in stereoscopic vision and in monocular observation, the occurrence of contours without gradients is due to the same general mechanism. This factor is the "stratification" of the total configuration in separate planes at different depths. He arrives at this conclusion after having shown that in all cases of the formation of contours without gradients, one can detect the presence of depth cues.

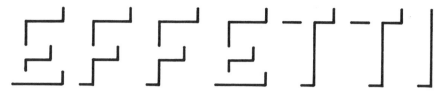

Figure 12.15 Shading as a cue for depth.

According to this hypothesis, in the patterns I conceived the "interposition cue" occurs, while in Figure 12.15, where a word is visible even though half of the borders are not present in the stimulus, there is the pictorial cue of shading. In other situations (for example, in Coren's Fig. 7), the cues of "perspective" and of "texture" are both present. A clear demonstration of the perceptual reality of the stratification in depth of the planes created in these configurations is given by another figure of Coren's (Figure 12.16). The two black rings are objectively identical, subtending the same visual angle, but since they are located on planes situated at phenomenally different distances, they seem to be of

Figure 12.16 The two black rings subtend the same visual angle; nevertheless, the phenomenal difference in depth produces a phenomenal difference in size (from Coren 1972).

different sizes: the one on the background, and thus the more distant, seems larger than the one lying on the triangle that is apparently closer.

The line of reasoning followed by Coren seems to me convincing. The formation of contours without gradients is usually connected with the generation ex novo of surfaces and their stratification. On the other hand, one should note that in all the cases examined by Coren, the stratification depends on the "completion" of some structure. When there is no need for completion, the scission of a surface from the background does not occur, there is no stratification of this surface, and there are no contours without gradients. Once more the primary factor seems to be the tendency to completion, and the displacement in depth seems to occur as a function of this completion.

J. M. Kennedy (1973) has argued, with demonstrations like those of Figure 12.12, that stratification in depth is not the primary factor. In his

Figure 12.17 The contours without gradients undergo the Zoellner illusion (after Pastore 1971).

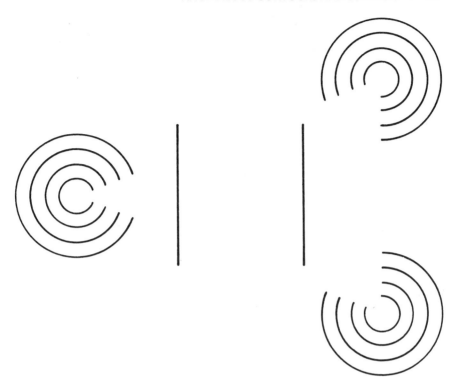

Figure 12.18 The contours without gradients produce the Ponzo illusion (from Farné 1968).

figures there is an impression of adjacent surfaces in the same plane that are separated ("shared") by contours without gradients, or of surfaces that differ in slant, like the walls of corners. Therefore, according to Kennedy, it is not necessary to have a steplike stratification in depth on either side of contours without gradients.

FUNCTIONAL REALITY OF ANOMALOUS CONTOURS

Some have posed the problem of whether contours without gradients are similar to ordinary contours, not only at the purely phenomenological level but also at the level of the functional effects that they exert or undergo.

An area of research in which the reciprocal action of lines on one another can be ascertained with great clarity is that of the so-called optical-geometrical illusions. Some researchers have shown that such illusions can be obtained by using contours without gradients. N. Pastore (1971) has demonstrated this with the Zoellner illusion (Figure

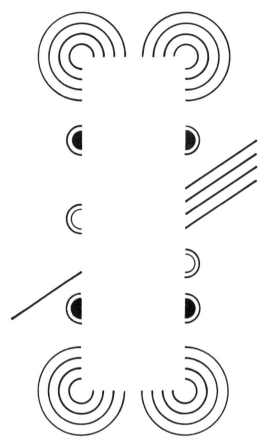

Figure 12.19 The contours without gradients produce the Poggendorff illusion (after Gregory 1972).

12.17), M. Farné (1968) with the Ponzo illusion (Figure 12.18), and R. L. Gregory (1972) with the Poggendorff illusion (Figure 12.19).

The situations illustrated by these configurations are not, however, of exactly the same kind, since in the case of the loss of parallelism, illustrated by Pastore, the contours without gradients *undergo* the effects of the rest of the field, while in the other two cases the contours without gradients *induce* deformations or displacements of other elements in the field. But these examples are not sufficient to prove that contours without gradients have the capacity to influence the normal lines in a configuration. In fact, analogous effects are obtained even without the presence of contours without gradients. For example, the Poggendorff illusion can be seen even when there are no parallel lines (Figure 12.20), and the Ponzo illusion occurs as well in a configuration such as Figure 12.21 in which the three black points are not linked by lines without gradients but, rather, at the most by virtual lines without a modal character.

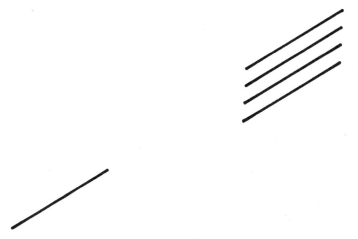

Figure 12.20 The Poggendorff illusion without the inducing lines.

Another method for bringing out possible functional effects of margins without gradients involves the use of figural aftereffects. Farné (1968), for example, used a display like that shown in Figure 12.22. The complex of stimulation is roughly equal on the right and left halves of the display; but, while on the left a triangular contour without gradient is phenomenally present, on the right there is no such contour. If one presents such configuration for 200 milliseconds and immediately afterward replaces it with two test squares T1 and T2 (also presented for 200 milliseconds), one can observe that square T1 clearly appears to be lower than square T2. Thus, this is an aftereffect that might be due to the presence of the contour without gradient. A. Smith and R. Over (1975) have shown that the tilt aftereffect, in which a vertical line appears displaced clockwise after exposure to a line tilted counterclockwise, can be induced with contours without gradients as well as with edges defined in terms of luminance discontinuity. In addition, exposure to a real contour results in a tilt aftereffect when the orientation of a contour without gradient is subsequently judged, and vice versa. Analogously, M. Stadler and J. Dieker (1969; 1972), by means of a rigorous psychophysical procedure, measured the extent of the divergence from parallelism of two lines presented after Figure 12.1a was fixated, and were able to show very strong aftereffects.

On the basis of their research, Stadler and Dieker formulated a hypothesis about the nature of the physiological correlates of contours without gradients, according to which the contours are produced by the action of only partially excited "contour detectors" that also activate contiguous cortical areas. That the activation induced by such

Figure 12.21 The Ponzo illusion using just three points.

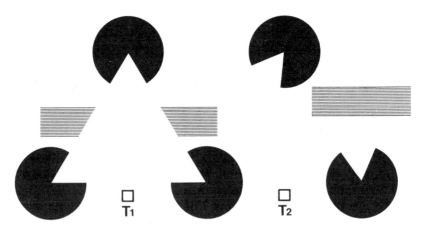

Figure 12.22 The inspection figure (without the test squares T1 and T2) is exposed for 200 milliseconds. The small squares are exposed immediately afterward for 200 milliseconds. The aftereffect occurs for T1 but not for T2 (from Farné 1968).

areas might have a phenomenal correlate would not be, according to Stadler and Dieker, completely unlikely, given that, in the neurological integration, even minimal differences in the intensity of the sensory excitation are reinforced by lateral inhibition.

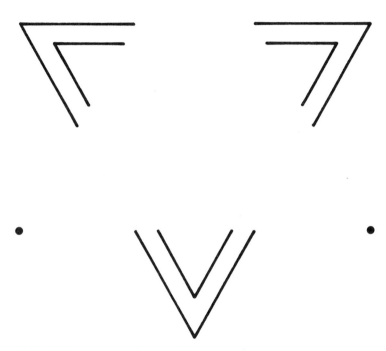

Figure 12.23a The contours without gradients are not oriented in the same direction as the black contours. (See Figure 12.23b).

Such an identification of neurophysiological correlates of contours with gradients and contours without gradients, albeit suggestively economical, gives rise to problems because it is constructed on the basis of examples like Figure 12.1a, in which *by chance* the direction of the contours without gradients coincides with that of some of the borders produced by sharp brightness gradients. But situations can be quite readily constructed in which the "partial activation of the contour detectors" gives rise not to the appearance of contours that continue in the same direction but, rather, to contours without gradients that have an entirely different direction, one without a linear stimulus that might support their appearance on the basis of a process of coactivation. Figure 12.10 is an example, as are Figures 12.23a and b, and 12.24. In such situations the rectilinear and curvilinear line segments are joined, but

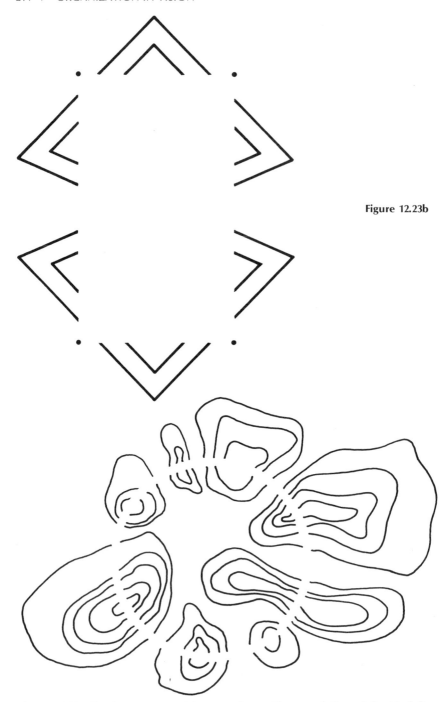

Figure 12.23b

Figure 12.24 Circular contours without gradients. The completion of the black lines occurs beneath the anomalous white ring.

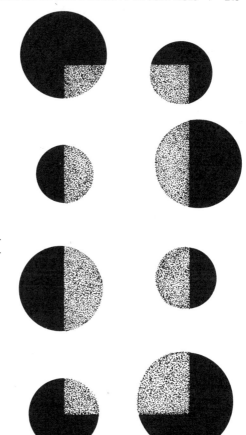

Figure 12.25 Contours without gradients in an anomalous transparent figure.

always "amodally," behind the induced surface, which itself possesses contours without gradients that have orientations completely different from those of the normal contours that are amodally joined. In fact, these are the typical cases where the formation of borders without gradients occurs, cases in which such borders always have as a necessary condition the "amodal completion" of some structure.

The real problem, then, is not so much that of the formation of the contours as it is that of the conditions in which *surfaces* are created that cover parts of other figures. In the cases that we have been examining, such surfaces are opaque because the completion is amodal, but it is just as easy to create transparent surfaces when the conditions for modal completion exist, as in Figure 12.25 (Kanizsa 1955b). In both cases the contours without gradients that are produced are a consequence of the formation of surfaces that are interposed between the observer and the figures and background surfaces.

In Figure 12.1a, and in those analogous to it with solid black areas, the completion is the primary factor in giving rise to the appearance of the triangular surface; the latter has some contours that by chance partially coincide with the direction of some edges that have gradients.

COGNITIVE CONTOURS

Gregory (1972) thinks it unlikely that contours without gradients are due to the partial activation of systems of feature detector cells in the striate cortex. In fact, for him the effect is of particular interest from a theoretical point of view because it permits a confrontation between two kinds of equally plausible but very different explanations: one physiological and the other cognitive. The latter characterizes perceptions as "hypotheses about objects" constructed on the basis of the information given in the sense data. In the case of contours without gradients, the illusory object (for example, the central triangle in Figure 12.1a) is postulated in order to account for the gaps present in the figures (in the case of Figure 12.1a, the black sectors and the breaks in the contour triangle). But to explain processes by postulating objects from sensory evidence requires, according to Gregory, concepts beyond those of classical physiology—that is, cognitive concepts. This is why he calls such formations "cognitive contours."

There are no good reasons to reject either such a label or the theory from which it is derived. It is a theory that has the support of a long and respectable tradition, since it represents a reformulation of Hermann von Helmholtz's theory, with the appropriate modernizations made possible by developments in information theory and in computer programming. The explanatory hypothesis that I proposed in 1955

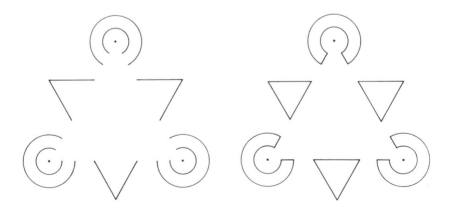

Figure 12.26a Open figures that have a tendency to closure. An anomalous triangle having contours without gradients is the result.

Figure 12.26b Closed figures having no tendency to amodal completion. There is no formation of contours without gradients.

Figure 12.27 There is no need for the figures that are amodally completed to be regular.

seems to coincide with Gregory's in spite of the difference in terminology. Essentially, I maintain that in the phenomenal field there arises just that opaque surface that permits the amodal completion of the figures with gaps in them; for Gregory the opaque surface is created in response to a perceptual hypothesis that postulates an object that, when superimposed on the other object, accounts for their gaps.

But the agreement probably is only apparent. Everything seems to me to depend on the meaning given to the term "gap." For the perceptual system (for the brain) what does "gap" mean? In other words, why for the perceptual system are some figures complete and others incomplete? I have the impression that Gregory does not even raise this problem, at least not explicitly, whereas for me it is the central problem. According to Gregory the sense data are used by the brain according to certain strategies, in order to decide which object has the highest probability of being present. But then, comparing the perceptual effects of Figures 12.26a and 12.26b, one should conclude that for the brain $\mathcal{C}$ is more probable than $\mathcal{C}$, a conclusion that seems to

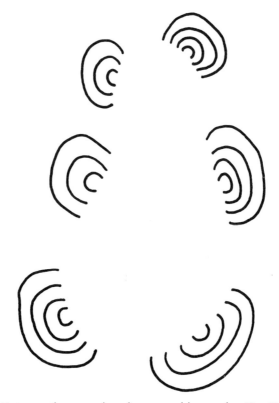

Figure 12.28 Not even the anomalous figure need be regular. (See Figures 12.29b and 12.29c).

me rather implausible. For me the first figure is a closed structure, isolated from the outside by the margin, while the second is an open structure. Only in the second is there an "autonomous" tendency to closure, to completion.

For this reason it is preferable not to call these contours "cognitive" but, rather, to continue to use a theoretically more neutral term that refers only to the conditions of stimulation: "contours without gradients."

SOME MORE OBSERVATIONS AND OPEN PROBLEMS

In my 1955 article I implicitly suggested that a tendency to maximal regularity was an important factor in completion. This is evident from the types of figures that I selected to illustrate the phenomenon; all of them are figures that, being completed, become regular, symmetric, balanced: triangles, circles, squares, octagons, crosses. But regularization, as I established later (Chapter 5), is a favorable but not at all necessary condition. Optimal contours without gradients can be obtained with completions that yield irregular figures (Figures 12.27 and 12.28). The decisive factor seems, then, to be not so much the tendency to geometric regularity as the tendency to closure of open structures.

In the same way that the question about the functional effects of contours without gradients was raised, one can also ask what degree of "reality" they have. That is, what resistance do they show in the face of interference by physically real stimulation? In examining Figures 12.29a, 12.29b, and 12.29c, one can see that in the regions where lines with gradients intersect the contour without gradients, the latter disappears, just as it disappears when one fixates it attentively. However, the amodal surface retains a surprisingly strong reality, sometimes "passing

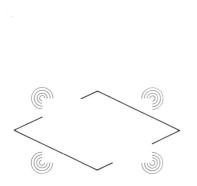

Figure 12.29a The anomalous surface "passes under" the sides of the black frame.

Figure 12.29c

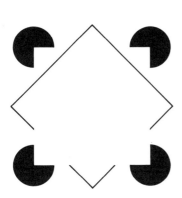

Figure 12.29b

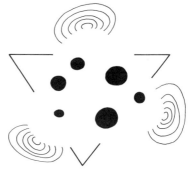

Figure 12.29d The anomalous, induced area maintains itself despite the superposition of other structures. (See Figure 12.29e).

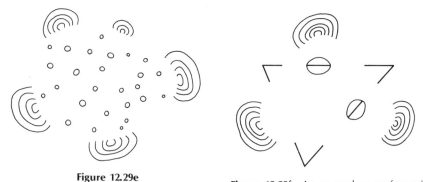

Figure 12.29e

Figure 12.29f An anomalous surface with holes.

under" the sides of the black frame, at other times "passing over" them.

Such resistance is shown even in the face of interference like that in Figures 12.29d and 12.29e which does not abolish the perception of the amodal surface. The appearance of an opaque surface is obviously reinforced if, as in Figure 12.29f, other indications of amodal completion taking place behind it are added.

In all the preceding situations there is a discontinuity in the stimulus corresponding to the corners of the anomalous figures, except those that are completely curvilinear. Sometimes this discontinuity is minimal, as in Figures 12.23a and 12.23b where in places it consists of simply a black point. Sambin (1974) has asked whether (and under what conditions) it is possible to produce surfaces with two contours without

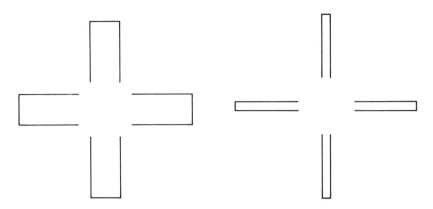

Figure 12.30a An anomalous surface with a corner (from Sambin 1974).

Figure 12.30b When the arms of the cross are narrowed, a circular surface having contours without gradients prevails (Sambin 1974).

gradients that meet and form a corner. He has obtained such results with outline figures such as 12.30a. 90 percent of his subjects saw a square in this situation, though the angles appeared a little rounded. Such a result is interesting inasmuch as the configuration, from a geometric point of view, could also be seen as involving a circular interposition surface—that is, a pattern having greater simplicity and *Pragnanz*. According to Sambin, the rectilinear path of the contours without gradients is due to the resistance of the arms of the cross to an "invasion" by the interposed figure, as would occur if the latter were a circle. The validity of this hypothesis is demonstrated by the fact that by progressively narrowing the arms of the cross, the response "square" is given less often and that of "circle" more often, to a point such that in Figure 12.30b, where the invasion of the internal area by the circumference is minimal, 90 percent of the subjects see a circular figure over the cross. A different explanation to account for the generation of corners in contours without gradients is given by S. Ullman (1976), who proposes a network model for generating the shape of anomalous contours.

13

ENVIRONMENTAL AND RETINAL FRAMES OF REFERENCE IN VISUAL PERCEPTION

THE PROBLEM

We are usually able to recognize objects or pictures without difficulty, regardless of their orientation. But this is not always so. The appearance of certain pictures changes so much when their orientation is varied that their recognition becomes impossible. The problem has been studied in a number of ways, in an attempt to discover the factors responsible for these radical changes in appearance.

The usual approach to this problem, involving the presentation of pictures or objects in various orientations, has been too limited. There are other factors that should be taken into consideration. For example, one should ask whether the phenomenal orientation of the visual objects depends on the environmental frame of reference or on the retinal one.

In order to ascertain the relative influence of these factors, experimental situations have sometimes been devised in which they conflict with each other. One way to obtain this effect consists in having the subjects bend forward and look at the pictures between their slightly spread legs. The head is thus upside down with reference to the

---

G. Kanizsa and G. Tampieri. 1976. "Environmental and Retinal Frames of Reference in Visual Perception." *Italian Journal of Psychology* 3: 317-32.

environment and the light rays reflected by the upper part of the environment stimulate the retinal area usually stimulated by the rays coming from the lower part, and vice versa.

One should be able to infer which frame of reference is the more influential from an observer's capacity to recognize an object or a picture when its orientation corresponds to one of the two frameworks. Research to date, however, has yielded conflicting results. Some of the studies have shown, for example, that the appearance of the pictures depends greatly on the environmental frame of reference (W. James 1890; T. Miyakawa 1950; C. Gajzago and R. H. Day 1972). However, these results are apparently contradicted by the observations of Hermann von Helmholtz (1867) and W. Koehler (1940) and by a series of experiments done by R. H. Thouless (1947).

Figure 13.1 Thouless (1947).

Both of the above types of results were questioned by I. Rock (1956; 1973) who performed a number of experiments from which he inferred that the appearance of the pictures depends on the *expectation* that the observer has of seeing the picture oriented in a given way (usually in the orientation corresponding to the environmental frame of reference).

In contrast with Rock's emphasis on the perceiver, we propose to try to reconcile the conflicting studies by emphasizing properties of the displays. Since in all of the studies the experimental conditions were quite similar, the only difference being the kind of pictures presented to the subjects, the key to the solution should lie in some feature that differentiates the pictures.

Of those who have maintained that the retinal influences predominate, Koehler used the photograph of a friend's face and tried to determine in which orientation of the photo it was possible for the observer to recognize the person. Thouless used a caricature of a human face, drawn to look like a sailor if seen in one orientation and like the Nazi stereotype for Jews in the other (Figure 13.1). Subjects were asked simply to describe the figure they saw.

In an experiment performed by Rock, using the same observation procedure as Koehler's, the pictures were those reproduced in Figure 13.2. Each was presented twice to the subjects, who were asked to observe them carefully, in order to be able to recognize them later among others. Soon afterward the subjects looked at three cards, one at a time, between their legs. On each card six figures were drawn, four of which were of approximately the same kind as one of the previously inspected figures. The remaining two were identical to that previously seen figure, and were oriented so that one yielded a "retinal image" like that of the inspected figure, while the other yielded an inverted "retinal image." The subjects were asked to point to the previously inspected figure.

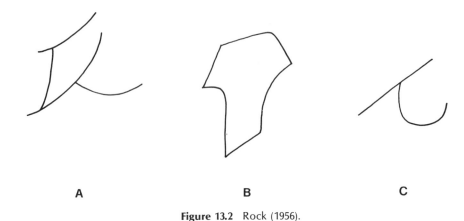

A   B   C

Figure 13.2 Rock (1956).

The pictures used by Koehler and Thouless, on the one hand, and by Rock, on the other, seem to me to differ with regard to an important feature, a difference that may be the cause of their apparently conflicting results. The pictures of faces used by Koehler and by Thouless (whose results support the retinal framework) have two quite different expressions in the two orientations, whereas Rock's designs (for which the retinal frame was irrelevant) do not change their appearance so radically with the change of orientation. Indeed, many features of Rock's patterns remain unaffected by the change of orientation: features such as "having branches," or "being thick at one end and thin at the other," or "being formed by a straight line and an arc." It may be that it is precisely these invariant features that make it possible to recognize Rock's designs no matter what their orientation. (Further, it is possible that expectations can play a role in Rock's studies precisely because of the invariance, which minimizes retinal-environmental effects, rather than because expectation generally has an important influence on perceptual organization.)

I think therefore, that Rock's patterns are not appropriate for resolving the question about the prevalence of either of the two frames. On the contrary, patterns should be used that have quite distinctive appearances in different orientations as a result of the various figural organizations that result when the relative positions of the pattern's individual elements are changed. This criterion is apparently met in Thouless' "double face," but in my opinion this picture has the disadvantage of being a kind of compromise between the two persons, so that neither is well-drawn. It is also possible that one of the interpretations prevails over the other simply because it is better-drawn.

To test this hypothesis we have performed a series of experiments using pictures better suited to the problem.

EXPERIMENTS WITH ADULTS

The main pictures employed for this research are reproduced in Figures 13.3 and 13.4 The first, which is more realistic, represents a "double face" of the kind used by Thouless. In the depicted orientation it represents an "old woman"; when inverted, it becomes a "princess." The other picture, representing a stylized human face, consists of a few lines within a circle that are so arranged that the small arc that in one orientation represents the mouth turns into the (unified) eyebrows in the other. Similarly, the small dots that in one orientation represent the eyes become the nostrils in the other. In the orientation depicted in Figure 13.4, this face has a sad, downhearted expression; in the inverted orientation it is smiling, though the eyebrows are frowning a bit.

Figure 13.3 Turn the page upside down.
(See Figures 13.4–13.9).

Condition 1

The old woman-princess figure (Figure 13.3) was individually presented to 40 adult subjects. It was held in one orientation for half of the
subjects and inverted for the others. The card was held two meters from
their eyes. In order to observe the figure the subjects had to bend
forward and look at it through their slightly spread legs. They were
asked what they saw, and if the answer was simply: "a face" or "a
woman's face," they were asked how old she might be, and sometimes
what she had on her head.

From the data shown in Table 13.1, we can see that all subjects to

TABLE 13.1

Frequencies of the Environmental, Retinal, and Uncertain Impressions in the First Three Experimental Conditions

Frame of Reference	Condition 1 Full Drawing			Condition 2 Schematic Face			Condition 3 Schematic Face plus Body		
	Princess (N = 20)	Old Woman (N = 20)	Total (N = 40)	Smiling Face (N = 20)	Sad Face (N = 20)	Total (N = 40)	Smiling Face (N = 20)	Sad Face (N = 20)	Total (N = 40)
E	—	—	—	1	—	1	—	4	4
R	20	17	37	19	19	38	20	13	33
U	—	3	3	—	1	1	—	3	3
R percent	100	92	96	95	97	96	100	72	86

E = environmental.
R = retinal.
U = uncertain.

$$R \text{ percent} = \frac{100}{N}\left(R + \frac{u}{2}\right).$$

Source: G. Kanizsa and G. Tampieri 1976, p. 322.

227

whom the figure was so presented as to have the "princess" corresponding to the retinal coordinates and the "old woman" to the environmental ones saw the "princess." Among those to whom the figure was presented in the opposite orientation, two subjects reported that they could see both faces, although the "old woman" prevailed; one subject reported that half of the face was that of an old woman and half of it was that of a young woman; and the rest saw only the old woman's face.

Thus, 37 out of 40 subjects described only the face corresponding to the retinal coordinates; nobody described only the one corresponding to the environmental coordinates.

Afterward, again with the subject's head upside down, the card was slowly rotated twice. The first time the subject was asked to report what was seen during the rotation; and at the beginning of the second rotation, to try to preserve the original impression, if possible, until the end of the rotation. If subjects were unable to do this, the retinal-frame hypothesis would receive strong support.

Even though this procedure gave an advantage to the appearance corresponding to the environmental coordinates, that appearance was never reported. A rotation of the card through about 90 degrees usually sufficed to yield a sudden transformation of the figure's appearance, in both the first (free observation) and the second (constrained observation) experimental conditions.

The amelioration of the Thouless figure thus led to results that support the retinal hypothesis even more clearly.

Condition 2

In this experiment the stylized face in Figure 13.4 was presented to 40 adult subjects in exactly the same observation conditions as in experiment 1. After having ascertained that they recognized a human face, in the pattern, they were asked: "What is the expression on his face?" or "How does he feel?"

From Table 13.1 it can be seen that in both orientations 19 subjects out of 20 perceived the expression corresponding to the retinal coordinates; only 1 subject reported the expression corresponding to the environmental coordinates; the report of 1 subject was too unclear to ascertain what he saw.

In the final test, in which the subjects observed the card while it was rotating, none of the 38 subjects who originally saw the expression corresponding to the retinal coordinates was able to willfully continue to see it until the card was upside down. All of them, and the uncertain subject as well, noticed an abrupt change in the expression after the card had rotated about 90-135 degrees.

Figure 13.4

The results are therefore quite similar to those of the first experiment and further strengthen the retinal hypothesis.

Condition 3

In the pictures used for experiments 1 and 2, the "top" and the "bottom" of the faces were undetermined; in effect both areas could play the role of the forehead as well as of the chin. As we have seen, however, their roles were determined without exception by "top" and "bottom" of the retina.

We performed a series of control experiments aimed at determining the effect of providing additional clues to the locations of these parts of the face. In experiment 3 an additional clue was provided by adding a stylized body to the stylized face (see Figure 13.5). Each picture was presented to 20 subjects with the same procedure as experiment 2 (both figures had their feet toward the floor of the room).

Figure 13.5

The "sad" man was described as such by 4 out of 20 subjects; 3 others gave descriptions from which it was impossible to ascertain what they saw. The "smiling" man was never so described (see Table 13.1). The prevalence of the retinal factor is, however, not significantly weaker here, than in experiment 2 ($X^2 = 2.50$; not significant). It manifests itself in a paradoxical way, however: the figures's head is seen as if it were reversed with respect to its body. That is, the figure looks as if its forehead were connected to its neck! This means that adding an "external" clue for the orientation of the face exerts scarcely any influence on perceptual organization. The organization seems to be bound to the retinal coordinates despite the clues to the contrary.

The 40 subjects were also shown the card while it was being rotated. As in experiment 2, none of the subjects who initially saw the facial expression corresponding to the retinal coordinates was able to obtain the expression corresponding to the environmental coordinates by means of preserving, with or without effort, the first impression until the card was upside down.

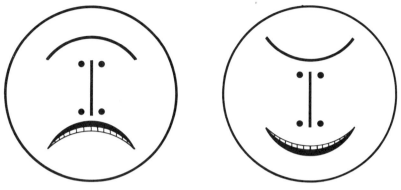

Figure 13.6

Condition 4

Our results emphasize the retinal orientation even when a paradoxical head-body relation ensues. If there are conflicts of features within the head and face itself, will the retinal orientation still prevail? Special clues can point out the forehead and the chin more clearly, modifying parts of the stylized face used in experiment 2.

The modifications are as follows:

- The mouth is emphasized by drawing in the teeth (condition T).
- The eyebrows are emphasized by drawing two separate arcs, which no longer look like a mouth when in the reversed position (condition E).
- The points representing the nostrils are omitted, while those representing the eyes remain (condition N).

For each of these modifications two pictures were prepared, one representing the "smiling" expression, the other the "sad" one (see figures 13.6-13.8); a fourth pair of pictures was prepared in which the three modifications were combined (see Figure 13.9).

The procedure for these experiments was exactly the same as for experiment 2: each picture was presented to 20 subjects. All the pictures were held so as to have the "chins" toward the floor of the room.

As can be seen from Table 13.2, the pictures obtained with the three modifications still yielded a prevalence of "retinal" impressions. The binomial test, however, reveals a significant deviation from an equal distribution for condition T ($p < .01$), whereas the deviations for

Figure 13.7

Figure 13.8

Figure 13.9

TABLE 13.2

Frequencies of the Various Kinds of Impressions in Four Experimental Conditions

Frame of Reference	Condition T Teeth Emphasized			Condition E Eyebrows Emphasized		
	Smiling Face (N = 20)	Sad Face (N = 20)	Total (N = 40)	Smiling Face (N = 20)	Sad Face (N = 20)	Total (N = 40)
EE	3	—	3	6	2	8
ER	2	4	6	—	6	6
RE	2	—	2	4	—	4
RR	10	16	26	10	12	22
U	3	—	3	—	—	—
R percent	67	80	74	70	60	65

Frame of Reference	Condition N Nostrils Omitted			Condition E + N + T Composite		
	Smiling Face (N = 20)	Sad Face (N = 20)	Total (N = 40)	Smiling Face (N = 20)	Sad Face (N = 20)	Total (N = 40)
EE	2	—	2	7	3	10
ER	6	6	12	2	12	14
RE	—	—	—	1	—	1
RR	12	14	26	9	5	14
U	—	—	—	1	—	1
R percent	60	70	65	52	25	39

Note: In Frame of Reference the first letter refers to the first impression; the second, to the impression after rotation of the picture.
E = environmental frame.
R = retinal frame.
U = uncertain impression.
R percent = percent of subjects reporting retinal frame initially.
Source: G. Kanizsa and G. Tampieri 1976, p. 327.

conditions E and N are not significant (p = .08). Furthermore, in all instances the prevalence of "retinal" impressions is less than for the standard face (experiment 2). In fact, the decrease in the proportion of those impressions proves to be highly significant for all situations (condition T: $X^2 = 7.94$, p < .01; conditions E and N: $X^2 = 12.46$; p < .001).

Also, a striking fact must be mentioned. In the earlier studies, during the rotation of the picture there was a sudden transformation of the impression, revealing the constancy of the frame of reference. But in all the present conditions about a quarter of the subjects preserved the same impression throughout the rotation, and therefore for them the frame of reference rotated with the figure. Most of these subjects (24 out of 30) were those who originally perceived the impression corresponding to the environmental frame of reference, and thus obtained the impression corresponding to the retinal frame (ER).

The picture with all of the modifications combined is the only one that yields a prevalence of environmental impressions. However, the deviation from an equal distribution is not statistically significant (binomial test: p = .10), though the deviation from the three other situations is highly significant (from conditions E and N: $X^2 = 5.52$, $p < .02$; from condition T: $X^2 = 9.55$, $p < .01$).

Figure 13.9 is the one that least often transforms when rotated: more than one-third of the subjects preserved the same impression throughout the rotation, and most of them (14 out of 15) originally had the impression corresponding to the environmental framework (ER).

EXPERIMENTS WITH CHILDREN

All the experiments thus far described were performed with adult subjects. In addition, we showed two of the faces to children 4-5 years old. The theoretical interest here is that children are said to be "indifferent" to orientation in visual space. This opinion has been confirmed by a number of experiments (including F. Oetjen 1915; C. R. Rice 1930; H. P. Davidson 1934, 1935; S. M. Newhall 1937).

According to these researchers, preschool children can easily recognize any figure in any orientation, so that frames of reference seem not to have any influence on their perceptual organization. For these subjects, then, neither the retinal nor the environmental frame should determine the kind of phenomenal organization that occurs in models like those we are discussing. Either both expressions should be seen with equal ease by all observers, or half of them should see one expression and half of them the other. It is precisely because Thouless supposed that such a result should be established that he did not show his pattern to children less than 5 years old.

However, studies by V. D. Hunton (1955), L. Ghent (1960), and R. M. Brooks and A. G. Goldstein (1965) have yielded clear evidence against this thesis. They have shown that the recognition of pictures by preschool children is even more affected by changes in orientation than is the case with older children and adults. According to these latter studies, then, the frame of reference should exert a strong influence on children's perceptual organization.

However, these studies leave unanswered the central point: Which frame exerts the key influence?

R. H. Thouless (1947) undertook to answer the question, but none of his child subjects were under five; and his figure was, as noted above, suspect. L. Ghent et al. (1960) showed the importance of retinal orientation for subjects younger than five, but the task involved preference judgments and perception of orientation, not the kind of organization concerning us here.

An experiment of the kind outlined by us has not yet been done with children younger than five. We decided, therefore, to perform two such experiments. One of these has already been reported elsewhere (G. Tampieri 1968): for it the princess/old woman figure from condition 1 was used.

The procedure was exactly the same as for the adult subjects. As can be seen from Table 13.3, all 40 subjects who saw the princess/old woman figure described only the face corresponding to the retinal frame of reference, and all of them experienced the sudden transformation during the rotation of the picture.

TABLE 13.3

Frequencies of the Various Kinds of Impressions Relative to the Experimental Conditions Presented to Preschool Children

| Frame of Reference | Condition 1 Full Drawing | | | Condition T Teeth Emphasized | | |
	Princess (N = 20)	Old Woman (N = 20)	Total (N = 40)	Smiling Face (N = 20)	Sad Face (N = 20)	Total (N = 40)
EE	—	—	—	7	2	9
ER	—	—	—	2	—	2
RE	—	—	—	3	—	3
RR	20	20	40	8	14	22
U	—	—	—	—	4	4
R percent	100	100	100	55	80	67

Note: In Frame of Reference the first letter refers to the first impression; the second, to the impression after rotation of the picture.
E = environmental frame.
R = retinal frame.
U = uncertain impression.
R percent = percent of subjects reporting retinal frame initially.
Source: G. Kanizsa and G. Tampieri 1976, p. 328.

For the second experiment the mouth-with-teeth face from condition 4 was chosen. From Table 13.3 we can see that the frequency of the retinal impressions is reduced to two-thirds (a little less frequently than with adult subjects).

CONCLUSIONS

Our findings concerning the adult subjects can be summarized as follows:

• A face that has quite different appearances in different orientations clearly receives its orientation from the retinal frame of reference.
• If we add some clues to the stylized face that indicate more clearly its forehead and chin in contrast with the retinal frame, three cases may be distinguished:
1. An "external" clue (a stylized body is shown instead of only the face) hardly reduces the prevalence of the retinal frame.
2. An "internal" clue (the mouth is emphasized by drawing in the teeth; or the nostrils are omitted, thus emphasizing the eyes as clearly being eyes; or the eyebrows are separated, thus distinguishing them from the mouth) has a strong influence against the retinal framework.
3. A combination of three internal clues results in a display where the environmental impressions are at least as frequent as the retinal ones.

From our findings we think the following conclusions may be drawn:

• When one looks at a face that has quite different appearances in different orientations, the appeerence corresponding to the retinal frame of reference is far more likely to be seen than that corresponding to the environmental frame.
• The mere awareness of the "proper" orientation of the face (mediated through the added presence of the body) is usually insufficient to yield the nonretinal organization of the face.
• The conflict between an absurd face, retinally determined, and a correct face, environmentally determined, weakens the prevalence of the retinal frame of reference to such a degree that the retinal impressions are at times no more frequent than environmental ones.

Therefore it seems to me that if proper patterns are used—that is, pictures that completely change their appearance in the two orientations—the environmental frame of reference (floor and ceiling of the room) or the subject's perceptual assumptions are overwhelmed by the retinal frame.

As for the children's results, substantially the same conclusions may be drawn: that is, no significant differences from the adult results were found. It was noted, however, that once a frame of reference prevails in their visual organization, children are more unlikely than are adults to report a change in their perception (due to the rotation of the card).

The prevalence of the retinal framework argues against the hypothesis of infantile indifference toward orientation in visual space, since most of the children reported two different impressions in the two orientations of the picture.

I think, however, that the problem should not be posed in this way and that the apparently conflicting results may receive a unitary interpretation. G. Tampieri (1963) has noted that the possibility of recognizing a given picture in different orientations depends on whether or not the phenomenal relationships among the figural elements, on which the picture's appearance depends, remain unchanged when they are put in different reciprocal or absolute positions in the visual field. Younger children, however, perhaps see any picture only in a rather blurred way—that is, not all the relationships among the figural elements that are phenomenally present in an adult's perceptual field are present for children. If the critical relationships, which alter the appearance of a rotated picture, are not phenomenally present, the appearance of the picture is not modified; if, on the contrary, those critical relationships are present for the child, the picture's appearance is modified for him or her, even more so than for adults.

Our findings with children are in agreement with this hypothesis, and show that these relationships are effective in the children's visual field, for their reaction to the picture depended on the retinal factor (as with adults).

It is in this same direction that the solution of the controversy between prevalence of retinal and environmental frames of reference should be sought. Since our findings show that the appearance of a pattern that looks radically different in different orientations does depend on the retinal framework, we propose that this frame exerts the fundamental influence in visual organization. Patterns that do not change their appearance, or do so only slightly, simply do not set this factor working, and therefore in these cases secondary factors can freely exert their influence: the "expectation to see the picture in a particular orientation"—detected by Rock—is simply one, though perhaps the most important, of these secondary factors.

14

"PRÄGNANZ" AS AN OBSTACLE TO PROBLEM SOLVING

DOES THE SOLUTION ALWAYS FOLLOW FROM THE "REQUIREDNESS" OF THE STRUCTURE?

According to Max Wertheimer, the problem-solving process is started and fed by forces inherent in the structure of the problem field, by the "requirements" that issue from such a structure, and by the tendency to *Prägnanz*. When one becomes aware of the existence of a problem, it is likely that the structural features of the situation will determine the tensions and the conflicts in the cognitive field from which vectors for eliminating disturbances and restoring equilibrium arise.

> When one grasps a problem situation, its structural features and requirements set up certain strains, stresses, tensions in the thinker. What happens in real thinking is that these strains and stresses are followed up, yield vectors in the direction of improvement of the situation, and change it accordingly. The situation in which the problem is solved is a state of affairs that is held together by inner forces as a good structure in which there is harmony in the mutual requirements, and in which the parts are determined by the structure of the whole, as the whole is by the parts. The process does not involve merely the given parts and their transformations. It works in conjunction with material that is structurally relevant but is selected from past experience, from previous knowledge and orientation (Wertheimer 1959, pp. 239-40).

However, it is evident that this thesis is valid only in principle, as an ideal model of a productive thought process; otherwise we could not explain the great number of errors, blockages, and failures. What is the nature of these obstacles that so often prevent thought from proceeding more swiftly, drive it away from the solution, and lead it to a dead end?

K. Duncker (1945) pointed out the hindering role of functional fixedness and of implicit self-instructions; G. Katona (1940) emphasized the consequences of structurally blind teaching and of a prevailing mnemonic and passive way of learning. A. Luchins (1942) made a comprehensive analysis of the blinding effect of set or *Einstellung* on the "mechanization" of problem-solving procedures.

It is interesting that Wertheimer himself pointed out that we can ascribe to the organizational factors both the function of promoting and facilitating the solution, and preventing it.

> Often the subject is lacking in breadth of view. Even when he has it at the beginning, he may lose it in the process because he is busy with or falls into a piecemeal attitude. Under these circumstances closure may tend to occur in regions that are too narrow (Wertheimer 1959, p. 240).
>
> Various conditions, forces, factors may determine a structure for the subject factors which often include inertia of habits, piecemeal attitudes, and the working of the very *Prägnanz* tendency in the direction of premature closure. The subject then falls victim to a seductive simplification (Wertheimer 1959, p. 243).

If one conceives the problem-solving process as essentially a series of restructurings of the cognitive material, one may expect that the difficulty encountered in restructuring a given situation will be directly proportional to the solidity of the structure. In other words, the resistance to reorganization is likely to depend on the degrees of closure, of equilibrium, and of "goodness" of the structure to be transformed.

For example, in Gauss's problem, an essential step in the solution process is the moment at which the direction of the numerical series splits into two equal and opposite movements, one ascending and the other descending, with rhythms of increase and decrease that counterbalance each other—that is, when one grasps the splitting of the single direction into two symmetrical and complementary ones, from ⟶ to

Gaetano Kanizsa. 1975. "Pragnanz as an Obstacle to Problem-Solving." *Italian Journal of Psychology* 2: 417–25.

⇌. The main difficulty consists precisely in this transformation, since the *uni*directional structure is psychologically very strong and resists the splitting.

And so, if we say to a subject, "Swimming under a bridge there are two ducks in front of two ducks, two ducks behind two ducks, and two ducks in the middle. How many ducks are there in all?" The first spontaneous answer is six ducks, with the following formation

•   •

•   •

•   •

According to M. R. Harrower (1932), the correct solution—four ducks, swimming in single file—would not cross one's mind immediately because the expression "two ducks" would imply "a pair of ducks"; and, since pairedness implies equality, a pair of ducks is likely to be imagined as equidistant from the observer—that is, equal from the point of view of the spatial localization with regard to the observer. For the same reasons, each spatial position referred to "requires" a pair of ducks. Moreover, in the "wrong" solution the pairs remain constant for each of the three stated relations, while in the "right" solution each of the two middle ducks is successively part of a different couple. P. Legrenzi (1975, pp. 527-28), who repeated Harrower's experiment, varying the verbal formulation of the task, confirmed her analyses, since the "wrong" solutions Harrower obtained seem to be a direct consequence of the structure in which the problem situation is imagined as a function of the formulation of the task.

Commenting upon Harrower's experiment, K. Koffka (1935) suggested the advantage of creating situations in which, from a dynamic point of view, the correct solution is not the only possible one, as the distribution of the operating forces favors wrong solutions.

In research on perception, important laws of perceptual organization were discovered by using situations that, a priori, may give rise to several perceptual organizations, even though in reality they give rise to only one, or to a small number of them, thus revealing the operating factors. For instance, in Figure 14.1 picture *a* may be seen either as the conjunction of two identical figures (*b*) that are perfectly symmetrical or as two figures (*c*) that are less symmetrical and partially overlapping. The latter perceptual solution is usually stronger, thus showing the superior organizational strength of the factor of continuity in comparison with the tendency to maximal symmetry (see Chapter 5).

In the same way a systematic use of this method could be very

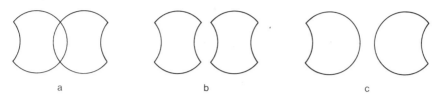

Figure 14.1 Picture *a* theoretically may be seen as *b* or as *c*. The latter solution is preferred according to the superior organizational strength of continuity in comparison with symmetry.

useful in research on productive thinking, and might lead to the discovery of factors that determine the organization of thought processes.

REQUIREMENTS OF THE STRUCTURE MAY BLOCK THE PROBLEM-SOLVING PROCESS

I have tried to contribute to this line of research by means of a series of experiments, some of whose results I think have a certain methodological interest. If the difficulty of a problem is a function of the strength with which certain organizational factors operate in the objectively dead-end direction, we should be able to hinder or to facilitate the solution by manipulating a structural variable of the initial situation in suitable fashion.

One of the tasks proposed consisted of building a square by putting together the six pieces of cardboard (four right-angled isosceles triangles and two trapezoids) represented in Figure 14.2.

The problem has proved to be surprisingly difficult. Even very intelligent subjects strive for many minutes without being able to find the solution, represented in Figure 14.3.

The cause of the difficulty seems to lie in the action of a structural

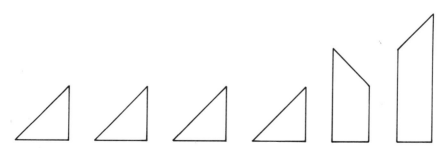

Figure 14.2 The six pieces of cardboard necessary to build up Figure 14.3.

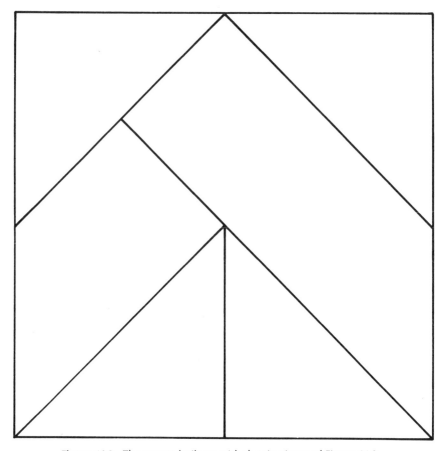

Figure 14.3 The square built up with the six pieces of Figure 14.2.

factor that has proved to be extremely strong. To build a square means to build a figure with four right angles: this "reformulation" of the task leads to an arrangement of the two trapezoids that is so frequent and persistent as to be regarded as the real barrier to the solution. One can obtain a right angle starting with the trapezoids, by arranging them as in a or as in b of Figure 14.4. The former arrangement is *pro-structural*, while the latter is much less so. In fact, the results we obtained show that the two pieces "require" the arrangement shown in a of Figure 14.4.

I examined 30 subjects individually and registered their attempts at arrangement during the first two minutes, at the end of which period they were given some "hints," the first of which consisted in showing the trapezoids as in b of Figure 14.4.

On the first attempt there were 15 kinds of arrangements. While 13

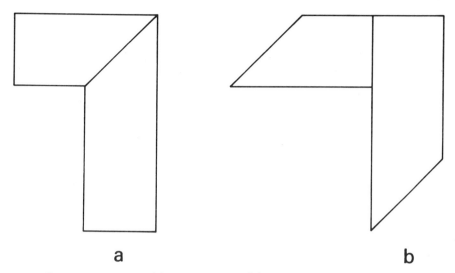

a   b

Figure 14.4 Two possible arrangements of the two trapezoids of Figure 14.2.

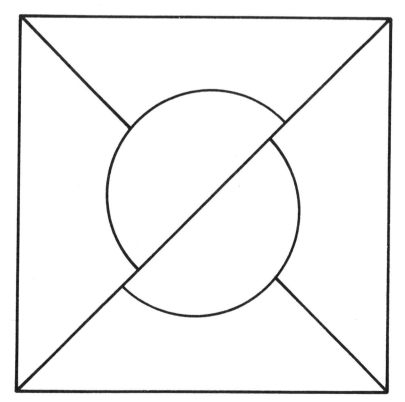

Figure 14.5 A square made up of six pieces and difficult to build because people tend to start with a disk.

of these arrangements were made by 21 different subjects, 9 subjects started directly with the arrangement in *a* of Figure 14.4. Of the 21 subjects, 10 changed on the second attempt to this arrangement. Therefore, during the first 2 attempts, 19 subjects out of 30 (63 percent) arranged the two pieces in the prostructural way represented in *a* of Figure 14.4.

I obtained analogous results with other patterns that I prepared in order to verify the extent to which the organizational tendencies suggested by the material may hinder a swift solution. For example, when subjects were asked to make a square from the six pieces of Figure 14.5, given to them in random order, 19 subjects out of 20 (95 percent) started by building a disk.

FACILITATION FROM ABOVE OR FROM BELOW

Most problems are not solved immediately, with a single act of understanding; usually the final solution is reached after a series of attempts, each of which is not, for some reason, completely satisfactory. According to Duncker (1945), the various stages of this problem-solving process may be considered as a continuous development, or *transformation of the problem*. In fact, each attempt is the "concretization" of a functional solving principle, but the discovery of a general functional principle is always equivalent to a *reformulation of the original problem*—that is, to a more or less radical restructuring of it.

Thus, in the problem of the tumor analyzed by Duncker, the formulation of the functional principle "avoid contact between radiation and sound tissues" represents an important reformulation of the original problem in terms of the more specific one "find an approach to the stomach which is free from tissues," with the resultant focusing on the esophagus.

What distinguishes a person who is capable of reaching a solution is, therefore, the capacity to reformulate the problem in ever more productive ways. This capacity is shown in the adoption (either spontaneous or programmatic) of procedures of thought that—because of their capacity to produce effective restructurings of the problem situation, and therefore to favor the discovery of the solution—are called heuristic.

The analysis of the problem situation can take various forms. First, it may be an *analysis of the conflict*—that is, it may consist in the search for what prevents the solution ("What's wrong?") and in the attempt to eliminate the cause of the conflict thus located ("What must I change?"). If I must carry a cumbersome table from one room to another, and I cannot do it because the doorway is too narrow, the cause of the conflict is immediately located in the collision or intersection between the top of the table and the door jambs. To eliminate the conflict, I must either enlarge the doorway or saw the table; or, more wisely, I can turn the table so that its shorter dimensions can pass through. The first procedure is not a solution if the task is to carry the whole table, and in rejecting this hasty operation I take into account an appropriate *analysis of the objective* ("What is really required?"). The second procedure is discovered through *an analysis of the material—* that is, through the examination of the properties of the material that can be used to solve the problem ("What is given? What can I use?").

The analysis of the material leads to the discovery of the functional values that are incorporated in the objects or in the available data. When the discovery of the functional principle precedes the discovery, in what is given, of the property that "concretizes" that principle, we can say that the solution has been reached *from above.* But the contrary may also occur. In the case of the problem of the tumor, we may come to consider the esophagus because we have already tried to find "an approach to the stomach which is free from tissues"—that is, we already have in mind a general solution principle that is ready to be "concretized." But it may also happen that, during a still relatively indeterminate exploration of the data of the situation, "one comes across" the esophagus, and the latter discovery may suggest *from below* the functional value "free approach to the stomach."

These two different strategies followed by thought in reaching the solution may also be adopted by the experimenter to help the subject find the solution. The suggestions that are supplied during an experiment on productive thinking may be either suggestions *from above* or suggestions *from below.* In the first case the decisive principle, as far as the solution is concerned, is supplied explicitly, although expressed in general terms. In the second case the emergence of the solving principle is facilitated by means of an intervention in the structure of the material, or by drawing the attention of the subject to certain characteristics of the available material that have a functional value in the context of the problem.

Duncker studied the effectiveness of the two kinds of suggestions by using the following problem: "Why are all numbers of the kind abcabc (such as 276276; 591591; 112112) divisible by 13?" (Solution: abcabc = abc × 1,001; 1,001 is divisible by 13; therefore abcabc also is divisible by 13).

The suggestions *from above* that he used were of the following kind: "If a common divisor of some numbers is divisible by 13, then all these numbers are divisible by 13" or "If the divisor of a number is divisible by p, then the number itself is divisible by p." The suggestions *from below* contained a hint directed to 1,001: "The numbers are divisible by 1,001" or "1,001 is divisible by 13."

The suggestions of the first kind were of no help at all, although they contained the enunciation of the general rule from which the solution must issue.

In contrast, the solution was greatly facilitated by suggestions from below. Duncker likewise obtained positive effects by slightly modifying the structure of the material. Instead of giving as examples numbers like 276276; 591591; 112112, he gave the series 276276; 277277; 278278. In this case the consecutiveness of the numbers oriented the "analysis of the situation" toward the constant difference 1,001, and thus suggested the

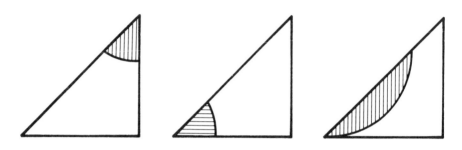

relationship that forms the basis of the solution: "If a number a and the difference $a - b$ are divisible by q, then b also is divisible by q."

These results, which seem to indicate that suggestions from below have a greater heuristic value, in my opinion have a certain importance also for their pedagogic implications, and have induced me to undertake research to check their validity.

The Role of Nonessential Features of the Material

In order to check whether the construction of the square in Figure 14.3 may be facilitated by adding suitable structural features, I have modified the six pieces of Figure 14.2 by painting a selected portion of each piece red (see Figure 14.6a). The assembly of their portions leads to the completed disk shown in Figure 14.6b.

The task of building a square with the pieces of Figure 14.2 was given to a control group of 20 subjects, while the other 20 subjects of the experimental group had to build the square with the material Figure 14.6a.

Table 14.1 presents the number of correct solutions reached by the subjects after 2, 5, and 15 minutes. In the control group (material Figure 14.2) none of the subjects reached the solution in the first two minutes,

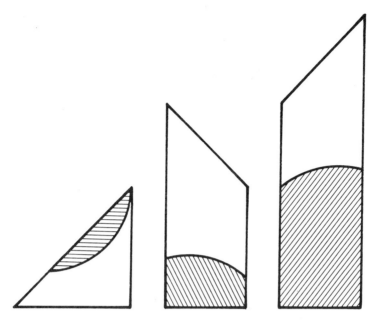

Figure 14.6a The six pieces of cardboard necessary to build up Figure 14.6b.

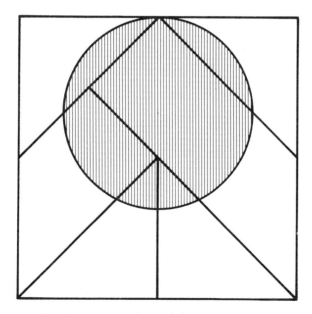

Figure 14.6b The square made up of the pieces of Figure 14.6a.

TABLE 14.1

Number of Subjects in the Control and Experimental Groups Who Reached the Solution After 2, 5, and 15 minutes

Time	Control Group (N = 20) (material of Fig. 14.2)	Experimental Group (N = 20) (material of Fig. 14.6a)
2 minutes	0	8
5 minutes	1	13
15 minutes	6	17

Source: G. Kanizsa 1975, p. 423.

only one after five minutes, and six after a quarter of an hour. In the experimental group (material of Figure 14.6) there were, respectively, 8, 13, and 17 solutions ($p < .001$, two-tail Fisher and Yates test). Moreover, the difference in difficulty of building up a square with the two kinds of material is demonstrated by the difference between the mean times of solution. The mean time of the 6 solutions obtained with the material of Figure 14.2 is 8 minutes, 43 seconds, while the 17 solutions obtained with the material of Figure 14.6a have a mean time of 3 minutes, 26 seconds ($t = 3.06$, $p < .001$).

These results show that the action of a structural factor may make the solution easier in a difficult task. Indeed, many subjects in the experimental group reached the solution by replacing the instructions given by the experimenter ("build up a square with the six pieces") with other instructions suggested by the material ("build up a disk with the six pieces"). One may suppose that, in the same way, it could be possible to make an easy task difficult by introducing into the material features that require the subject to start with a strategy that delays or removes the solution.

I have investigated additional ways to favor the solution of a difficult problem through a structural modification of the material (Kanizsa and Grubissa 1976). The next sections describe two experiments in that research.

The Role of Spatial Orientation

In the first experiment we used a problem that had already been analyzed by Max Wertheimer (1920) to demonstrate the role of perceptual reorganization in solving geometrical problems. The subject was shown Figure 14.7 and the problem was expressed orally in the following way:

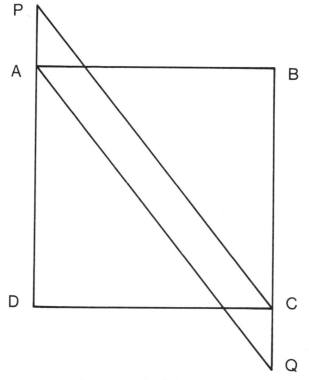

Figure 14.7 Wertheimer (1920).

ABCD is a square.
Side AB is known.
AP = CQ is known.
Find the area of the square ABCD
and of the parallelogram   APCQ.

Since the area of the square is practically known, the "difficulty" consists in calculating the area of parallelogram APCQ, until one notices that the side of the square is also the height of the parallelogram. This demands a reorganization of the original data of the problem, which, for a nonmathematician, may be rather difficult. In fact, it means that an element that has been given with a certain function (side) must assume a new function (height).

This difficulty is confirmed by the results of our experiment, in which only 2 subjects out of 20 (10 percent obtained the exact solution within the maximum time allowed, 5 minutes.

The facilitation from below that we introduced in this case con-

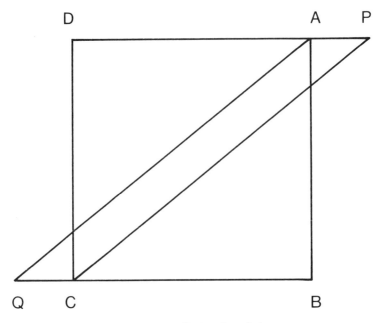

Figure 14.8 Facilitation from below.

sisted of rotating the design by 90 degrees, as in Figure 14.8 Thus we thought to favor the transformation of the side of the square into the height of the parallelogram.

The effect of such a simple modification of the experimental situation was considerable: we obtained 10 solutions out of 20 tests—that is, the problem was solved correctly in the allowed time in half of the cases (see Table 14.2).

TABLE 14.2

Success in Solving Figures 14.7 and 14.8

Figure	Number Subjects	Number Solvers	Percent Solvers
A	20	2	10
B	20	10	50

Significance: A – B: $X^2 = 7.62$; $p < .01$.
Source: G. Kanizsa and B. Grubissa 1976, p. 427.

Thus, with the same verbal instructions the orientation of the critical element of the figure proved to be an efficient facilitation from below, probably because it makes it less difficult to "see" the side of the square as the height of the parallelogram, since the height is normally "lowered" so as to appear vertical with regard to the observer.

The Role of Structural Salience of the Terms

The problem we used, which at first sight may seem very easy, is really rather difficult, so much so that many people are not able to produce the right answer even after 10 or 20 minutes of reflection. It was proposed to the first group of 30 subjects, who were examined individually, as formulation A: "A brick weighs one kilo plus half a brick. How much does the brick weigh?" The question was presented on a sheet of paper, on which the subject was asked to write the answer. After five minutes the test was interrupted and the experiment continued as a conversation, during which the experimenter tried to understand the nature of the subject's difficulty in tackling the problem.

Two other groups, of 42 and 35 subjects, respectively, were presented with the two following formulations, each of which contains a modification of a different kind. Formulation B was "A brick weighs one kilo plus half a brick. How much does the brick weigh? Keep in mind that *the two halves of a whole are always equal*." Formulation C was "A brick weighs half a brick plus one kilo. How much does the brick weigh?"

In formulation B the problem, proposed exactly as in formulation A, is given with the a priori axiomatic statement of the fundamental logical relation implicit in the problem itself; therefore it is a facilitation from above. In formulation C the statement is slightly modified: we made a simple commutation of the terms, which should leave the substance of the problem unchanged. Actually, it is a reformulation that radically changes the structural salience of the terms: *half* a brick comes to the foreground and *one* kilo recedes. The "wholeness" that dominated in the first formulation gives way to an "incomplete" structure that induces one to search for its completion. "Half a brick" calls for the other half-brick, and thus can lead to the discovery that "half a brick" and "one kilo" are the same thing said in two different ways. It is therefore a structural simplification that corresponds to a facilitation from below, just like the introduction of consecutive numbers in the problem of 13.

Table 14.3 presents the results concerning the number of subjects who answered correctly within the first five minutes.

As one can see, the a priori enunciation of the logical relation that is fundamental as far as the solution is concerned, had practically no influence on the number of successes, while formulation C had considerable influence.

TABLE 14.3

Success in Solving Formulations A, B, and C

Formulation	Number Subjects	Number Solvers	Percent Solvers
A	30	14	47
B	42	19	45
C	35	30	84

Significance: χ^2

A – B	0.14	$p > .50$
A – C	11.20	$p < .001$
B – C	8.60	$p < .01$

Source: G. Kanizsa and B. Grubissa 1976, p. 425.

Therefore in this case, too, a facilitation from below, consisting of making the structure of the problem situation more "transparent," was more effective.

DISCUSSION

If the organizational factors may lead, as in our examples, to a premature closure, delaying or hindering the solution, what does it mean to say that these same factors promote the process of solution? It is clear that when Wertheimer speaks of factors that arise from the structure and lead to the solution, he has in mind the problem-solving situation as a whole—that is, the system constituted by the goal toward which the mind strives and the means the mind has at its disposal. In our first example the goal is the construction of a square (see Figure 14.3) with its specific requirements, while the features of the material require their being handled in such a way that achievement of the solution is hindered. Usually in a difficult problem the organizational features of the available material do not facilitate their use in reaching the solution. There is a conflict between the requirements of the goal and the requirements of the material. The strains and tension provoked by this conflict generate the vectors that lead to the productive restructuring. To be dominated by the features and the requirements of the material is tantamount to narrowing the field of vision, to losing sight of the goal and its requirements, thus leading to a premature closure. In our example of Figure 14.6a, it is *only by chance* that following the demands of the material (to build up a disk) leads blindly to the correct solution (to build up a square). In the case of Figure 14.5, the same requirement of the material (to build up a disk) does not lead to the correct solution; on the contrary, it hampers it, so that we are obliged to make a useless step.

Wertheimer's interest was mainly in the analysis of the thought processes when we are truly productive, when we are able to be really free from the immediate requirements of the material. His attention was directed more to the processes that lead to success than to the causes of errors. Nevertheless, he clearly recognized that errors may be due to organizational factors that lead to a premature closure. It is for this reason that too often, in the literature, Wertheimer's theses were misunderstood and cited in an oversimplified and unilateral way.

BIBLIOGRAPHY

Aarons, L. 1964. "Visual Apparent Movement Research: Review 1935–1955 and Bibliography 1955–1963." *Perspectual and Motor Skills, Mono. Supplement* 18:239–74.

Ames, A. 1946. *Some Demonstrations Concerned with the Origin and Nature of Our Sensations: A Laboratory Manual.* Hanover, N.H.: Dartmouth Eye Institute.

Andrews, D. P. 1967a. "Perception of Contour Orientation in the Central Fovea. I: Short Lines." *Vision Research* 7:975–97.

———. 1967b. "Perception of Contour Orientation in the Central Fovea. II: Spatial Integration." *Vision Research* 7:999–1013.

Arnheim, R. 1949. "The Gestalt Theory of Expression." *Psychological Review* 46:156–71.

———. 1969. *Visual Thinking.* Berkeley and Los Angeles: University of California Press.

———. 1974. *Art and Visual Perception.* Berkeley: University of California Press.

Asch, S. 1952. *Social Psychology.* New York: Prentice-Hall.

———. 1968. "Gestalt Theory." In *International Encyclopedia of the Social Sciences,* ed. D. L. Sills. New York: MacMillan.

Attneave, F. 1955. "Symmetry, Information and Memory for Patterns." *American Journal of Psychology* 68:209–22.

———. 1959. *Applications of Information Theory to Psychology.* New York: Holt, Rinehart and Winston.

Bahnsen, P. 1928. "Eine Untersuchung über Symmetrie und Asymmetrie bei visuellen Wahrnehmungen." *Zeitschrift für Psychologie* 108:129–54.

Beck, J. 1972. *Surface Color Perception.* Ithaca, N.Y.: Cornell University Press.

Benary, W. 1924. "Beobachtungen zu einem Experiment ueber Helligkeitskontrast." *Psychologische Forschung* 5:131–42.

Benussi, V. 1925. *La suggestione e l'ipnosi come mezzi di analisi psichica reale.* Bologna: Zanichelli.

Berman, P. and Leibowitz. 1965. "Some Effects of Contour on Brightness Contrast." *Journal of Experimental Psychology* 69:251–56.

Birenbaum, G. 1930. "Das Vergessen einer Vornahme. Isolierte seelische Systeme und dynamische Gesamtbereiche," *Psychologische Forschung* 13:218–84.

Boring, E. G. 1921. "The Stimulus Error." *American Journal of Psychology* 32:449–71.

Bosinelli, M., R. Canestrari, and G. F. Minguzzi. 1960. "Beitrag zum Problem der gekreuzten und ungekreuzten Bewegungen." *Psychologische Beiträge* 5:8–12.

Bozzi, P. 1969. "Direzionalità e organizzazione interna della figura." *Memorie dell'Accademia Patavina di Scienze, Lettere ed Arti* 81:135–70.

_____. 1972. "Cinque varietà di errore dello stimolo." *Rivista di Psicologia* 66:131–41.

Bradley, D., and S. Dumais. 1975. "Ambiguous Cognitive Contours." *Nature* 257:582–84.

Bradley, D., and S. Petry. 1977. "Organizational Determinants of Subjective Contours: The Subjective Necker Cube." *American Journal of Psychology* 90:253–62.

Braine, L. G. 1965. "Disorientation of Forms: An Examination of Rock's Theory." *Psychonomic Science* 3:541–42.

Brigner, W., and M. Gallagher. 1974. "Subjective Contours: Apparent Depth or Simultaneous Brightness Contrast?" *Perceptual and Motor Skills* 38:1047–53.

Brooks, R. M., and A. G. Goldstein. 1965. "Recognition by Children of Inverted Photographs of Faces." *Child Development* 34:1033–40.

Brown, J. F. 1933. "Ueber die dynamischen Eigenschaften der Realitäts-und Irrealitätsschichten." *Psychologische Forschung* 18:2–26.

_____. 1936. *Psychology and the Social Order.* New York: McGraw-Hill.

Bruner, J. 1957a. "On Perceptual Readiness." *Psychological Review* 64:123–52.

_____. 1957. "Going Beyond the Information Given." in Bruner et al., *Contemporary Approaches to Cognition.* Cambridge, Mass.: Harvard University Press.

Bruner, J., and A. Minturn. 1955. "Perceptual Identification and Perceptual Organization." *Journal of General Psychology* 53:21–28.

Brunswik, E. 1934. *Wahrnehmung und Gegenstandswelt.* Vienna: Deuticke.

Burke, L. 1952. "On the Tunnel Effect." *Quarterly Journal of Experimental Psychology* 4:121–38.

Coren, S. 1969. "Brightness Contrast as a Function of Figure-Ground Relations." *Journal of Experimental Psychology* 80:517–24.

_____. 1972. "Subjective Contours and Apparent Depth." *Psychological Review* 79 (4):359–67.

Coren, S., and L. Theodor. 1977. "Neural Interactions and Subjective Contours." *Perception* 6:107–11.

Davidson, H. P. 1934. "A Study of Reversals in Young Children." *Journal of Genetic Psychology* 45:452–65.

_____. 1935. "A Study of the Confusing Letters B, D, P and Q." *Journal of Genetic Psychology* 47:458–68.

Dembo, T. 1931. "Der Aerger als dynamisches Problem." *Psychologische Forschung* 15:1–144.

Dinnerstein, D., and Michael Wertheimer, 1957. "Some Determinants of Phenomenal Overlapping." *American Journal of Psychology* 70:21–37.

Duncker, K. 1945. "On Problem Solving." *Psychological Monographs* 58, 5.

Ellis, W. D. 1938. *A Sourcebook of Gestalt Psychology.* New York: Harcourt Brace.

Engel, P. 1928. "Tachistoscopische Expositionen und Scheinbewegungen." *Zeitschrift für Psychologie* 107:273–313.

Ertel, S., L. Kemmler and M. Stadler, eds. 1975. *Gestalttheorie in der modernen Psychologie*. Darmstadt: Steinkopf.

Farné, M. 1965. "Contributo alla misura psicofisica della 'buona forma'" *Bollettino della Società italiana di biologia sperimentale* 41:1506–09.

_____. 1968. "Alcune osservazioni con linee virtuali e margini quasi percettivi." *Bollettino della Società Italiana di biologia sperimentale* 44 (19):1613–16.

Fieandt, K. von. 1938. *Über das Sehen von Tiefengebilden bei wechselnder Beleuchtungsrichtung*, Helsinki: Psychologisches Institut Universität Helsinki.

_____. 1949. "Das phänomenologische Problem von Licht und Schatten." *Acta Psychologica* 6:337–57.

Flores d'Arcais, G. 1975. "Einflusse der Gestalttheorie auf die moderne kognitive Psychologie." In *Gestalttheorie in der modernen Psychologie*, ed. S. Ertel, L. Kemmler, and M. Stadler, pp. 45–57. Darmstadt: Steinkopf.

Flores d'Arcais, G., ed. 1975. *Studies in Perception*. Florence: Martello—Giunti.

Fry, G. A. 1931. "The Stimulus Correlate of Bulky Color." *American Journal of Psychology* 43:618–20.

Fuchs, W. 1923. "Experimentelle Untersuchungen über das simultane Hintereinandersehen auf der selben Sehrichtung." *Zeitschrift für Psychologie* 91:145–235.

Gabassi, P. G., and L. Zanuttini. 1978. "Il ruolo dei fattori di organizzazione percettiva nel completamento amodale." *Giornale italiano di psicologia* 5:207–16.

Gajzago, C., and R. H. Day. 1972. "Uprightness Constancy with Head Inversion in Young Children and Adults." *Journal of Experimental Child Psychology* 14:43–52.

Galli, A., and A. Zama, 1931. "Untersuchungen über die Wahrnehmung ebener geometrischen Figuren die ganz oder teilweise von anderen geometrischen Figuren verdeckt sind." *Zeitschrift für Psychologie* 123:308–48.

Gerbino, W. 1975. "Perceptual Transparency and Phenomenal Shrinkage of Visual Objects." *Italian Journal of Psychology* 2:403–15.

Ghent, L., L. Bernstein, and A. M. Goldweber. 1960. "Preferences for Orientation of Form Under Varying Conditions." *Perceptual and Motor Skills* 11:46.

Gibson, J. J. 1971. "The Legacies of Koffka's 'Principles.'" *Journal of the History of the Behavioral Sciences* 7:3–9.

Gibson, J. J., J. Purdy, and L. Lawrence. 1955. "A Method of Controlling Stimulation for the Study of Space Perception: The Optical Tunnel." *Journal of Experimental Psychology* 50:1–14.

Gibson, J. J., and R. D. Walk. 1960. "The Visual Cliff." *Scientific American* 202, 4:64–71.

Ginsburg, A. 1975. "Is the Illusory Triangle Physical or Imaginary?" *Nature* 257:219–20.

Giovanelli, G. 1966. "Stati di tensione e di equilibrio nel campo percettivo." *Rivista di psicologia* 60:327–36.

Goldmeier, E. 1972. *Similarity in Visually Perceived Forms*. New York: International Universities Press.

Goldstein, K. 1939. *The Organism*. New York: American Book Co.

Gottschaldt, K. 1926. "Über den Einfluss der Erfahrung auf die Wahrnehmung von Figuren." *Psychologische Forschung* 8:261–317.

———. 1929. "Ueber den Einfluss der Erfahrung auf die Wahrnehmung von Figuren, II." *Psychologische Forschung* 12:1–79.

Gregory, R. L. 1966. *Eye and Brain*. London: Weidenfeld and Nicolson.

———. 1972. "Cognitive Contours." *Nature* 238 (5358):51–52.

Hajos, A. 1968. "Psychophysiologische Probleme der 'Farbenkonturen' und 'Konturfarben'" *Studia psychologica* 10:254–66.

Harrower, M. R. 1929. "Some Experiments on the Nature of Gamma Movement." *Psychologische Forschung* 13:55–63.

———. 1932. "Organization in Higher Mental Processes." *Psychologische Forschung* 17:56–120.

Heider, F. 1958. *The Psychology of Interpersonal Relations*. New York: Wiley.

———. 1970. "Gestalt Theory: Early History and Reminiscences." *Journal of the History of the Behavioral Sciences* 6:131–39.

Heinemann, E. G. 1955. "Simultaneous Brightness Induction as a Function of Inducing- and Test-Field Luminance" *Journal of Experimental Psychology* 50:89–96.

Helmholtz, Hermann von. 1867. *Handbuch der physiologischen Optik*. Leipzig: Voss

Helson, H. 1963. "Studies on Anomalous Contrast and Assimilation." *Journal of the Optical Society of America* 53:179–84.

———. 1969. "Why Did Their Precursors Fail and the Gestalt Psychologists Succeed?" *American Psychologist* 24:1007–11.

Henle, M. 1965. "On Gestalt Psychology." In *Scientific Psychology*, ed. B. Wolman, pp. 276–92. New York: Basic Books.

———. 1977. "The Influence of Gestalt Psychology in America." *Annals of the New York Academy of Sciences* 291:3–12.

Henle, M., ed. 1961. *Documents of Gestalt Psychology*. Berkeley: University of California Press.

Henneman, R. H. 1935. "A Photometric Study of the Perception of Object Color." *Archives of Psychology* 179.

Hering, E. 1920. *Grundzüge der Lehre vom Lichtsinn*. Leipzig: J. Springer.

———. 1964. *Outlines of a Theory of the Light Sense*. Cambridge, Mass.: Harvard University Press.

Hess, C. and H. Pretori. 1894. "Messende Untersuchungen ueber die Gesetzmässigkeit des Simultanen Helligkeits-Contrast." *Archiv für Opthalmologie* 40:1–27.

Hillebrand, F. 1922. "Zur Theorie der stroboscopischen Bewegungen." *Zeitschrift für Psychologie* 89:209–72.

Hochberg, J. E. 1957. "The Effects of the Gestalt Revolution: The Cornell Symposium on Perception." *Psychological Review* 64:73–84.

———. 1974. "Perception." In *Woodworth and Schlosberg's Experimental Psychology*, ed. J. Kling, and A. Riggs, pp. 395–546. London: Methuen.

Hochberg, J. E., W. Triebel, and G. Seaman. 1951. "Color Adaption Under Conditions of Homogeneous Visual Stimulation (Ganzfeld)." *Journal of Experimental Psychology* 41:153–59.

Hochberg, J. and V. Brooks. 1960. "The Psychophysics of Form: Reversible-Perspective Drawings of Spatial Objects", *American Journal of Psychology* 73:237–354.

Hornbostel, E. M. von. 1925. "Die Einheit der Sinne." *Melos* 4.

_____. 1930. "Gestaltpsychologisches zur Stilkritik." In *Festschrift für G. Adler*. Leipzig: Engelmann.

Hubel, D. H., and T. N., Wiesel. 1959. "Receptive Fields of Single Neurons in the Cat's Striate Cortex." *Journal of Physiology* 148:574–91.

_____. 1962. "Receptive Fields, Binocular Interaction and Functional Architecture in the Cat's Visual Center." *Journal of Physiology* 160:106–54.

Hunton, V. D. 1955. "The Recognition of Inverted Pictures by Children." *Journal of Genetic Psychology* 86:281–88.

Hurvich, L. and D. Jameson. 1966. *The Perception of Brightness and Darkness*. Boston: Allyn and Bacon.

James, William. 1890. *Principles of Psychology*. New York: Henry Holt.

Jenkins, J. G. 1930. "Perceptual Determinants in Plain Designs." *Journal of Experimental Psychology* 13:24–46.

Julesz, B. 1960. "Binocular Depth Perception of Computer-Generated Patterns." *Bell System Technical Journal* 39:1125–61.

_____. 1964. "Binocular Depth Perception Without Familiarity Cues." *Science* 145:356–62.

Kanizsa, Gaetano. 1951. "Sulla polarizzazione del movimento gamma." *Archivio di Psicologia, Neurologia e Psichiatria* 3:224–67.

_____. 1954a. "Il gradiente marginale come fattore dell'aspetto fenomenico dei colori." *Archivio di psicologia, neurologia e psichiatria* 15 (3):251–64.

_____. 1954b. "Linee virtuali e margini fenomenici in assenza di discontinuità di stimolazione." *Atti 10° Convegno degli psicologi italiani*. ed. V. Lazzeroni, Firenze: Editrice Universitaria.

_____. 1955a. "Margini quasi-percettivi in campi con stimolazione omogenea." *Rivista di psicologia* 49 (1):7–30.

_____. 1955b. "Condizioni ed effetti della trasparenza fenomenica." *Rivista di psicologia* 49 (3):3–19.

_____. 1956. "Il fattore empirico nella percezione." *Rassegna di psicologia generale e clinica* 1:3–9.

_____. 1957. "Gradient marginal et perception Chromatique." In *Problèmes de la couleur*, ed. I. Meyerson, pp. 107–14. Paris: SEVPEN.

_____. 1969. "Perception, Past Experience and the Impossible Experiment." *Acta psychologica* 31:66–96.

_____. 1970. "Amodale Ergänzungen und Erwarfungsfehler' des Gestaltpsychologen." *Psychologische Forschung* 33:325–44.

_____. 1972a. "Schrumpfung von visuellen Feldern bei amodaler Ergänzung." *Studia psychologica* 14 (13):208–10.

_____. 1972b. "Errore dei gestaltista ed altri errori-da-aspettativa." *Rivista di psicologia* 66:3–18.

_____. 1975a. "Prägnanz as an Obstacle to Problem Solving." *Italian Journal of Psychology* 2:417–25.

_____. 1975b. "The Role of Regularity in Perceptual Organization." In *Studies in Perception*, ed. G. Flores d'Arcais, pp. 48–66. Florence: Martello-Giunti.

_____. 1975c. "Amodal Completion and Phenominal Shrinkage of Surfaces in the Visual Field." *Italian Journal of Psychology* 2:187–95.

_____. 1976. "Subjective Contours." *Scientific American* 234 (4):48–52.

Kanizsa, G. and G. Tampieri. 1968. "Nuove osservazione sull'orientamento retinico ed ambientale." In *Ricerche sperimentali sulla percezione*, ed. G. Kanizsa and G. Vicaro, pp. 49–68. Trieste: Edizioni Universita degli Studi.

Kanizsa, G. and G. Vicario, eds. 1968. *Ricerche sperimentali sulla percezione.* Trieste: Edizioni Universita degli Studi.

Kanizsa, G., P. Legrenzi, and P. Meazzini. 1975. *I processi cognitivi.* Bologna: Il Mulino.

Kanizsa, G. and W. Gerbino. 1976. "Convexity and Symmetry in Figure-Ground Organization." In *Art and Artefacts*, ed. M. Henle, pp. 25–32. New York: Springer.

Kanizsa, G. and B. Grubissa. 1976. "Facilitation from Above and Facilitation from Below in Solving a Problem." *Italian Journal of Psychology* 3:421–30.

Kanizsa, G. and G. Tampieri. 1976. "Environmental and Retinal Frames of Reference in Visual Perception." *Italian Journal of Psychology* 2:317–32.

Kanizsa, G. and R. Luccio. 1978. "Espansione fenomenica di superfici in condizioni di completamento amodale." *Reports of the Institute of Psychology, Trieste.*

Kardos, L. 1934. "Ding und Schatten." *Zeitschrift für Psychologie* (spec vol.) 22.

Karsten, A. 1928. "Psychische Sattigung." *Psychologische Forschung* 10:142–54.

Katona, G. 1940. *Organizing and Memorizing.* New York: Columbia University Press.

Katz, D. 1911. "Die Erscheinungsweisen der Farben und ihre Beeinflussung durch die individuelle Erfahrung." *Zeitschrift für Psychologie* (spec. vol.) 7.

_____. 1935. *The World of Color.* London: Kegan Paul.

Kenkel, F. 1913. "Untersuchungen über den Zusammenhang zwischen Erscheinungsgrösse und Erscheinungsbewegung bei einigen sogennanten optischen tauschungen." *Zeitschrift für Psychologie* 67:358–449.

Kennedy, J. M. 1973. "Depth at an Edge, Coplanarity, Slant Depth, Change in Direction and Change in Brightness in the Production of Subjective Contours." In *Conference on Structural Learning.* Philadelphia: University of Pennsylvania Press.

Kennedy, J. 1974. *A Psychology of Picture Perception.* San Francisco: Jossey-Bass.

Knops, L. 1947. "Contribution à l'étude de la "naissance" et de la "permanence" phénoménales dans le champ visuel." In *Miscellanea Psychologica A. Michotte*, ed. J. Nuttin, pp. 562–610. Louvain: Edition Institut Supérieur de Philosophie.

Koehler, W. 1920. *Die physischen Gestalten in Ruhe und im stationären Zustand.* Brunswick: Vieweg.

_____. 1921. *Intelligenzprufüngen an Menschenaffen.* Berlin: Springer.

_____. 1938. *The Place of Value in a World of Facts.* New York: Liveright.

_____. 1940. *Dynamics in Psychology.* New York: Liveright.

_____. 1947. *Gestalt Psychology.* New York: Liveright.

_____. 1958. "The Present Situations in Brain Psychology." *American Psychologist* 13:150–54.

_____. 1959. "Psychologie und Naturwissenschaft." In *Proceedings of the XV International Congress of Psychology,* ed. W. Metzger, pp. 37-50. Amsterdam: North Holland.

_____. 1965. "Unsolved Problems in the Field of Figural After-Effects." *Psychological Record* 15:63-83.

_____. 1969. *The Task of Gestalt Psychology.* Princeton: Princeton University Press.

_____. 1971. *Selected Papers.* ed. M. Henle. New York: Liveright.

Koffka, K. 1928. *The Growth of the Mind.* London: Harcourt.

_____. 1935. *Principles of Gestalt Psychology.* New York: Harcourt.

Kohler, I. 1951. *Über Aufbau und Wandlungen der Wahrnehmungswelt.* Vienna: Rohrer.

Kolers, P. 1972. *Aspects of Motion Perception.* Oxford: Pergamon Press.

Kopfermann, H. 1930. "Psychologische Untersuchungen über die Wirkung zweidimensionaler Darstellung körperlicher Gebilde." *Psychologische Forschung* 13:293-364.

Korte, A. 1915. "Kinematoskopische Untersuchungen." *Zeitschrift für Psychologie* 72:194-296.

Krech, D., and R., Crutchfield. 1948. *Theory and Problems of Social Psychology.* New York: McGraw-Hill.

Lauenstein, L. 1938. "Über räumliche Wirkungen von Licht und Schatten." *Psychologische Forschung* 19:267-319.

Lawson, R. B., and W. L., Gulick. 1967. "Stereopsis and Anomalous Contours." *Vision Research* 7:271-97.

Legrenzi, P. 1975. *Forma e contenuto dei processi cognitivi.* Bologna: Il Mulino.

Lehmann, H. 1939. "Wesen und Entstehung der Scheinbewegung im Lichte neuer Versuche." *Archiv für die gesamte Psychologie* 102:51-94.

Lewin, K. 1931. "Environmental Forces in Child Behavior and Development." In *Handbook of Child Psychology,* ed. C. Murchison, pp. 94-127. Worcester, Mass.

_____. 1935. *Dynamic Theory of Personality.* New York: McGraw-Hill

_____. 1936. *Principles of Topological Psychology.* New York: McGraw-Hill.

_____. 1951. *Field Theory in Social Science.* New York: Harper and Row.

Liebmann, S. 1927. "Ueber das Verhalten farbigen Formen bei Helligkeitsgleichkeit von Figur und Grund." *Psychologische Forschung* 9:300-53.

Lindemann, E. 1922. "Experimentelle Untersuchungen über das Entstehen und Vergehen von Gestalten." *Psychologische Forschung* 2:5-60.

Luchins, A. 1942. "Mechanization in Problem Solving: The Effect of Einstellung." *Psychological Monographs* 54 (6).

_____. 1951. "An Evaluation of Current Criticism of Gestalt Psychological Work on Perception." *Psychological Review* 58:69-95.

_____. 1975. "The Place of Gestalt Theory in American Psychology." In *Gestalttheorie in der modernen Psychologie,* ed. S. Ertel, L. Kemmler, and M. Stadler, pp. 21-44. Darmstadt: Steinkopf.

Macleod, R. B. 1947. "The Effects of 'Artificial Penumbrae' on the Brightness of Included Areas." In *Miscellanea Psychologica A. Michotte.* ed. J. Nuttin, pp. 138-54. Louvain: Editions Institut Supérieur de Philosophie.

Metelli, Fabio, 1960. "Morfologia dei fenomeni di completamento nella percezione visiva. In *Gestalthaftes Sehen*, ed. F. Weinhandl, pp. 266–78. Darmstadt: Wissenschaftliche Gesellschaft.

———. 1967. "Zur Analyse der phänomenalen Durchsichtigkeitserscheinungen." In *Gestalt and Wirklichkeit*, ed. R. Mühlher and J. Fischl, 50–71. Berlin: Duncker und Humblot.

———. 1970. "An Algebraic Development of the Theory of Perceptual Transparency." *Ergonomics* 13:59–66.

———. 1974a. "The Perception of Transparency." *Scientific American* 230, 4:90–98.

———. 1974b. "Achromatic Color Conditions in the Perception of Transparency." In *Perception, Essays in Honor of James J. Gibson*, ed. R. Macleod and H. Pick, pp. 95–116. Ithaca, N.Y.: Cornell University Press.

Metzger, W. 1930. "Optische Untersuchungen am Ganzfeld." *Psychologische Forschung* 13:6–29.

———. 1931. "Gestalt und Kontrast", *Psychologische Forschung* 15:374–86.

———. 1934. "Beobachtungen über phänomenale Identität." *Psychologische Forschung* 19:1–60.

———. 1954. *Psychologie*. Darmstadt: Steinkopf.

———. 1962. *Schöpferische Freiheit*. Frankfurt-am-Main: Kramer.

———. 1966. "Figural-Wahrnehmung." In *Handbuch der Psychologie*, vol. I, ed. W. Metzger, pp. 693–744. Göttingen: Hogrefe.

———. 1974. *Gesetze des Sehens*. Frankfurt-am-Main: Kramer.

Micali, G., O. Giurissevich, and M. Seriani. 1978. "Il completamento amodale come fattore della espansione fenomenica di superfici." *Reports of the Institute of Psychology*, Trieste.

Michels, K. M., and L. Zusne. 1965. "Metrics of Visual Form." *Psychological Bulletin* 63:72–86.

Michotte, A. 1946. *La perception de la causalité*. Louvain: Publications Universitaires de Louvain.

———. 1962. *The Perception of Causality*. London: Methuen.

Michotte, A., and L. Burke. 1951. "Une nouvelle énigme de la psychologie de la perception: Le 'donné amodal' dans l'expérience sensorielle." In *Proceedings and Papers of the XIIIth International Congress of Psychology at Stockholm*, ed. G. Ekman, pp. 179–80. Stockholm: Broderna Lagerström.

Michotte, A., G. Thinés, and G. Crabbé. 1966. "Die amodalen Ergänzungen von Wahrnehmungsstrukturen." In *Handbuch der Psychologie*, vol. I, ed. W. Metzger, pp. 978–1002. Göttingen: Hogrefe.

Mikesell, W. H. and M., Bentley. 1930. "Configuration and Contrast." *Journal of Experimental Psychology* 13:1–23.

Miyakawa, T. 1950. "Experimental Research on the Structure of Visual Space when We Bend Forward and Look Backward Between the Spread Legs." *Japan Journal of Psychology* 20 (2):14–23.

Moore Heider, G. 1933. "New Studies in Transparency, Form and Color." *Psychologische Forschung* 17:13–55.

Musatti, Cesare L. 1924. "Sui fenomeni stereocinetici." *Archivio italiano di psichologia* 3:105–20.

———. 1953. "Colore e luce." *Archivio di psicologia, neurologia e psichiatria* 14 (5):544–77.

_____. 1964. "Struttura ed esperienza nella fenomenologia percettica." In C. L. Musatti, *Condizioni dell'esperienza e fondazione della psicologia*, pp. 351–67. Florence: Editrice Universitaria.

Neisser, U. 1967. *Cognitive Psychology*. Englewood Cliffs, New Jersey: Prentice-Hall.

Newhall, S. M. 1937. "Indentification by Young Children of Differentially Oriented Forms." *Child Development* 8:105–11.

Newman, E. B. 1934. "Versuche über das Gamma Phänomen." *Psychologische Forschung* 19:102–24.

Oetjen, F. 1915. "Die Bedeutung der Orientierung des Lesestoffs für das Lesen und der Orientierung von sinnlosen Formen für das Wiedererkennen derselben." *Zeitschrift für Psychologie* 71:321–55.

Pastore, N. 1949. "Need as a Determinant of Perception." *Journal of Psychology* 28:457–75.

_____. 1956. "An Examination of One Aspect of the Thesis That Perceiving Is Named." *Psychological Review* 63:309–16.

_____. 1960. "Perceiving as Innately Determined." *Journal of Genetic Psychology* 96:93–99.

_____. 1971. *Selective History of Theories of Visual Perception 1650–1950*. New York: Oxford University Press.

Penrose, L. S. and R. Penrose. 1958. "Impossible Objects: a Special Type of Illusion." *British Journal of Psychology* 49:31.

Petter, G. 1956. "Nuove ricerche sperimentali sulla totalizzazione percettiva." *Rivista di psicologia* 50:213–27.

Piggins, D. 1975. "Cognitive Space." *Perception* 4:337–40.

Pritchard, R. M., M. Heron, and D. O. Hebb. 1960. "Visual Perception Approached by the Method of Stabilized Images." *Canadian Journal of Psychology* 14:67–77

Ratliff, F., H. K. Hartline, and W. H. Miller. 1963. "Spatial and Temporal Aspects of Retinal Inhibitory Interaction." *Journal of Optical Society of America* 53:110–20.

Renvall, P. 1929. "Zur Theorie des stereokinetischen Phänomens." *Annales Universitatis Aboensis* (ser. B) 10.

Restorff, H. von. 1933. "Ueber die Wirkung von Bereichsbildung im Spurenfeld." *Psychologische Forschung* 18:299–342.

Rice, C., 1930. "The Orientation of Plane Figures as a Factor in Their Perception by Children." *Child Development* 1:111–43.

_____. 1956. "The Orientation of Forms on the Retina and in the Environment." *American Journal of Psychology* 69:513–28.

Rock, I. 1973. *Orientation and Form*. New York and London: Academic Press.

Rubin, E. 1921. *Visuell wahrgenommene Figuren*. Copenhagen: Gyldendals.

Sambin, M. 1974. "Angular Margins Without Gradients." *Italian Journal of Psychology* 1:355–61.

Sander, F. 1928. "Experimentelle Ergebnisse der Gestaltpsychologie." *Bericht ueber den 10 Kongress für experimentelle Psychologie*, Jena.

Schultz, D. P. 1965. *Sensory Restriction*. New York: Academic Press.

Schumann, F. 1904. "Beiträge zur Analyse der Gesichtswahrnehmungen: 1°. Einige Beobachtungen über die Zusammenfassung von Gesichtseindrücken zu Einheiten." *Zeitschrift für Psychologie* 23:1–32.

Sherif, M., and C. W. Sherif. 1969. *Social Psychology*. New York: Harper and Row.

Shipley, T. 1965. "Visual Contours in Homogeneous Space." *Science* 150:348-50.

Smith, A., and R. Over. 1975. "Tilt Aftereffects with Subjective Contours." *Nature* 257:581-82.

Spillmann, L. 1975. "Perceptual Modification of the Ehrenstein Illusion." In *Gestalttheorie in der modernen Psychologie*, ed. S. Ertel, L. Kemmler, and M. Stadler, pp. 210-18. Darmstadt: Steinkopf.

Stadler, M. 1972. "Untersuchungen zum Problem virtueller Konturen in der visuellen Wahrnehmung." *Zeitschrift für experimentalle und angewandte Psychologie* 19 (2):325-50.

Stadler, M., and J. Dieker. 1969. "Margini quasi percettivi e after-effects figurali." *Rivista di psicologia* 63 (1):95-104.

Tampieri, G. 1956. "Sul completamento amodale di rappresentazioni prospettiche di solidi geometrici." *Atti dell'XI Congresso degli psicologi italiani*, ed. L. Ancona, pp. 1-3. Milano: Vita e Pensiero.

――――. 1963. "Il problema dell'indifferenza infantile per l'orientamento nello spazio visivo." *Rivista di psicologia* 57:125-77.

――――. 1965. "Un esperimento intorno alla cosiddetta indifferenza infantile per l'orientamento nello spazio visivo." *Atti del XIV Congresso degli psicologi italiani*, ed. G. Iacono, pp. 569-73. Florence: Editrice Universitaria.

――――. 1968. "L'influenza dei sistemi di riferimento ambientale e retinico sull'organizzazione percettiva nei bambini." *Rivista di psicologia* 62:263-70.

Tampieri, G. 1978. "The Shrinkage of Amodally Completed Surfaces in Figure-Ground Situations." *Italian Journal of Psychology* 5.

Thouless, R. H. 1947. "The Experience of 'Upright' and 'Upside-down' in Looking at Pictures." In *Miscellanea Psychologica A. Michotte*, ed. J. Nuttih, pp. 130-37. Louvain: Institut Supérieur de Philosophie.

Titchener, E. B. 1905. *Experimental Psychology Vol. II. Quantitative*. New York: Macmillan.

Tudor-Hart, B. 1928. "Studies in Transparency, Form and Color." *Psychologische Forschung* 10:255-98.

Tyler, C. 1977. "Is the Illusory Triangle Physical or Imaginary?" *Perception* 6:603-04.

Ullman, S. 1976. "Filling-in the Gaps: The Shape of Subjective Contours and a Model for Their Generation." *Biological Cybernetics* 25:1-6.

Varin, D. 1971. "Fenomeni di contrasto e diffusione cromatica nell'organizzazione spaziale del campo percettivo." *Rivista di psicologia* 65 (1):101-28.

Vurpillot, E. 1959. "Vers une psychophysique de la forme." *Année Psychologique* 39:117-42.

Wallach, H. 1935. "Über visuell wahrgenommene Bewegungsrichtung." *Psychologische Forschung*, 20:323-80.

Wertheimer, Max. 1912. "Experimentelle Studien über das Sehen von Bewegungen." *Zeitschrift für Psychologie* 61:161-265.

――――. 1920. *Über Schlussprozesse im produktiven Denken*. Berlin: De Gruyter.

――――. 1923. "Untersunchungen zur Lehre der Gestalt." *Psychologische Forschung*, 4:301-50.

_____. 1925a. *Drei Abhandlungen zur Gestalttheorie*. Erlangen: Verlag der Philosophischen Akademie.

_____. 1925b. "Ueber Gestalttheorie." *Symposion* 1:1–24.

_____. 1959. *Productive Thinking*. New York: Harper.

Wolff, W. 1933. "Ueber die Kontrasterregende Wirkung der transformierten Farben." *Psychologische Forschung* 18:90–97.

_____. 1934. "Induzierte Helligkeitsveränderung." *Psychologische Forschung* 20:159–94.

Wulf, F. 1922. "Ueber die Veränderung von Vorstellungen." *Psychologische Forschung* 1:333–89.

Zapparoli, G. and F. Ferradini. 1963. *Introduzione allo studio della percezione del movimento*. Milano: Edizioni Instituto Gemelli.

Zeigarnik, B. 1927. "Ueber das Behalten von erledigten und unerledigten Handlungen." *Psychologische Forschung* 9:1–85.

Zuckerman, C. B., and I. Rock. 1957. "A Reappraisal of the Role of Past Experience and Innate Organizing Processes in Visual Perception." *Psychological Bulletin* 54:269–94.

NAME INDEX

ABOUT THE AUTHOR ⎯⎯⎯⎯⎯

GAETANO KANIZSA is professor of psychology at the University of Trieste. He received his doctorate in psychology from the University of Padua, where, he was influenced by the European Gestalt tradition. Since then he has dedicated himself to the phenomenology of visual perception and thought processes. He carried on his work in Florence and Milan before returning to his native city of Trieste in 1953 to take up his present post. In addition to his psychological research he is also interested in the relation between science and the visual arts and is actively engaged in painting.